Medical Law in Luxembourg

Medical Law in Luxembourg

Mike Schwebag

Herman Nys

This book was originally published as a monograph in the International Encyclopaedia of Laws/Medical Law.

Founding Editor: Roger Blanpain
General Editor: Frank Hendrickx
Volume Editor: Herman Nys; Associate Editor: Tom Goffin

Wolters Kluwer

Published by:
Kluwer Law International B.V.
PO Box 316
2400 AH Alphen aan den Rijn
The Netherlands
E-mail: lrs-sales@wolterskluwer.com
Website: www.wolterskluwer.com/en/solutions/kluwerlawinternational

Sold and distributed by:
Wolters Kluwer Legal & Regulatory U.S.
920 Links Avenue
Landisville, PA 17538
United States of America
E-mail: customer.service@wolterskluwer.com

ISBN 978-94-035-1239-6

e-Book: ISBN 978-94-035-1249-5
web-PDF: ISBN 978-94-035-1259-4

This title is available on www.kluwerlawonline.com

The Authors

Mike Schwebag (born 16 October 1974) studied Law at Luxembourg University and at Université Robert Schuman Strasbourg, France. In 2001, he completed the complementary training in Luxembourgish law and accessed the Bar as a trainee lawyer. From 2003 to 2015, Mike worked as a legal and policy advisor at the Ministry of Health. His main areas of activity were bioethics, patient rights, drugs and pharmaceuticals, data protection, eHealth and biomedical research. He has been assisting in regulatory work at national level, including end-of-life legislation (2009) and patient rights and duties (2014). Mike has been the national coordinator for eHealth policy and representative at the EU eHealth Network. He has been taking part in the work of the Council of Europe bodies (including DH-BIO) and is a former board member of European Monitoring Centre for Drugs and Drug Addiction and the European Medicines Agency. Mike is an accredited mediator and currently holds the position of 'Médiateur de la Santé', heading the National Patient Information and Mediation Service since its creation in 2015. Mike is an adjunct teacher at the University of Luxembourg. He has published several articles on health law issues and is a member of the editorial board of the *Revue luxembourgeoise Droit & Santé (RLDS)*. He is further a national contact point of the European Association of Health Law.

Emeritus Professor Dr Herman Nys (born on 20 January 1951) studied Law at the K.U. Leuven, Belgium (1969–1974) and at the K.U. Nijmegen, the Netherlands (1974–1975). From 1975 to 1980, he worked as an assistant, specialising in healthcare law, at the Centre for Hospital Sciences in Leuven, where in 1980 he received his doctoral degree for his thesis on 'Legal Aspects of Health Care Planning'. From 1981 through 1989, he was affiliated with the law school in Leuven, first as Lecturer in Medical Law and since 1985 as an associate professor. He has been the director of the Centre of Biomedical Ethics and Law in Leuven from 1989 until 2015. In 1992, he was appointed as a professor, and he retired on 1 October 2016.

The Author

Between 2000 and 2006, he has also been Professor of International Health Law at the University of Maastricht, the Netherlands. Professor Nys is the author of over 700 articles and books on medical law and healthcare policy. He is a member of the editorial boards of several learned journals and the editor-in-chief of the *European Journal of Health Law (EJHL)*.

He is co-founder and director of the European Association of Health Law (2008–2017) and vice-president of the World Association of Medical Law (2010–2012).

He is a member of the European Group of Ethics in Science and New Technologies (2021–2025).

Table of Contents

The Authors 3

List of Abbreviations 17

Acknowledgements 21

General Introduction 23

Chapter 1. General Background of the Country 23

§1. Geography and Climate 23

§2. Population and Cultural Composition 24

§3. Political and Judicial System 25
I. Political System and Government 25
II. Judicial System 27

§4. Social and Cultural Values Regarding Health 28

Chapter 2. General Description of the Healthcare System 30

§1. General Overview of the Luxembourg Healthcare System 30
I. Hospital Establishments and Hospital Care 30
A. Historical Background 30
B. Overview of the Hospital Sector 32
II. Independent Medical Practices and Private Out-of-Hospital Healthcare 35
III. Medical Laboratories and Pharmacies 37
IV. Long-Term Care 38
V. Cross-Border Healthcare 39
VI. Patient Organisations and Representation 41

§2. Regulation and Governance of the Healthcare System 41

§3. Financing of Healthcare and Health Insurance 45

Chapter 3. Sources of Medical Law 49

§1. International Sources of Medical Law 49
I. Instruments Protecting Fundamental Human Rights 49
II. European Union Law and Policy 52

§2. National Sources 54
I. Constitution 54
II. Laws ('Lois') 56
III. Grand-Ducal Regulations ('Règlements Grand-Ducaux') 57
IV. Further Sources 58

Part I. The Medical Profession 61

Chapter 1. Access to the Medical Profession 61

§1. Medical Training 61

§2. Freedom of Establishment, Recognition of Qualifications and Manpower Planning 62

§3. Authorisation to Practise Medicine and Temporary Service Provision 63
I. Standard Authorisation to Practise 63
II. Specific Temporary Authorisations 65
III. Duration and Lapsing 66
IV. Suspension and Revocation 66
V. Judicial Review 67
VI. Temporary Service Provision 67

Chapter 2. Practice of Medicine 69

§1. Legal Monopoly to Practise Medicine 69

§2. Medical Practices 69

§3. Professional Obligations and Rules of Conduct 70
I. Continuity of Care and Mandatory Duty Service 70
II. Insurance Coverage 70
III. Rules of Professional Conduct 71

§4. Use of Professional and Academic Titles 71

§5. Compliance with Social Security Legislation 72

§6. Professional Freedom 72

Chapter 3. Illegal Practice of Medicine 73

§1. ILLEGAL PRACTICE BY A NON-PROFESSIONAL 73

§2. ILLEGAL PRACTICE BY A HEALTHCARE PROFESSIONAL 75
I. Physicians and Dentists Assisting in Illegal Practise 75
II. Physicians Without a Regular Entitlement 76

§3. NON-CONVENTIONAL PRACTICES AND PROFESSIONS NOT RECOGNISED 76

§4. SANCTIONS 77

Chapter 4. Control over the Practice of Medicine 78

§1. MEDICAL COLLEGE AND RULES OF PROFESSIONAL CONDUCT 78
I. Introduction 78
II. Composition, Attributions and Functioning 78
III. Registration on the Ordinal Register 79
IV. Rules of Professional Conduct 80
A. Legally Determined Rules of Professional Conduct 80
B. Code of Medical Ethics 80
V. Disciplinary Action 82
A. Introduction 82
B. Scope and Nature of Disciplinary Action 82
C. Preparatory Phase of Disciplinary Action 83
D. Prescription Period and Interruption Thereof 84
E. Disciplinary Jurisdictions 84
1. Disciplinary Council of the Medical College 84
2. Superior Disciplinary Council of the Medical College 85
3. Cassation 86
F. Disciplinary Sanctions 86

§2. PROFESSIONAL LIABILITY 87
I. Civil Liability 88
A. Introduction 88
B. Legal Nature of Medical Liability: Tort or Contract? 89
C. Duties of the Physician 90
1. Physicians Have a Duty to Care in Conformity with Best Practice 90
2. Physicians Have a Safety Obligation with Regard to Certain Risks 90
3. Liability for Failure to Inform 91
4. Liability for Acts of Employees and Assistants 91
D. Liability of Hospitals 92
E. Damage and Causation 92
F. Prescription Period 93
II. Criminal Liability 94

§3. Quality Assurance 95

§4. Medical Ethics Committees 96
I. National Ethics Commission (Commission Nationale d'Ethique) 96
II. Ethics Committees in Hospitals 97
III. Ethics Committees for Long-Term Care 98
IV. Research Ethics Boards 98
A. National Research Ethics Committee (Comité National d'Ethique de Recherche) 98
B. University of Luxembourg Bodies 99
C. Luxembourg Agency for Research Integrity 99

§5. Social Security Jurisdictions 100

Part II. The Physician-Patient Relationship 101

Chapter 1. General Rights and Obligations of the Patient 101

§1. Introduction 101

§2. Scope of the Law on the Rights and Obligations of the Patient 102

§3. Privacy, Dignity and Respect of Religious and Philosophical Values (Article 3, §1) 103

§4. Patient Obligations 104

§5. Free Choice of Provider and Second Opinion 106
I. General Right to Free Choice 106
II. Second Opinion 107
III. Limitations 107

§6. Refusal of Care by the Physician 107

§7. Patient Companion 108

§8. Person of Trust 109

§9. Equal Access to Quality Care 109

§10. Right to Information about the State of Health 111
I. General Right to Information 111
II. How to Inform 111
III. Right Not to Know about One's State of Health 112
IV. Therapeutic Exception 113
V. Announcement Consultation 113

§11. Informed Consent and Decision-Making Process 113
I. Informed Consent: A Precondition to Healthcare Provision 113
II. Content of Adequate Prior Information 114
III. Expression and Proof of Informed Consent 115
IV. Shared Decision-Making 116
V. Presumed Consent in Cases of Emergency 117

§12. Refusal or Withdrawal of Consent 117
I. General Right to Refuse Care 117
II. Advance Refusal for Future Care 117
III. Mandatory Care Imposed by Law 117

§13. Patient File 118
I. Right to a Carefully Kept Patient File 118
II. Access Rights and Right to a Copy of the Patient File 119
III. Conservation of Patient Files 120
IV. Access by Next of Kin after the Death of a Patient 121
V. Patient File in Hospital 121

§14. Complaints and Mediation 122

Chapter 2. Medical Secrecy, Confidentiality and Data Protection 124

§1. Introduction 124

§2. Protection of Professional Secrecy under Article 458 of the Criminal Code 124
I. Scope of Article 458 of the Criminal Code 124
A. Persons Covered by the Duty of Secrecy 125
B. Professional Knowledge 125
C. Personal and Secret Information 126
II. Shared Professional Secrecy 126
III. Consent of the Patient or Waiver of Medical Secrecy 127
IV. Accompanying Person, Person of Trust, and Relatives 127
V. Testimony 128
VI. Reporting to Judicial or Police Authorities 129
VII. Statutory Obligations to Disclose 130
VIII. Consequences of an Infringement 130

§3. Complementary Protection of Confidentiality 131

§4. General Data Protection Regulation 131
I. Introduction 131
II. General Rule for Processing of Personal Health Data and Genetic Data 132

III. Derogation from the Prohibition on Processing of Data Regarding Health and Genetic Data 134
A. Compliance with the Principles Relating to Processing of Personal Data 134
B. One of the Following Justifications Applies 134
1. The Data Subject Has Given Explicit Consent 134
2. Necessity to Protect the Vital Interests of the Data Subject or of Another Natural Person 135
3. Necessary for Reasons of Substantial Public Interest 135
4. Necessary for Health-Related Purposes 135
5. Necessary for Reasons of Public Interest in the Area of Public Health 136
C. Comply with Member States Further Conditions 137
IV. Rights of the Data Subject 137
A. The Right to the Protection of Personal Data 137
B. Information to Be Provided Where Personal Data Are Collected from the Data Subject 137
C. The Right of Access by the Data Subject 138
D. Right to Rectification 139
E. Restricted Right to Erasure of Personal Health Data or Genetic Data ('Right to Be Forgotten') 139
F. Right to Restriction of Processing 140
G. Restricted Right to Portability of Health Data or Genetic Data 141
H. Right Not to Be Subject to Automated Individual Decision-Making, Including Profiling 141
I. Right to Transparent Information and Communication Concerning Rights of the Data Subject 142
J. Right to Lodge a Complaint and to an Effective Judicial Remedy 142
K. Right to Be Represented 143
L. Right to Compensation and Liability 143
V. Modalities for the Exercise of the Rights of the Data Subject 144
VI. Data Protection by Design and by Default 144
VII. Communication of a Personal Data Breach to the Data Subject 145
VIII. Data Protection Impact Assessment 145
IX. Designation of a Data Protection Officer When Health Data or Genetic Data Are Processed on a Large Scale 146

Chapter 3. End-of-Life Care (Palliative Care and Euthanasia) 147

§1. INTRODUCTION 147

§2. PALLIATIVE CARE 148
I. Introduction 148
II. Definition, Access, and Promotion of Palliative Care 149
III. Life-Shortening Effect of Pain Relief 150

IV. Cessation of Treatment at the Patient's Actual Request 150
V. Presumed Patient Will, Advance Directive and Person of Trust 150
VI. Cessation of Treatment Without Prospect 152
VII. End-of-Life Support Leave 152

§3. EUTHANASIA AND ASSISTED SUICIDE 153
I. Introduction 153
II. Definition of Euthanasia and of Assisted Suicide 153
III. Actual Request for Euthanasia or Assisted Suicide: Requirements and Procedure 154
A. Substantive Requirements 154
B. Formal and Procedural Requirements 155
IV. Advance Request for Euthanasia (End-of-Life Provisions) 157
A. Scope and Drafting of End-of-Life Provisions 157
B. Euthanasia Based on End-of-Life Provisions 158
V. Role and Functioning of the National Control and Evaluation Commission 159
A. Composition of the Commission 159
B. Mandatory Notification to the Commission 159
C. Functioning and Control by the Commission 160
D. Bi-annual Report 161
VI. Objection of Conscience 162
VII. Insurance Contracts 163

Chapter 4. Patients Not Capable to Exercise Their Rights (Autonomously) 164

§1. MINOR PATIENT 164
I. Introduction 164
II. Rights and Obligations Assigned to the Holder(s) of Parental Authority 164
III. Gradual Involvement and Autonomy of the Minor Patient 165
IV. Conflictual Situations 166
V. Urgent Need for Care 166

§2. ADULT PATIENT UNDER PROTECTIVE MEASURES 167
I. Introduction 167
II. Influence of Protective Regimes on the Exercise of Patient Rights 167
III. Urgent Need for Care 168

§3. PATIENTS DE FACTO NOT CAPABLE OF EXERCISING THEIR PATIENT RIGHTS 168

§4. PSYCHIATRIC PATIENTS AND HOSPITALISATION WITHOUT CONSENT 169
I. Introduction 169
II. Hospitalisation at the Request of a Third Party 170

A. Justifying Condition: Constitute a Danger to Oneself or to Others 170
B. Application for Admission 170
C. Initial Observation Period 171
D. Judicial Decision on Release or Placement 172
E. Treatment and Conditions of Stay 172
1. Involuntary Treatment 172
2. Permission to Leave 173
3. Visits 173
F. End of Hospitalisation Without Consent 173
G. Oversight 174
1. Supervisory Judge 174
2. District Court and Court of Appeal 174
3. Supervisory Commission 174
4. External Control of Places of Deprivation of Liberty 175
5. Information on Rights 175
III. Judicial Placement Order 175
A. Special Commission 175
B. District Court and Court of Appeal 176

Chapter 5. Specific Activities and Issues 177

§1. Preventive Medicine 177
I. Introduction 177
II. Perinatal Care, Childcare and School Medicine 177
III. Occupational Health 178
IV. Preventive Medicine Measures in Collaboration with CNS 179
V. Public Health Action Plans and Other Initiatives 180

§2. Prenatal Diagnosis, Genetic Testing and Genetic Counselling 180

§3. Medically Assisted Procreation 182
I. Introduction 182
II. Current Legislation and Soft Law 182
III. Regulatory Outlook 183

§4. Termination of Pregnancy (Abortion) 184
I. Introduction 184
II. Legal Conditions for Termination of Pregnancy 185
A. Termination Before the 12th Week of Pregnancy 185
B. Therapeutic Termination of Pregnancy 186
C. Prior Consultation of a Physician Specialised in Gynaecology and Obstetrics 186
D. Psychosocial Consultation 187
E. Termination of Pregnancy 187
F. Non-emancipated Minor Women 188

III. Objection of Conscience 188
IV. Illegal Termination of Pregnancy 188

§5. Vaccination 189

§6. Removal, Donation and Use of Human Bodily Material 190
I. Human Organs 191
A. Introduction 191
B. Scope of the Law on Organs Intended for Transplantation 191
C. Donation and Removal from Living Persons 192
D. Organ Removal from Deceased Persons 194
E. Gratuity of Donation and Prohibition of Financial Gain 195
F. Further Provisions 195
II. Tissues and Cells Intended for Human Applications 196
A. Scope of the Law on Human Tissues and Cells Intended for Human Applications 196
B. Removal for Donation from Living Persons 197
C. Surgical Leftovers 198
D. Removal from Deceased Persons 198
E. Allowed Purposes 198
F. Gratuity of Donation and Prohibition of Financial Gain 199
G. Further Provisions 199
III. Blood and Blood Components 199

§7. Digital Health (eHealth) 200
I. Introduction 200
II. National eHealth Agency and Services Platform 200
III. Electronic Healthcare Record ('Dossier de Soins Partagé') 201

§8. Biomedical Research 202
I. Introduction 202
II. Authorisation and Evaluation Pursuant to Article 27 of the Law on Hospitals 203
A. Field of Application 203
B. General Authorisation Process 204
III. Clinical Trials on Medicinal Products for Human Use 205
A. Grand-Ducal Regulation of 30 May 2005 205
B. Clinical Trials Regulation (Regulation 536/2014/UE) 206
1. Field of Application 206
2. Protection of Subjects of a Clinical Trial 207
3. Clinical Trials on Incapacitated Subjects 212
4. Clinical Trials on Minors 213
5. Clinical Trials on Pregnant or Breastfeeding Women 214
6. Clinical Trials on Other Vulnerable Subjects 214
7. Clinical Trials in Emergency Situations 215
IV. Medical Devices 216
V. Human Bodily Material 216

A. Organs 216
B. Tissues and Cells 216
C. Supernumerary Embryos, Gametes and Stem Cells 217

§9. Declaration of Death and Causes of Death, Autopsies and Mortal Remains 217
I. Declaration of Death and Causes of Death 217
II. Autopsies 218
III. Burial, Cremation and Mortal Remains 219

Part III. The Physician in Relation to the Healthcare System 221

Chapter 1. Collegial Relationships 221

§1. Professional Duties Towards Colleagues 221

§2. Associations of Physicians 222

Chapter 2. Relationship with Other Professions 224

§1. Pharmacists 224

§2. Psychotherapists 226

§3. Law on the Practice and Revalorisation of Certain Health Professions 227
I. Introduction 227
II. Healthcare Professions Covered 228
III. Overview of the Legal Framework 229

Chapter 3. Relationship with Healthcare Institutions 230

§1. Hospitals 230
I. General Overview 230
II. Practice of Hospital Medicine 231

§2. Private Healthcare Centres and Hospital Antennas 233

§3. Long-Term Care Institutions 236

Chapter 4. Relations with Social Security 238

§1. Mandatory Contracting with Social Security 238

§2. Convention for Physicians and Dentists 238

§3. Medical Fees and Nomenclature of Medical Fees 239

§4. Social Security Litigation 242
I. Social Security Supervisory Commission 242
II. Social Security Jurisdictions 243

Selected Bibliography 245

Index 247

List of Abbreviations

AMMD	Association des Médecins et Médecins-Dentistes (Union of Physicians and Dentists)
Ann. dr. lux.	Annales du droit luxembourgeois
BLQS	Bulletin luxembourgeois des questions sociales
C. Const.	Cour Constitutionnelle (Luxembourg Constitutional Court)
CA	Cour administrative (Luxembourg Administrative Court)
Cass.	Cour de Cassation (Luxembourg Court of Cassation)
CD	Conseil de Discipline du Collège Médical (Disciplinary Council of the Medical College)
CE	Conseil d'Etat (Council of State)
CGI	Comité de gestion interhospitalière (Interhospital Management Committee)
CHD	Chambre des Députés (Chamber of Deputies)
CHdN	Centre Hospitalier du Nord
CHEM	Centre Hospitalier Emile Mayrich
CHL	Centre Hospitalier de Luxembourg
CHNP	Centre Hospitalier Neuro-Psychiatrique
CJEU	Court of Justice of the European Union
CMSS	Contrôle médical de la sécurité sociale (Social Security Medical Board)
CNE	Commission Nationale d'Ethique (National Ethics Commission)
CNER	Comité National d'Ethique de Recherche (National Research Ethics Committee)
CNPD	Commission nationale pour la protection des données (National Commission for Data Protection)
CNS	Caisse nationale de Santé (National Health Fund)
CoE	Council of Europe
Cour	Cour d'appel (Court of Appeal)

List of Abbreviations

CPH	Commission Permanente du Secteur Hospitalier (Permanent Commission of the Hospital Sector)
CSD	Conseil Supérieur de Discipline du Collège Médical (Superior Disciplinary Council of the Medical College)
CSS	Code de la Sécurité Sociale (Social Security Code)
CSV	Chrëschtlech Sozial Vollekspartei (Christian Social People's Party)
CTIS	Clinical Trials Information System
DP	Demokratesch Partei (Democratic Party)
DSP	Dossier de Soins Partagé (Electronic Healthcare Record)
ECHR	European Convention on Human Rights
ECSC	European Coal and Steel Community
ECtHR	European Court of Human Rights
EEA	European Economic Area
EEC	European Economic Community
EJHL	European Journal of Health Law
EMA	European Medicines Agency
EU	European Union
FHL	Fédération des Hôpitaux Luxembourgeois (Luxembourg Federation of Hospitals)
GDPR	General Data Protection Regulation
GP	General Practitioner
HRS	Hôpitaux Robert Schuman
IGSS	Inspection générale de la sécurité sociale (General Inspectorate of Social Security)
JT	Journal des Tribunaux, Luxembourg
LARI	Luxembourg Agency for Research Integrity
LNS	National Health Laboratory
M3S	Ministère de la Santé et de la Sécurité sociale (Ministry of Health and Social Security)
MAP	Medically Assisted Procreation
NCG	National Centre of Genetics
OJEU	Official Journal of the European Union
Pas. lux.	Pasicrisie luxembourgeoise
PID	Paiement Immédiat Direct (Immediate Direct Electronic Payment)
RLDS	Revue luxembourgeoise Droit & Santé
TA	Tribunal administratif (Administrative Tribunal)

Trib. Lux.	Tribunal d'Arrondissement de Luxembourg (District Court of Luxembourg)
UN	United Nations (Organisation des Nations Unies)
WHO	World Health Organization (Organisation mondiale de la Santé)

List of Abbreviations

Acknowledgements

The authors would like to thank V. Besch, M. Harpes, J.-A. Marot, L. Mertz, M. Poos, K. Rausch, P. Schmit and M. Walch, who contributed to this book by their advice and availability to review it.

Acknowledgements

General Introduction

Chapter 1. General Background of the Country

§1. Geography and Climate[1]

1. The Grand Duchy of Luxembourg is lying at the heart of Western Europe. It covers an area of 2,586 km^2 (998 square miles) and measures 82 km (51 mi) long and 57 km (35 mi) wide.

2. The country's territory is divided into two geographical regions: the Oesling up north and the Guttland in the centre and south. In the east, Luxembourg is bordered by the Moselle, Sûre and Our rivers that form 135 km of natural border between the Grand Duchy and Germany. The Southern border with France is 73 km long and the Western border with Belgium is 148 km.

The Oesling ('Éislek'), in the northern part of the country, forms part of the Ardennes massif and borders the German Eifel region. It is a very green area covering 828 km^2, approximately one-third of the territory. The highest point in the Grand Duchy is situated in the Oesling in Wilwerdange (560 m). The main towns in this North are Wiltz, Clervaux and Vianden.

The Guttland, literally the 'good country', lies in the south and centre of the country. Together with the capital, it occupies the remainder of the country (68%, or 1.758 km^2). The Guttland is essentially made up of the capital, the countryside, forests and, in the south, mining regions. The City of Luxembourg is the largest city of Luxembourg with approx. 130,000 inhabitants. Luxembourg City is the capital of the Grand Duchy and a European capital. The old town of Luxembourg City has a long history and is a UNESCO World Heritage site. The origins and the name of Luxembourg, as a country as well as a city, go back to the acquisition of 'Lucilinburhuc' by Count Siegfried in the year 963.[2] To the east of the Guttland, the Moselle valley ('Musel') is the Grand Duchy's most impressive valley, both in terms of size and variety of landscapes. It is one of the country's main tourist attractions and a winemaking area. The lowest point in the Grand Duchy lies in Wasserbillig (130 m). The Mullerthal region ('Mëllerdall') lies in the northeast of the Guttland, bordering Germany. This region's particular appellation, 'Little Luxembourg Switzerland', is owed to the many rocky hills amidst which watercourses wind their way. The Land

1. Based on Luxembourg Government web portal, https://luxembourg.public.lu/en.html.
2. *History of Luxembourg City,* Luxembourg City Tourist Office (2022), https://www.luxembourg-city.com/en/about-luxembourg-city/presentation/history.

of the Red Rocks (or 'Minett') lies in the south of the country. The area has been moulded by industry where iron ore was extracted from the red earth. Today, former industrial wastelands have been urbanised or converted into nature reserves. The Minett is the most densely populated region of Luxembourg. The second largest city, Esch-sur-Alzette (36.177 inh.), and larger towns lie here (Bettembourg, Differdange, Dudelange, Kayl, and Schifflange). Esch-Belval also welcomes the University of Luxembourg. The young campus of the University in Esch-Belval attracts scientific and research activities in the fields of biomedicine.

3. Luxembourg enjoys a moderately continental climate, with generally mild winters and mild summers. Over the past few years, the number of summer days with over 30°C (86°F) has risen significantly.

§2. Population and Cultural Composition[3]

4. Luxembourg has a population of 660.809 inhabitants on 1 January 2023 and an average of 255.5 inhabitants per km^2. It is thus one of the most densely populated regions of Europe (average European Union (EU): 118). In the Grand Duchy, the City of Luxembourg (132.780 inhabitants) and the town of Esch-sur-Alzette (36.625 inhabitants) are the most populous.

The population has been steadily growing since 1945, mainly through immigration. Today, Luxembourg hosts large foreign communities, including descendants of nineteenth and twentieth-century migrants and expats.

Almost half of the population is of foreign nationality (47.4%). On 1 January 2023, 313.407 foreign nationals were living in the Grand Duchy, of whom 12.9% were born in Luxembourg. Nationals of EU Member States alone account for 78.4% of the foreign population in Luxembourg. There is a diversification of immigration and the share of people with a non-EU-27 nationality is on the rise. Over 170 nationalities are present. The largest foreign communities are Portuguese (13.9% of pop.), French (7.4%), Belgian (2.9%) and German (1.9%) nationality.

5. In the last quarter of 2022, around 224.000 cross-border commuters journey to Luxembourg from France, Germany and Belgium to work and contribute to the country's wealth. They form about 47% of domestic employment (+/– 479.000).[4] There are further over 10.000 international officials and civil servants present in Luxembourg. The importance of cross-border commuters explains the high number of persons affiliated with social security. In 2022, there were 936.254 affiliates to the Luxembourg health insurance, amongst which 336.733 were non-residents.[5]

3. *La démographie luxembourgeoise en chiffres – Edition 2023*, Statec (2023), https://statistiques.public.lu/dam-assets/catalogue-publications/en-chiffres/2023/demographie-en-chiffres-2023.pdf.
4. *Regards 06/23 – Panorama sur le monde du travail luxembourgeois à l'occasion du 1er Mai*, Statec (2023).
5. *Rapport annuel 2022*, CNS (2023).

6. The linguistic situation in Luxembourg is characterised by the practice and recognition of three official languages: French, German, and the national language, Luxembourgish, which was recognised in 1984. These three official languages are the three administrative languages. For historical and legal reasons, French enjoys a preferential position in Administration and the judicial system. For legislative texts, the French language version is used. At the same time, citizens can apply to the administration in any of the three administrative languages, and officials are requested to respond in the language used by the citizens.[6] English is frequently used in a professional context.

As of 2018, 98% of the population was able to speak French at more or less a high level (usually as a second language), 78% spoke German, and 77% Luxembourgish.[7]

7. Luxembourg's population is ageing; immigration explains that the proportion of elderly people is, however, lower in Luxembourg than in its European neighbouring countries. In 2021, the share of the population aged 65 and over was 14.6% in Luxembourg, compared with 20.7% in France, 19.3% in Belgium and 22.0% in Germany.

Luxembourg has seen a continuous increase in life expectancy up to 2019, and life expectancy continues to increase after a moderate fall in 2020 due to COVID-19 deaths.[8] In 2021, life expectancy at birth was 80.7 years for men and 84.90 years for women.

§3. Political and Judicial System

I. Political System and Government

8. After occupation by Revolutionary France, the 1815 Vienna Congress transformed Luxembourg into a Grand Duchy that was constitutionally distinct but in personal union with the Sovereign of the Netherlands. Luxembourg remained at the same time within the German Confederation, and a Prussian military garrison was established in the capital. The 1867 Treaty of London confirmed independence. The Prussian garrison was withdrawn, and the fortress was dismantled. The personal union with the Netherlands remained until 1890 when Grand Duke Adolphe ascended to the throne.[9]

---

6. *About … Languages in Luxembourg*, Information and Press Service of the Luxembourg Government (2022), https://sip.gouvernement.lu/en/publications/minist-etat/sip/brochure/a-propos/A_propos_Langues.html.
7. *TNS-ILRES Survey*, Press Release, Luxembourg Government (2018), https://gouvernement.lu/fr/actualites/toutes_actualites/articles/2018/06-juin/07-luxembourgeois.html.
8. *Après une légère surmortalité en 2020, la mortalité retrouve un niveau plus normal en 2021*, Regards No. 7, Statec (2022).
9. At the death of William III of the Netherlands (1890), by virtue of the Nassau Family Pact applicable to Luxembourg but not to the Netherlands, inheritance by females was not allowed. As a result, Adolphe of the branch of Nassau-Weilburg, ascended to the Luxembourg throne. Wilhelmina, the only surviving child of King William III, ascended the throne of the Netherlands.

9. The Grand Duchy of Luxembourg is today a representative democracy in the form of a constitutional monarchy, and sovereign power resides in the nation. The Constitution sets out the rights and liberties, the organisation and separation of powers, the role of the Grand Duke and the country's main institutions (*See:* General Introduction, Chapter 3., §2., I., Constitution).

10. The Grand Duke and the Parliament exercise the legislative power collectively; the executive power is vested in the Grand Duke and his ministers; and the judicial power is in the hands of the Courts and Tribunals.

11. The Grand Duke,[10] currently Grand Duke Henri, is the Head of State but does not rule. This means that although he appoints and dismisses his ministers, his person is inviolable, and his ministers are responsible. No act of the Grand Duke is effective unless a minister countersigns it.

12. Luxembourg's parliament, the Chamber of Deputies ('Chambre des Députés' (CHD)),[11] exercises legislative power. It is composed of sixty Deputies, elected through a direct election conducted in the four electoral circumscriptions (South – twenty-three seats; Centre – twenty-one seats; North – nine seats; and East – seven seats).

13. Following the October 2023 general elections, Luxembourg is governed by a two-party coalition composed of the Christian Social People's Party ('CSV – Chrëschtlech Sozial Vollekspartei') with twenty-one seats and the Democratic Party ('DP – Demokratesch Partei') with fourteen seats, totalling a majority of thirty-five seats in the sixty seats Chamber of Deputies. The main opposition party is the Luxembourg Socialist Workers Party ('LSAP – Lëtzebuerger Sozialistesch Aarbechterpartei') with eleven seats, followed by the Alternative Democratic Reform Party ('ADR – Alternativ Demokratesch Reformpartei') with five seats, the Greens ('Déi Gréng') with four seats, the Pirate Party ('Piratepartei') with three seats and the Left Party ('Déi Lénk') with two seats.

The current Prime Minister of Luxembourg is Luc Frieden (CSV), seconded by Vice-Prime Minister Xavier Bettel (DP). The current Minister of Health and Social Security is Martine Deprez (CSV).

14. The Council of State ('Conseil d'Etat' (CE))[12] was established in 1856 as an unelected advisory organ. It acts as a second chamber with a suspensive veto right for legislative matters. It is composed of twenty-one councillors nominated by the Grand Duke upon an alternate proposal by the Government, the Chamber of Deputies, and the Council of State. The Council of State acted as Administrative Court until 1996

10. Official website: https://monarchie.lu/en.
11. Official website: https://www.chd.lu.
12. Official website: https://conseil-etat.public.lu.

when this function was transferred to a newly created administrative branch of jurisdictions.[13]

15. The Government and the Parliament are further aided in the execution of their duties by consultative bodies. In the domain of medical law, the main consultation bodies are the Medical College ('Collège Médical'), the Superior Council of Certain Health Professions ('Conseil Supérieur de Certaines Professions de Santé') and the Permanent Commission of the Hospital Sector ('Commission Permanente du Secteur Hospitalier') (CPH). Consultation is mandatory for any normative act affecting their domain of competence.

The consultation of the Union of Physicians and Dentists ('Association des Médecins et Médecins-Dentistes' (AMMD)), as the most representative union for physicians, is mandatory in certain domains[14] and generally observed for norms affecting the medical profession.

There is no obligation to consult patient organisations in the legislative and regulatory process. Patient organisations are, however, frequently asked to issue a statement or take the initiative to formulate a statement.

16. The Ombudsman of the Grand Duchy ('Ombudsman')[15] is an independent institution dealing with complaints concerning the functioning of central and municipal administrations and other appertaining public institutions or bodies, including the social security institutions. The Ombudsman has further been designated as a national preventive mechanism performing regular visits to places where people are deprived of their liberty, including in closed psychiatric units.

II. Judicial System[16]

17. Luxembourg shares with France and Belgium a common legal tradition and legal principles originating from the Napoleonic codifications.[17] The legal system is based on written legislation, mainly Laws and Grand-Ducal Regulations. The French language is used for legislation.

Luxembourg law can be divided into two principal areas: private law and public law. Private law includes civil law and criminal law. Public law includes administrative law and constitutional law.

---

13. The administrative branch of jurisdictions was established following the ECtHR questioning of the double role of the Council of State in the case of *Procola v. Luxembourg* (ECtHR, 28 Sep. 1995, No. 14570/89).
14. Health legislation partly requests the consultation of the 'most representative union for physicians' prior to regulate certain matters by a Grand-Ducal Regulation. Generally, consultation of AMMD is however not mandatory, whereas the consultation of the Medical College is generally mandatory.
15. Official website: https://www.ombudsman.lu.
16. Based upon the official website (in French): https://justice.public.lu/fr/organisation-justice.html.
17. All five Codes adopted under Napoleon between 1804 and 1810 applied to Luxembourg. In Luxembourg, the 'Code Civil' (1804) and the 'Code de commerce' (1807) are still in force, although frequently amended. The Belgian Criminal Code (1867) inspired the Luxembourg Criminal Code (1879).

18. Courts and Tribunals are organised into two main juridical branches: an ordinary judicial branch, which deals with civil, commercial, and penal disputes, and an administrative branch. These are completed by specialised jurisdictions, in particular, the social jurisdictions when it comes to matters concerning social security.

Within the ordinary judicial branch, the Grand Duchy is divided into two judicial districts with a District Court ('Tribunal d'arrondissement') in Luxembourg City and a second District Court in Diekirch. There are three Justices of the Peace ('Justices de Paix'): Luxembourg City, Esch/Alzette, and Diekirch. The Justices of the Peace are the first instances jurisdictions for civil and commercial disputes over minor value (below EUR 15,000) and unlimited competence for some specific matters (housing leases; attachment of earnings). Appeal of the judgments of the Justices of Peace is before the District Courts. Appeal of first instance decisions of the District Courts is before the Court of Appeal. Cassation is always before the Court of Cassation.

The administrative branch, which rules on disputes with central and local authorities, is composed of an Administrative Tribunal ('Tribunal administratif' (TA)). Appeal is before the Administrative Court ('Cour administrative'). Cassation is before the Court of Cassation.

The social jurisdictions are composed of the 'Arbitration Council for Social Security' ('Conseil arbitral de la sécurité sociale') and the 'Superior Council for Social Security' ('Conseil supérieur de la sécurité sociale'). Cassation is before the Court of Cassation.

At the top of the hierarchy stands the Supreme Court of Justice ('Cour supérieure de Justice') which comprises the Court of Cassation ('Cour de Cassation') and the Court of Appeal ('Cour d'Appel') for the ordinary judicial branch and the social jurisdictions. It further comprises the Supreme Prosecutor's Office ('Parquet Général)'. The Supreme Court of Justice is based in Luxembourg City.

The Court of Cassation has general authority (judiciary, social and administrative matters), and it is the Court of last instance for questions arising from the infringement of a law or substantial procedural or regulatory violation under penalty of nullity. It is judging the legality, but it does not judge the merits of the case.

The Constitutional Court, established in 1997, performs an *a posteriori* control of the constitutionality of Laws. It gives a preliminary ruling on the compatibility with the Constitution when a case is referred to it by ordinary courts. It does not judge the merits of the case and does not have the power to invalidate *a priori* legislative acts. The effect of a decision invalidating a legal disposition may be postponed in time to avoid a legal vacuum.

§4. Social and Cultural Values Regarding Health

19. Fundamental values which guide Luxembourg healthcare and social security system are universal access, solidarity, and equitable access to high-quality care.

20. Luxembourg health law has, over the last twenty years, shifted from a moderately conservative approach towards a progressive liberal and patient-centred approach. Health law currently highly values personal autonomy, including when it comes to controversial bioethical issues. Luxembourg legalised euthanasia and assisted suicide in 2009. The 1979 abortion law was liberalised in 2011 and 2014. An autonomy-based patient rights law was adopted in 2014. A high value is further attributed to the patient's right to choose the preferred healthcare provider, including direct access to specialised care.

This shift in health law values parallels a shift in societal values. Over 80% of the population approved in a 2020 survey a liberal approach on bioethical issues such as euthanasia or artificial insemination and favoured cultural liberalism on other fundamental societal issues, such as same-sex marriage.[18]

21. The right to healthcare and long-term care is ensured through a mandatory public insurance scheme for health, accident and long-term care that covers nearly the entire population. There is a comparatively low level of cost-sharing by patients.

Luxembourg has a 'Bismarck' social health insurance system based on compulsory contributions from the working population, with a relatively high statal contribution to social security. Social partners (representatives of employers and employees) play an important role in the governance of the mandatory insurance regime, pursuant to the principle of autonomy of social partners.

22. A central role is attributed to self-employed physicians and other self-employed private healthcare providers. At the same time, mandatory contracting of physicians and most other categories of private healthcare providers, in conjunction with mandatory fee schedules, are an important characteristic of the social security system, ensuring solidarity and equal access to healthcare.

18. 'Studialux 2021' data, *Les valeurs de la société luxembourgeoise,* interview Prof. Ph. Poirier, Chamber Aktuell, 13 mars 2022, Chambre des Députés (2022), https://www.chd.lu/fr/node/515.

Chapter 2. General Description of the Healthcare System

§1. General Overview of the Luxembourg Healthcare System

23. State played historically only a minor role when it comes to public health issues. The first public health laws date from the late nineteenth century and early twentieth century and are concerned with the fight against infectious diseases (cholera and plague) and poor hygiene conditions at a local level.[19] Until 1945, public health competencies were mainly exercised by regional medical inspectors ('médecins inspecteurs cantonaux') and the Medical College.[20] No ministry dedicated to public health existed until 1945.[21]

24. Currently, given the size of the country, the healthcare system is relatively centralised. When it comes to the organisation, the legal regime and the financing of healthcare, differences exist. We will briefly give a general overview of healthcare provision, focussing on the following subdivisions:

(I) hospital establishments and hospital care;
(II) independent medical practices and private out-of-hospital healthcare;
(III) medical laboratories and pharmacies;
(IV) long-term care;
(V) cross-border healthcare.
To complete the overview, we will focus on the role of patients and patient organisations (VI).

I. Hospital Establishments and Hospital Care

A. Historical Background

25. The first hospitals in Luxembourg were established by religious orders. After the French Revolution, hospitals started to be run by municipalities as 'Hospice Civil'. With industrialisation and societal changes linked to it, steel companies started creating industry infirmaries and hospitals within or near their industrial sites

19. Loi du 25 mars 1885, concernant les mesures à prendre pour parer à l'invasion et à la propagation des maladies contagieuses, Mém. A – 20 du 04.04.1885, https://legilux.public.lu/eli/etat/leg/loi/1885/03/25/n2/jo; Loi du 18 mai 1902 concernant l'institution des médecins-inspecteurs et l'exercice de leurs attributions, Mém. A – 33 du 25.05.1902, https://legilux.public.lu/eli/etat/leg/loi/1902/05/18/n4/jo; Loi du 27 juin 1906, concernant la protection de la santé publique, Mém. A – 40 du 02.07.1906. https://legilux.public.lu/eli/etat/leg/loi/1906/06/27/n3/jo.
20. Loi du 18 mai 1902 concernant l'institution des médecins inspecteurs et l'exercice de leurs attributions, Mém. A – 3 du 24.05.1902, https://legilux.public.lu/eli/etat/leg/loi/1902/05/18/n4/jo.
21. Nati, R., *Etapes essentielles de l'organisation sanitaire, médicale et hospitalière au Luxembourg*, in: *Le Conseil d'État face à l'évolution de la société luxembourgeoise*, pp. 195–214, Conseil d'Etat (2006).

and participated in the creation of hospitals by municipalities.[22] Even for such hospitals created by lay initiatives or run by municipalities, collaborations were generally put in place with religious orders and nuns were charged to care of the sick.[23] Physicians were nearly exclusively self-employed external physicians, operating on a fee-for-service basis paid by the patient. In 1901, mandatory health insurance was introduced for workers[24] and quickly expanded to cover almost the entire population.[25]

26. The first direct statal initiative, in 1855, concerns the creation of a central asylum, 'Hospice Central' to lock away vagabonds, child orphans, the 'insane', and other forms of marginality in the area of former barracks in the town of Ettelbruck. In 1901, the name of the 'Hospice Central' was changed to 'Maison de Santé' and the institution was transformed into an exclusively psychiatric asylum. The institution directly run by State changed its name to 'Hôpital Neuro-Psychiatrique de l'Etat' in 1974. The former asylum is currently a public establishment called 'Centre Hospitalier Neuro-psychiatrique (CHNP)' governed by the amended Law of 17 April 1998.[26] The focus of CHNP is today on active psychiatric rehabilitation, as well as on support for people with mental disabilities. The CHNP further runs a residential care setting for the elderly.

State acquired in 1886 the thermal bath of Mondorf-les-Bains, currently governed by a modified Law of 1987.[27] The sanatarium of Vianden opened in 1931, receiving mainly tuberculosis patients until it was converted into a facility for the elderly at the end of the 1970s.

One may further note that in 1877, a state midwifery school and a maternity clinic were created in Luxembourg City[28] and were integrated in 1975 into the then-newly created Centre Hospitalier de Luxembourg (CHL).

27. State gradually aspired and gained influence in oversight and governance of the hospital sector after 1945. The 1960s/1970s marked a turning point. In the early 1960s, the so-called Sunier Report evaluated psychiatric care. It was followed by a

22. *La santé publique dans le bassin minier. L'évolution de la santé publique dans le sud du Luxembourg (1870–2020)*, Mutations, No. 12, Fondation Bassin Minier (2022).
23. Consbruck, R., *A Brief History of Hospitals in the Grand Duchy of Luxembourg*, Ministère de la Santé (2010), https://sante.public.lu/fr/publications/h/histoire-succincte-hopitaux-lux-fr-de-en.html.
24. Loi du 31 juillet 1901 concernant l'assurance obligatoire des ouvriers contre les maladies, Mém. A – 53 du 08.08.1901, https://legilux.public.lu/eli/etat/leg/loi/1901/07/31/n1/jo.
25. *See:* §3. Financing of Healthcare and Health Insurance *infra*.
26. Loi du 17 avril 1998 portant création d'un établissement public dénommé centre hospitalier neuropsychiatrique, Mém. A – 31 du 27.04.1998, https://legilux.public.lu/eli/etat/leg/loi/1998/04/17/n1/jo; for a historical overview: Majerus, J.-M., *Das Centre Hospitalier Neuro-Psychiatrique*, in: Willems, H. et al. (dir.), *Handbuch der sozialen und erzieherischen Arbeit in Luxemburg*, Luxemburg (2009), pp. 113–125; De Smet, Y., *Histoire de la psychiatrie en Luxembourg – L'hospice Central d'Ettelbruck (1854–1904),* Ed. Phi, Luxembourg (2022).
27. Loi du 18 décembre 1987 organisant le centre thermal et de santé de Mondorf-les-Bains, Mém. A 101 – du 21.12.1987, https://legilux.public.lu/eli/etat/leg/loi/1987/12/18/n1/jo.
28. Loi du 15 avril 1877 concernant la création d'une école d'accouchement et d'un établissement de maternité. Mém. A – 25 du 05.05.1877, https://legilux.public.lu/eli/etat/leg/loi/1877/04/15/n1/jo.

modernisation of the 'Maison de Santé' (later CHNP) and the development of community psychiatry.[29] The 'Aujaleu-Rösch report'[30] of 1972 identified and prioritised the main public health problems of the time, drawing up a medium and long-term development plan. This report was followed by the creation of the public establishment called 'CHL' in 1975.[31] At the time, the CHL was innovative and aspired to establish a modern organisational form and encourage participation in research. It was the first – and to date only – hospital to operate under a 'closed regime' with salaried physicians and entirely lay paramedical staff. At the same time, in 1976, the first Luxembourg Law on hospitals planning and hospital organisation was adopted, inspired by the Belgian and French legislation of the time.[32] The same year saw the adoption of law allowing the state to finance hospital modernisation, as well as financial support to the establishment of physicians and health professionals.[33]

28. The hospital landscape has been modernised and concentrated in the years that followed. From the thirty-six hospitals that were still existing in 1986, many have been converted into facilities for the elderly, childcare centres, or dedicated to other purposes. There have further been fusions of hospitals and new modern hospitals have been built with public funding. This led to relative concentration of the actors around four general hospitals regionally distributed, complemented by specialised hospitals. This shift in the hospital landscape was facilitated by the rising influence of hospital planning and considerable State funding, even though public authorities tended to act as facilitators rather than as strong decision-makers.[34]

B. *Overview of the Hospital Sector*

29. There is currently a relatively dense regulation of the hospital sector in comparison to non-hospital healthcare. The amended Law of 8 March 2018 on hospital establishments and hospital planning,[35] hereinafter referred to as 'Law on hospitals', sets the general legal framework applicable to hospital establishments.

29. It was followed in the 1990/2000s by the 'Häfner report' and 'Rössler plan'. *See:* Part II., Ch. 4., §4. Psychiatric Patients and Hospitalisation without Consent.
30. Aujaleu, E. & Roesch, G., *Plan de développement des services de santé publique du Grand-Duché de Luxembourg. Rapport sur une mission, novembre-décembre 1971,* OMS – Bureau régional de l'Europe, Copenhague (1972).
31. Loi du 10 décembre 1975 créant un établissement public dénommé Centre hospitalier de Luxembourg, groupant la maternité Grande-Duchesse Charlotte, la clinique pédiatrique fondation Grand-Duc Jean et Grande-Duchesse Joséphine-Charlotte et l'Hôpital municipal, Mém. A – 83 du 19.12.1975, https://legilux.public.lu/eli/etat/leg/loi/1975/12/10/n1/jo.
32. Loi du 29 août 1976 portant planification et organisation hospitalières, Mem. A – 57 du 24.09.1976, https://legilux.public.lu/eli/etat/leg/loi/1976/08/29/n5/jo.
33. Loi du 17 décembre 1976 ayant pour objet de garantir un équipement médical et hospitalier ainsi qu'une répartition régionale des prestations médicales conformes aux besoins du pays, Mem. A – 80 du 24.12.1976, http://data.legilux.public.lu/eli/etat/leg/loi/1976/12/17/n2/jo.
34. Leist, A., *Luxembourg*, in: Immergut, E., et al. (eds), *Health Politics in Europe: A Handbook*, Oxford University Press (2021).
35. Loi modifiée du 8 mars 2018 relative aux établissements hospitaliers et à la planification hospitalière, Mém. A – 22 du 28.03.2018, https://legilux.public.lu/eli/etat/leg/loi/2018/03/08/a222/jo.

The hospital sector is subject to detailed planning; the Law on hospitals fixes the total number of hospitals and hospital services on a national level, as well as core standards and norms applicable to the different types of hospital services. It further lays down the general organisation and governance structures of hospitals. Grand-Ducal Regulations further implement the Law on hospitals.

30. The Law on hospitals foresees two sectorial bodies:

- The Permanent Commission of the Hospital Sector ('Commission Permanente du Secteur Hospitalier – CPH'). It is composed of representatives of the Ministry of Health and Social Security (Ministère de la Santé et de la Sécurité sociale (M3S)), the Ministry of Finance, the National Health Fund (Caisse nationale de Santé (CNS)), the Luxembourg Federation of Hospitals (Fédération des Hôpitaux Luxembourgeois (FHL)), the medical profession and of the non-medical healthcare professions. It must be consulted on issues related to the hospital legislation, on requests for authorisation of a hospital, for authorisation of a hospital service, or for modifications thereof, as well as for Government financial support for hospital investments.[36]
- The Interhospital Management Committee ('Comité de gestion interhospitalière – CGI'). It is composed of representatives of the hospital establishments and of their medical councils, of the non-medical healthcare professions, of the M3S, CNS, and comprises a patient representative. It is notably contributing to the establishment of integrated care networks and the national coordination of hospital quality insurance.[37]

31. Since the last hospital fusion in 2014, the hospital landscape has been composed of four regionally distributed general hospitals. There are a further nine entities with a specialised offer falling under hospital legislation.

The four general hospitals are regionally distributed, with a main hospital site and one or two secondary sites for each general hospital. The Centre Hospitalier du Nord (CHdN) is situated in the North with hospital sites in Ettelbruck and Wiltz. The Centre Hospitalier Emile Mayrich (CHEM) is situated in the South with sites in Esch/Alzette, Dudelange and Niederkorn. The CHL has two sites located in Luxembourg-Strassen and Luxembourg-Eich. Hôpitaux Robert Schuman (HRS) has one site in Luxembourg-Gare, one in Luxembourg-Kirchberg and a third one in Esch/Alzette. Since the amendment of the Law on hospitals adopted in 2023, general hospitals have been allowed to open 'hospital antennas' that exclusively provide ambulatory care out of the main or secondary hospital site.[38]

These general hospitals provide general medical, surgical and childbirth facilities to the population. They offer planned care, as well as acute emergency care. Every general hospital has a psychiatric department that treats adult psychiatric patients for short acute stays.

---

36. Article 22, Law on hospitals.
37. Article 28, Law on hospitals.
38. *See:* Part III., Ch. 3., §2. Private Healthcare Centres and Hospital Antennas *infra*.

If rehabilitation is necessary, psychiatric patients are referred to the CHNP. Child and juvenile psychiatry are centralised in a specialised unit of the HRS site in Luxembourg-Kirchberg. Several specialised services are available only in one general hospital, as so-called national hospital services. This is the case in the fields of paediatric surgery, neurosurgery, intensive neonatology, specialised ophthalmology, paediatric emergency services, intensive paediatric care and certain specific specialised paediatric services, as well as for the level 2 stroke unit. There is also one national assisted reproduction lab.

32. There are further specialised hospital establishments dedicated to each of the following specialised specific activities: invasive treatment of cardiac diseases; radiation therapy; psychiatric rehabilitation; functional re-education and re-adaptation; physical and post-oncology rehabilitation; geriatric rehabilitation; end-of-life care centre; thermal treatment.

The National Health Laboratory (LNS) operates the National Centre of Genetics (NCG), a centre falling under the hospital legislation that provides genetic counselling and diagnosis of genetic diseases and carries out molecular and genetic analysis of cancers.[39]

The establishment of a military hospital, to be run in cooperation with the existing general hospitals and available to civilians, is considered to strengthen urgency and disaster capacities while raising military spending required by international commitments.[40]

33. In 2021, Luxembourg had 2,667 hospital beds, including 2,042 acute beds and 558 medium stay beds.[41] This corresponds to a ratio of 4.2 hospital beds per 1,000 inhabitants in 2021, which is slightly below the EU average and lower than the neighbouring countries. In terms of acute beds, the ratio is 3.2 per 1,000 inhabitants, which is quite lower than in Germany and Belgium but higher than in Switzerland, France, or the Netherlands. Between 2015 and 2019, the annual occupancy rate of acute hospital beds varied between 72.9% and 78.1%.

Health policy has been promoting a switch towards ambulatory care for several years,[42] as soon as ambulatory care can be provided without a loss of quality of care for the patient. From 2010 to 2019, day hospitalisation has risen sharply and represents 44.8% of total admissions in 2019 compared to 31% in 2010. The rate of ambulatory surgery for tracer procedures increased from 58.9% in 2015 to 68.5% in 2019. Overall, from 2010 to 2019, hospital admissions have increased, but they are of shorter duration.[43]

39. *See:* Part II., Ch. 5., §2. Prenatal Diagnosis, Genetic Testing and Genetic Counselling *infra*.
40. *Luxembourg Government Coalition Agreement 2023–2028*, p. 31, https://gouvernement.lu/fr/publications/accord-coalition/accord-de-coalition-2023-2028/accord-de-coalition-2023-2028.html.
41. *Carte Sanitaire – mise à jour 2021,* Observatoire de la Santé (2022), https://sante.public.lu/fr/espace-obsante/carte-sanitaire.html.
42. Article 19 of the repealed Grand-Ducal Regulation of 13 Mar. 2009 establishing the hospital plan, Mém. A – 54 du 23.03.2009, https://legilux.public.lu/eli/etat/leg/rgd/2009/03/13/n6/jo.
43. *Carte Sanitaire – mise à jour 2021,* Observatoire de la Santé (2022), https://sante.public.lu/fr/espace-obsante/carte-sanitaire.html.

34. The installation of heavy medical equipment requires approval from the Minister of Health and Social Security and the total number of such heavy equipment is fixed by the hospital legislation. Furthermore, the acquisition of hospital equipment exceeding a value of EUR 250,000 needs prior approval.[44]

Luxembourg counts eleven scanners in general hospitals as well as twelve MRIs. There are further seven gamma cameras, eight mammography machines, one PET-CT and one prone-table. An authorisation for one scanner and one PET-CT are pending.[45]

(*See also:* Part III., Chapter 3., §1. Hospitals *infra.*)

II. Independent Medical Practices and Private Out-of-Hospital Healthcare

35. Luxembourg has the second lowest number of physicians in the EU, with approximately 3.0 physicians per 1.000 population in 2019 (compared to 3.9 across the EU) despite an increase of 39% since the year 2000. Over the same period, population increased by 42%. The share of physicians living outside the country but practising in Luxembourg nearly doubled between 2008 and 2017 (from 15.6% to 26.4%). General Practitioners (GPs) account for about one-third of physicians, which is higher than the EU average (21%). The physician workforce is ageing: more than half of practising GPs (54.4%) and nearly two-third of specialists (60%) were over the age of 50 in 2017. In contrast, the number of nurses in Luxembourg has increased continually over the last few years, and its density is one of the highest in the EU.[46]

36. GPs, or paediatricians for childcare, provide primary healthcare. Private dental practitioners provide primary dental care. GPs have no gatekeeper function. Patients have a free choice of the first doctor to contact, and specialists provide primary healthcare. There is accordingly a lack of a clear distinction between the roles of GPs and specialists. Luxembourg scores low in categories such as primary care governance and continuity of primary care, leading to a low ranking for the strength of the total primary care system in comparative studies.[47]

37. Most of the population has a regular GP; the share of patients without a regular GP is, however, growing. Traditionally, most GPs operated as a private practice without any staff, except perhaps a medical secretary. Group practices with several GPs are nowadays frequent.

44. Article 14, Law on hospitals.
45. Department of health data provided to the authors (03/2024).
46. OECD/European Observatory on Health Systems and Policies, *Luxembourg: Country Health Profile 2021*, State of Health in the EU, OECD Publishing, Paris/European Observatory on Health Systems and Policies, Brussels (2021), https://www.oecd.org/publications/luxembourg-country-health-profile-2021-3c147ce7-en.htm.
47. Berthet, F., et al., *Luxembourg: HiT in brief*, WHO Regional Office for Europe, European Observatory on Health Systems and Policies (2015).

So-called medical houses (maisons médicales) ensure a replacement service for GPs to provide primary healthcare at night, on weekends and on public holidays when medical practices are closed.

One centralised 'paediatric medical house' run by a shift of paediatricians is available in Luxembourg City within the CHL-KannerKlinik premises. The paediatric departments of the general hospitals further provide urgent paediatric care.

38. Self-employed medical specialists provide specialist medical care in private practices. Most medical specialists divide their time between their private practice and hospital work. Even when working in a hospital establishment, medical specialists are generally self-employed. Only one hospital (CHL) works mainly with physicians who are employees of the hospital.

Private specialist practices are generally operated independently, frequently regrouping several physicians of the same specialty admitted to practice in the same hospital. A growing number of specialist private practices are established within the premises of a hospital or in a nearby separate building operated by the hospital.

39. Private group practices traditionally regrouped only physicians active in the same field; this has, however, evolved over the last decade. Health centres regrouping GPs and specialists are more and more frequent. Specialised healthcare remains comparatively hospital-centric; there are, however, recent initiatives to offer a broader scope of ambulatory care through dedicated structures.[48]

40. The 2010 healthcare reform introduced a 'reference doctor' scheme ('médecin référent'), as well as a Electronic Healthcare Record ('dossier de soins partagé' or 'DSP') to strengthen coordination of care and facilitate access to essential information about the patient's state of health. The reference doctor scheme is defined by Article 19bis of the Social Security Code (*Code de la Sécurité Sociale* (CSS)) and currently targets patients with long-term health affection. The role of the reference doctor, who may be a GP or a paediatrician, is to guide his patient through the healthcare system. Patients that chose a reference doctor keep at the same time a direct access to all types of healthcare; the reference doctor has no formal gatekeeping function. The reference doctor is also responsible for updating the medical file and supervising the DSP of his patient. Having an active DSP is a precondition to enrolling on the reference doctor scheme. After more than ten years, the impact and take-up remain limited for both the reference doctor scheme and the DSP.[49]

41. Besides the medical profession, the provision of many other healthcare services is organised as a self-employed independent profession unless delivered within a hospital establishment. This is notably the case for dieticians, midwives, nurses, occupational therapists, physiotherapists, psychotherapists, and speech therapists.

48. *See:* Part III., Ch. 3., §2. Private Healthcare Centres and Hospital Antennas *infra*.
49. *See:* Part II., Ch. 5., §7., III. Electronic Healthcare Record *infra*.

42. Privately established midwives assist in the prenatal and postnatal period. Pregnant women may give birth at home and can be accompanied and supervised by a midwife during their delivery. Out-of-hospital childbirth is, however, relatively rare. Pursuant to the introduction of a specific nomenclature tariff for out-of-hospital delivery by midwives,[50] a birthing house operated by an association of midwives opened its doors in September 2022. This raised questions about the necessity of a specific legal framework for out-of-hospital birthing centres. Considering that this activity was a monopoly of hospital obstetrical units, the Ministry of Health ordered the concerned midwives to stop deliveries in their birthing house.[51] The Government elected in October 2023 agreed to assess the opportunity to legislate after a study of the benefits and possible risks of such birthing houses.[52]

III. Medical Laboratories and Pharmacies

43. The amended Law of 16 July 1984 on medical laboratories[53] sets the general legal framework for medical laboratories. The Minister of Health and Social Security must authorise the opening and operation of such a laboratory and the law foresees a check that there is an unmet need to be covered. There are further strict ownership rules with a prohibition of multiple activities to avoid possible conflicts of interest. Grand-Ducal Regulations implement the law by fixing criteria such as training requirements and minimum criteria concerning personnel, facilities, installations, and equipment. Medical laboratories are further required to participate in mandatory quality controls for biomedical analyses.

All four general hospitals dispose of internal medical laboratories. The LNS, a public establishment governed by the Law of 7 August 2012,[54] operates diagnostics in the fields of anatomic and molecular pathology, genetics, medical biology, microbiology, forensic medicine, and health protection. There are finally three major private laboratory groups, with collection centres all over Luxembourg, as well as sample collection at home or at the office.

44. Medicines are dispensed by pharmacies ‘open to the public’, which dispense medicines to the public through a retail outlet. On 1 April 2024, there were 102

50. Amended Grand-Ducal Regulation of 27 Oct. 2018 adopting the nomenclature of midwifery acts and services covered by health insurance, Mém A – 1008 du 08.11.2018, https://cns.public.lu/en/legislations/alsf/cns-alsf-tableau.html.
51. *Ausserklinesch Gebuerten zu Lëtzebuerg – D'Demande ass do, ma et feelt e legale Kader,* RTL Luxembourg (2022), https://www.rtl.lu/news/national/a/1988996.html; *Am Gebuertshaus zu Bartreng dierfe keng Kanner méi op d'Welt kommen,* RTL Luxembourg (2022), https://www.rtl.lu/news/national/a/2001971.html.
52. *Luxembourg Government Coalition Agreement 2023–2028*, p. 91, https://gouvernement.lu/fr/publications/accord-coalition/accord-de-coalition-2023-2028/accord-de-coalition-2023-2028.html.
53. Loi du 16 juillet 1984 relative aux laboratoires d'analyses médicales, Mém. A – 71 du 30.07.1984, http://data.legilux.public.lu/eli/etat/leg/loi/1984/07/16/n1.
54. Loi du 7 août 2012 portant création de l'établissement public Laboratoire national de santé, Mém. A – 167 du 13.08.2012, https://legilux.public.lu/eli/etat/leg/loi/2012/08/07/n1/jo.

pharmacies open to the public.[55] Two different legal regimes apply to these pharmacies. Seventy-six pharmacies operate as 'state concession' governed by the Law of 4 July 1973 on the pharmacy regime.[56] The allocation of statal pharmacy concessions is governed by a system attributing points calculated by considering the seniority of the pharmaceutical diploma, the years of experience and the qualifications of the applicant pharmacists. Another twenty-six pharmacies are privately owned pharmacies pre-existing to the creation of the 'state concessions' regime. These remain partly governed by the Royal Grand-Ducal Decree of 1841 organising the medical service.[57]

The Law on hospitals, as well as the amended Grand-Ducal Regulation of 1 March 2002 on hospital pharmacy and drug stocks, specify the legal regime of hospital pharmacies, which primarily dispense medicines to inpatients.

IV. Long-Term Care

45. The amended Law of 8 September 1998 regulating relations between the State and organisations working in the social, family, and therapeutic fields[58] applies to the providers of long-term care and submits such activities to an authorisation. The Minister of Family authorises residential long-term care providing facilities, day care institutions and home care networks. In addition, the providers sign a framework contract with CNS. Several care and assistance networks provide care at home. Home care is aimed at keeping patients at home while they receive care and can include preventive, curative, palliative, or informal care. There is a diverse offer of day care institutions, where the elderly or persons with a disability can be taken care of during the day but spend the night at home. Long-term care residential facilities are considered a home-replacing environment. The medical responsibility generally rests with a privately established GP, who visits patients regularly.

46. The Law of 19 June 1998 introduced long-term care insurance[59] ('assurance dépendance') and created a specific universal long-term care insurance as part of the mandatory social security scheme. This fourth pillar, inspired by the German long-term care insurance system, was introduced in response to the growing needs of persons for whom neither maternity, accident, nor health insurance provisions applied. It covers the needs of persons who regularly require assistance from another person to carry out basic day-to-day tasks owing to illness or a physical, psychological, or mental disability. It finances the provision of long-term care, either at home or in an

55. *Source*: Data provided to the authors by the Ministry of Health and Social Security (04/2024).
56. Loi du 4 juillet 1973 concernant le régime de la pharmacie, Mém. A – 43 du 28.07.1973, https://legilux.public.lu/eli/etat/leg/loi/1973/07/04/n2/jo.
57. Ordonnance royale grand-ducale du 12 octobre 1841, No. 16, portant organisation du service médical, Mém. A – 54 du 17.11.1841, http://data.legilux.public.lu/eli/etat/leg/ordr/1841/10/12/n3/jo.
58. Loi modifiée du 8 septembre 1998 réglant les relations entre l'État et les organismes œuvrant dans les domaines social, familial et thérapeutique, Mém. A – 43 du 28.07.1973, http://data.legilux.public.lu/eli/etat/leg/loi/1998/09/08/n4.
59. Loi du 19 juin 1998 portant introduction d'une assurance dépendance, Mém. A – 48 du 29 juin 1998, https://legilux.public.lu/eli/etat/leg/loi/1998/06/19/n1/jo.

institution. Long-term care insurance also covers the benefit of technical aids and home adaptations in the form of benefits in kind provided by a professional provider.

47. The recently adopted Law of 23 August 2023 on the quality of services for the elderly entered into force on 1 March 2024.[60] It regulates home care and long-stay accommodation for the elderly, as well as certain services for the elderly. Besides strengthening quality management and introducing specific control mechanisms, it creates an online register of providers, including the basic characteristics of their services. It establishes a Superior Council of the Elderly ('Conseil supérieur des personnes âgées') and a Permanent Commission for the Sector of the Elderly ('Commission permanente pour le secteur des personnes âgées') with missions comparable to those of the Permanent Commission for the Hospital Sector (*See above:* I. Hospital Establishments and Hospital Care), as well as a national information and mediation service in the field of services for the elderly, with missions comparable to those of its existing counterpart for healthcare.[61]

V. Cross-Border Healthcare

48. Luxembourg has, out of necessity and for historical reasons, a very generous policy for care abroad. Because of the limited size of the country, the healthcare system cannot always guarantee specialised treatments with adequate quality. There is, for example, no centre for severe burn victims. Furthermore, almost all physicians have been trained at university hospitals abroad, maintain ties with their former colleagues and tend to refer their patients to these specialised providers. Referrals to institutions abroad have thus a long tradition. Cultural, linguistic, and social ties further explain why patients with an immigration background tend to use healthcare in their country of origin.

49. Automatic reimbursement of non-hospital care was implemented early in comparison to other Member States, since the 1998 ECJ judgments in Decker and Kohll concerned patients insured in Luxembourg.[62]

A prior authorisation regime is required for planned inpatient hospital care in a Member State of the EU, the European Economic Area (EEA) and Switzerland. A request for prior authorisation must be submitted based on a specific request form. Out-of-hospital care generally does not need such prior approval, unless using equipment classified as highly specialised medical equipment. The request for prior

60. Loi du 23 août 2023 portant sur la qualité des services pour personnes âgées et portant modification de: (1) la loi modifiée du 16 mai 1975 portant statut de la copropriété des immeubles bâtis; (2) la loi modifiée du 8 septembre 1998 réglant les relations entre l'État et les organismes œuvrant dans les domaines social, familial et thérapeutique, Mém. A – 562 du 04.09.2023, http://data.legilux.public.lu/eli/etat/leg/loi/2023/08/23/a562/jo.

61. *See:* Part II., Ch. 1., §14. Complaints and Mediation *infra*.

62. *See:* para. 86 *infra*.

authorisation must be medically motivated by a physician and submitted to CNS. It may be subject to review by the Social Security Medical Board ('Contrôle Médical de la Sécurité Sociale – CMSS').

50. The Luxembourg healthcare system significantly provides healthcare to non-residents, mainly commuters insured in Luxembourg and co-insured family members. They represent more than one-third of the insured population and benefit from the same access as residents. According to the CSS, compliance with social security rules and tariffs is further mandatory for healthcare providers if a patient is insured in another EU Member State, Switzerland, an EEA country, or a country with which Luxembourg has signed a bilateral health insurance agreement.[63] As hospital costs are mainly financed through a complex budgeting system, a specific pricing model is applied to calculate non-medical hospital costs. The same pricing model is applied for treatment under the cross-border healthcare directive and for incoming patients covered by the EU social security coordination regulations. Hospital costs in Luxembourg are generally covered without upfront payment through S2, as all hospitals are contracted with social security. Only those costs not covered by Luxembourg social security (daily allowance; first class) are billed directly to the patient. Under the cross-border healthcare directive, the patient must pay upfront, and a bill is issued by the hospital.

51. In 2022, the costs for benefits in kind delivered abroad amounted to EUR 548 million (16.9%) out of a total cost of EUR 3,231.8 million for such benefits. Luxembourg granted 11.306 authorisation for treatment abroad. Most authorisations were granted as S2 (10.229), but only a minority were granted under Directive 2011/24 (1.077).[64]

Commuters typically seek healthcare in their country of residence; their use of Luxembourg hospitals has, however, moderately risen from 5.3% in 2010 to 8.0% of hospital stays in 2019. Commuters of working age are those that use healthcare in Luxembourg the most, the 25–64-year-olds, representing 74.4% of the hospital stays of non-residents in 2019. Some specific healthcare services are more frequently used: 14.7% of all deliveries in 2019 were deliveries by non-resident women.[65]

To sum it up, cross-border healthcare is a significant reality in Luxembourg. Healthcare abroad ensures the delivery of highly specialised healthcare that is not available within the limited territory. Treatment abroad is further generally less expensive, given the high-cost level in Luxembourg. The Luxembourg healthcare system is, at the same time, moderately used by non-residents, mainly by commuters affiliated with Luxembourg. Cross-border healthcare has the overall effect to

---

63. Article 64(1), CSS.
64. *Rapport annuel 2022*, CNS (2023), https://cns.public.lu/fr/publications/rapport-annuel/rp-2022.html.
65. *Carte sanitaire – mise à jour 2021*, Observatoire national de la santé, Luxembourg (2022), https://sante.public.lu/fr/espace-obsante/carte-sanitaire.html.

grant access to tertiary care not available in the country, as well as to reduce both healthcare costs and the pressure on the nationally available healthcare services.[66]

VI. Patient Organisations and Representation

52. The 'Representation of Patient' ('Patiente Vertriedung') carries out activities to support, inform and defend patients and their interests. A variety of non-profit organisations advocate for the interests and well-being of patients with a specific health condition and/or their families. In 2022, a Federation of Patient Organisation ('Cercle des Associations de Patients (CAPAT)') was created as an umbrella organisation.

53. Involvement of patients in the development and implementation of healthcare policy is progressing. Patient representatives are present in an increasing number of consultative bodies of the health system, such as the CGI. They also participate in the setting up and evaluation of numerous public health plans, such as the National Cancer Plan. Ensuring patient representation in the governing board of hospitals is intended by the Government elected in October 2023.[67]

54. The Higher Council for Disabled Persons must be consulted on issues related to the rights and conditions of persons with a disability.[68] The Higher Council for the Elderly must be consulted on issues concerning the elderly.[69] There is no further general obligation to consult patient organisations in the legislative and regulatory process. Patient organisations are, however, frequently asked to issue a statement and may take the initiative to formulate a statement.

§2. Regulation and Governance of the Healthcare System

55. Given the small territory, governance and regulation are relatively centralised. Luxembourg has a hundred communes and municipalities. These local authorities have competencies that mainly concern local hygiene and environmental health responsibilities, such as the supply of clean drinking water, sewage, and waste disposal. They further contribute to the financing of healthcare services to vulnerable residents through regional social welfare offices. These welfare offices are notably responsible for granting access to third-party social payment regimes (*See:* §3. Financing of Healthcare and Health Insurance). Communes and municipalities are further responsible for organising school medicine for nurseries, primary schools, and special education (*See:* Part II., Chapter 5., §1. Preventive

66. Leist, A., *Luxembourg*, in: Immergut, E., et al. (eds), *Health politics in Europe: A Handbook*, Oxford University Press (2021).
67. *Luxembourg Government, 2023–2028 Coalition Agreement*, p. 102, https://gouvernement.lu/fr/publications/accord-coalition/accord-de-coalition-2023-2028/accord-de-coalition-2023-2028.html.
68. Article 34, amended Law of 12 Sep. 2003 on disabled persons.
69. Article 95, Law of 23 Aug. 2023 on the quality of services for the elderly.

Medicine). Finally, a growing number of initiatives at local level promote prevention and information, for instance by organising events such as a 'Health Week'.

56. Following the October 2023 general elections, Martine Deprez has been nominated Minister of Health and of Social Security ('Ministre de la Santé et de la Sécurité sociale') with ministerial competencies over the Department of Health and the Department of Social Security. The M3S comprises a Department of Health and a Department of Social Security. Under the previous government, these two departments constituted two separate ministries.

57. The Department of Health develops health policy and elaborates legislation that applies to the healthcare sector. It authorises healthcare professionals, hospitals, medical laboratories, pharmacies, and other actors of the healthcare system. It further authorises medicines, medical devices, and other regulated healthcare products. It develops prevention and finances public health matters. It accomplishes its missions with the support of the Directorate of Health, a public administration under the supervision of the M3S.

Pursuant to the Law of 21 November 1980 on the organisation of the Health Directorate,[70] the Directorate of Health functions as an executive administration for public health. It has responsibilities to study and advise public authorities on public health matters, oversee the implementation of laws and regulations on public health, assume quality control missions and take immediate measures to protect public health in the face of any threat. Subdivisions of the Directorate of Health are in charge of specific domains:

- The Division of Sanitary Inspection is responsible for public health in the areas of environmental hygiene and the surveillance and control of communicable diseases.
- The Division of School Medicine, Child and Youth Health is responsible for all matters relating to school medicine, surveillance and health promotion of children and youth.
- The Division of Curative Medicine and Health Quality is responsible for the planning, organisation, performance evaluation and supervision of hospitals and primary care facilities, healthcare facilities and equipment, as well as quality in healthcare, including the prevention of healthcare risks and the quality control of laboratories.
- The Radiation Protection Division deals with protection against ionising and non-ionising radiation, nuclear safety, and the safe management of radioactive waste.
- The Occupational Health and Environment Division is responsible for all matters concerning the promotion of health and well-being at work. It supervises occupational health services and has competencies in the domain of environmental health in general and the domestic environment in particular.

70. Loi du 21 novembre 1980 portant organisation de la direction de la santé, Mém. A – 79 du 27.11.1980, https://legilux.public.lu/eli/etat/leg/loi/1980/11/21/n1/jo.

– The Division of Social Medicine, Addiction Diseases and Mental Health is responsible for planning, organisation, orientation and medical-social supervision of illnesses, addiction diseases, mental illnesses and medical-social problems.

58. As of today, the Minister of Health and Social Security issues marketing authorisations for medicines and regulated health products and licenses the actors of the distribution chain of such products (pharmacies; wholesalers). The Pharmacy and Medicines Division of the Directorate of Health oversees and assesses medicines, medical devices, narcotic drugs, and cosmetic products, as well as the practice of pharmacy or wholesale. It further has attributions in the domain of genetically modified organisms and other health products. A law proposal aiming to create a Medicines and Health Products Agency is currently pending in Parliament.[71]

59. In 2021, a National Health Observatory was established[72] to strengthen the quality and availability of data on public health issues, to support evaluation of health policy, and to support evidence-based governance of the healthcare system. It is placed under the authority of the Minister for Health and Social Security but enjoys scientific and professional independence in terms of its observation tools, findings, and proposals.

60. The Department of Social Security guarantees social security in the fields of illness, age, dependency, invalidity, and occupational accident. It accomplishes its missions with the support of the General Inspectorate of Social Security ('Inspection générale de la sécurité sociale (IGSS)'), a public administration under the supervision of the M3S. The IGSS collaborates in drafting the regulatory framework addressing social security issues. It further assists and supervises the social security institutions. Moreover, it carries out analyses and studies to assess and plan social welfare schemes.

61. Under the supervision of the M3S and of IGSS, the following social security institutions have responsibilities for financing and governance of the social security and healthcare system:

– The 'Caisse Nationale de Santé (CNS)' is the main public establishment in charge of sickness, maternity, and long-term care insurance. Since the 2008 law introduced a single status for the private sector, CNS has been competent for all private sector insured (salaried and non-salaried such as the self-employed) as well as for public-sector workers. CNS concludes mandatory agreements with professional groups and negotiates hospital budgets.[73] CNS further provides common

71. Projet de loi 7,532 portant création de l'établissement public 'Agence luxembourgeoise des médicaments et produits de santé (ALMPS)', https://www.chd.lu/fr/dossier/7523.
72. Loi du 2 mars 2021 portant création d'un Observatoire national de la santé et modification, Mém. A – 168 du 3.03.2021, https://legilux.public.lu/eli/etat/leg/loi/2021/03/02/a168/jo.
73. *See:* Part III., Ch. 4. Relations with Social Security *infra.*

centralised services to the public sector establishments in the domains of sickness, maternity, and long-term care insurance.
- Three public establishments manage health insurance in the public sector: the 'Caisse de Maladie des Fonctionnaires et Employés Publics (CMFEP)' for civil servants and public employees, the 'Caisse de maladie des fonctionnaires et employés communaux (CMFEC)' for communal civil servants and employees and the 'Entraide médicale des CFL' for the national railway company CFL. While not merged into CNS, the coverage is identical to the private sector and parts of the back office are provided to these entities by CNS (such as issuing certain prior authorisations, including authorisations for treatment abroad;).
- The 'Association d'assurance accident (AAA)' is the public establishment in charge of occupational accidents, including accidents on the way to and from work, as well as occupational diseases.
- The 'Centre commun de la sécurité sociale (CCSS)' is the public establishment in charge of voluntary and mandatory affiliation to the Luxembourg social security system, as well as calculating, collecting, and recovering contributions. It collects the contributions and distributes these amongst the social security institutions. It further provides centralised IT services to the different institutions.[74]

62. Under the supervision of the M3S and IGSS, two public administrations composed of physicians and other healthcare professionals are in charge of specific assessments and control missions:

- The 'CMSS' is mainly in charge of medical assessments and control missions in the domain of sickness, maternity, and occupational accident insurance, including prior authorisation of certain medical, dental, and pharmaceutical treatment expenses, including partly cross-border healthcare. CMSS provides opinions to CNS and to the different social security institutions, including binding advice on the registration of new products in the positive list of drugs. It has supervisory missions towards patients and healthcare providers.[75]
- The 'Administration d'évaluation et de contrôle de l'assurance dépendance (AEC)' is mainly in charge of medical assessments and control missions in the domain of long-term dependency insurance benefits.[76]

63. The Ministry for the Family, Solidarity, Living Together and Reception of Refugees ('Ministère de la Famille, des Solidarités, du Vivre ensemble et de l'Accueil') has responsibilities for family and social issues. The Ministry is notably in charge of authorising and supervising long-term care facilities, home care networks and care services for disabled persons. Under its supervision, the Children's Future Fund ('Caisse pour l'avenir des enfants (CAE)') is responsible for the management of family, birth, and back-to-school allowances. It is also responsible for managing parental leave. Furthermore, the National Office for Childhood ('Office

74. Articles 413–417, CSS.
75. Articles 418-421, CSS.
76. Articles 383–386, CSS.

National de l'Enfance (ONE)') is providing aid to children and their families. ONE handles the prevention and early management of situations of psychosocial distress in children, young adults, and families. It finances individual assistance provided predominantly by professionals in the socio-educational sector and partly by healthcare professionals where social security does not cover such services.

§3. Financing of Healthcare and Health Insurance

64. Spending on health is high in Luxembourg. Health expenditure per capita stood at EUR 4.182 in 2021 (adjusted for differences in purchasing power), which was about EUR 153 higher than the EU average. In contrast, Luxembourg spends only 5.7% of its GDP on health, the lowest share in the EU (11%). Public expenditure on health (including expenditure for long-term care and accident insurance) is the second highest in the EU, accounting for 86.0% of the total (compared to the EU average of 81.1%) – a share that has increased continuously since 2012. Due to the very broad coverage, out-of-pocket (OOP) spending is low, at 9% compared to the EU average of 15%. Complementary voluntary health insurance represents only 3.9% of health expenditure, although it is purchased by two-thirds of the population.[77]

65. Luxembourg has a 'Bismarck' social health insurance system based on compulsory contributions from the working population. Historically, the roots of the social security system lie in the mutual aid societies set up to provide support to workers and their families in case of illness or death. The first mutual aid society ('Arbeiter-Unterstützungs-Verein') was created in Luxembourg in 1848. Compulsory health insurance for manufacturing and industrial workers was introduced in Luxembourg in 1901. In 1925, sickness insurance, accident insurance and incapacity insurance were codified and merged into a harmonised system with increased benefits. Luxembourg retained some elements of the German insurance system from the German occupation in 1940–1944, most significantly the extension of insurance to cover pensioners. The scope of the compulsory insurance was further expanded from 1952 onwards. By 1973, the working population, their families, and all pensioners were covered by compulsory health insurance. In 1974, legislation was passed to allow significant injections of state resources, up to 40% of the total receipts. This law further standardised contribution levels across all sickness funds.[78]

66. Today, Luxembourg's compulsory insurance covers healthcare, sickness leave and dependency insurance. It covers insured persons and family members, including minors and students who have no occupation. Persons who only work

77. OECD/European Observatory on Health Systems and Policies, *Luxembourg: Country Health Profile 2023*, State of Health in the EU, OECD Publishing/European Observatory on Health Systems and Policies (2023), https://www.oecd.org/luxembourg/luxembourg-country-health-profile-2023-3cf98074-en.htm.

78. *100 ans de Sécurité sociale au Luxembourg,* BLQS, No. 10, ALOSS (2001), https://www.aloss.lu/bulletin-luxembourgeois-des-questions-sociales/.

occasionally in Luxembourg (i.e., less than three months per calendar year) are exempt but may choose to pay voluntary contributions. Other persons not covered by a social security scheme may also choose voluntary insurance.

The social health insurance covers around 92% of the resident population. This public health insurance system is financed through State contributions (40%), and the remaining 60% is equally shared between the insured population and employers.[79] Long-term dependency insurance is financed by the State to 40% of the total expenditure, a contribution rate from the insured persons and a small contribution of around 1% from electricity consumers of more than 1 million kW.[80] The overall budget of the health insurance system is determined each year for the following year based on multiannual expenditure forecasts.

Around 5% of the resident population are EU civil servants covered by the Joint Sickness Insurance Scheme (JSIS) as well as other persons covered by a specific non-domestic social security scheme.

67. Tariffs and fees are fixed in a mandatory fee schedule called 'nomenclature of acts and services'. For physicians and dentists, there is no distinction in the fee rates between whether the service is delivered in a hospital or to outpatients. The reimbursement rates, however, differ (*See:* Part III., Chapter 4., §3. Medical Fees and Nomenclature of Fees). For non-medical healthcare professions, the respective nomenclature tariffs do generally not apply for hospital care.

Luxembourg is amongst a minority of countries in the EU where patients generally pay independent medical practitioners and ambulatory care directly. Patients pay the entire amount due and provide the invoice ('mémoire d'honoraires') to be reimbursed by CNS or the competent public sector fund. The deployment of an immediate direct electronic payment ('paiement immédiat direct – PID') of medical fees started in September 2023. It is currently not mandatory for physicians to offer PID.

Inpatient hospital costs are covered by hospital budgeting. Hospital financing is mainly based on prospective budgets. Pursuant to the 2010 healthcare reform, the Government has fixed a global budget envelope delimiting the funds to be allocated to hospitals over a two-year period. The envelope relates to all acute and sub-acute hospitals. CNS negotiates an annual budget for operating costs individually with every hospital, bearing in mind the overall funding cap fixed by the global budget envelope. The so-called PRN workload calculation system, developed in Canada, is used to plan the human resources necessary to care for patients. An annual bonus of a maximum of 2% of the budget is awarded through a programme targeting quality, patient safety, efficiency, and transparency criteria. Hospital construction, modernisation or acquisition of heavy medical equipment receive direct State financing of up to 80% of the eligible costs. The remaining 20% are financed through social security budgets. The investments must fit with the national hospital planning as fixed by the Law on hospitals. An insured adult patient pays a daily participation (EUR 25,50) to the hospital. The bulk of the cost of treatment is covered. Daily participation is not required for children under the age of 18. Hospitals may request

79. Articles 28–43, CSS.
80. Article 375, CSS.

additional funding charged to patients for optional '1st class' single rooms and for auxiliary activities (parking fees, cafeteria, shops, etc.). These surcharges are typically covered by complementary voluntary health insurance.

Medical fees in hospitals are covered through third-party payment under certain circumstances (*See:* Part III., Chapter 4., §3. Medical Fees and Nomenclature of Fees).

68. For non-medical healthcare professions, the respective nomenclature tariffs generally apply only to outpatient care. It does not apply to hospital care. Like for physicians, a nomenclature negotiated between CNS and the union or grouping representing the profession regulates tariffs and reimbursement by social security for dieticians, midwives, nurses, occupational therapists, physiotherapists, psychotherapists, and speech therapists. Some recognised health professions, like orthoptists or ergo-therapists, are not covered by a nomenclature and services delivered by self-employed professionals are thus not reimbursed by social security. However, access to such services may be part of a budgeted hospital service or publicly funded through a not-for-profit organisation.

Paramedical treatment generally needs a prescription to be reimbursed. Coverage varies according to the profession of the service providers. For midwives, the coverage is 100% and the patient generally needs no medical prescription. A prescription is requested, and coverage is 88% for speech therapy, dietetics, nursing care, etc. The coverage is 70% and a prior validation process is in place for physiotherapy and psychotherapy. For psychotherapy, which is reimbursed at 70% of the tariff, third-party payment is currently not available. Further specific limitations and exceptions apply, according to the healthcare concerned.

Third-party payment is applied for physiotherapy (by choice) and midwives.

69. A specific nomenclature regulates tariffs and reimbursement of laboratory services by social security. Third-party payment is applied.

Pharmaceuticals and medical devices used or delivered within a hospital are part of the hospital financing system and delivered to patients as benefits in kind. Prices of medicines delivered to patients in pharmacies open to the public are approved by the Department of Social Security based on the price of the country of origin, generally Belgium. The reimbursement level is subject to the inclusion of the medicine in a positive list of medicines with fixed prices. The medicines on the positive list are classified into three different classes. For each of these classes, there is a specific rate of reimbursement: 40%, 80% or 100%. For medicines within a group of generics, the pharmacist may substitute the medicine indicated on the prescription with the cheapest available generic. The price of the cheapest available generic is used as a common reference price before applying the reimbursement rate. Third-party payment is applied for total or partial reimbursement of medicines in pharmacies open to the public and the patient only pays his part.

70. While compulsory health insurance provides significant reimbursement levels, pre-payment of medical fees and co-payment remain nevertheless a barrier to accessing healthcare. A third-party social payment regime ('tiers payant social') for medical fees was introduced in 2013 with the aim of facilitating access to healthcare for patients in economic hardship. The benefit of the third-party social payment regime must be applied for through the social welfare office competent for the commune where the patient resides. In case a resident is not affiliated with social security, the competent social welfare office may proceed to a voluntary affiliation and pay the fees. Eligible patients receive a certificate that exempts them from payment of medical fees. The physician sends the fee note to CNS who directly pays the physician. CNS recovers the patient's share of the cost from the competent social welfare office. The social welfare office may recover the costs if the beneficiary is able to repay. The deployment of an PID system of medical fees ('paiement immédiat direct') started in September 2023.

71. Compulsory health insurance generally provides a broad benefits package. Mandatory contracting of healthcare providers, in conjunction with fixed tariffs and generous reimbursement levels, ensures solidarity and broad equal access to healthcare.

Maintaining a fee schedule that adequately considers medical advances has, despite many efforts, proven challenging. The mandatory nomenclature of physicians is thus not always in line with the justified needs of patients. This may lead, in practice, to inequities, a questionable use of the existing nomenclature, or the unavailability of recognised innovative treatment options.[81]

72. Healthcare for regular asylum seekers, persons detained in prison and other specific groups is financed through specific State funding. Vulnerable populations, mainly homeless and immigrants without a valid residence permit, remain nevertheless partly excluded from the healthcare insurance system.[82] A pilot project ('CUSS') aiming to improve access to social insurance for these populations has been operational since April 2022.[83] The Government elected in October 2023 agreed to consolidate the benefits of the measure after evaluation of the CUSS pilot project.[84]

81. Collège médical, *Réflexions sur la nomenclature et la tarification des actes*, Info-Point, No. 22 (2017), http://www.collegemedical.lu/uploads/news/doc/37_1_Info%20Point%20No%2022.pdf.
82. *Invisibles, vulnérables et sans protection: les laissés pour compte du système de santé au Luxembourg*, Médecins du Monde Luxembourg (2022), https://medecinsdumonde.lu/sortie-du-1er-observatoire-de-lacces-a-la-sante/.
83. *Présentation de la Couverture universelle des soins de santé*, Press release, Luxembourg Government (2021), https://gouvernement.lu/fr/actualites/toutes_actualites/communiques/2021/10-octobre/27-cuss.html.
84. *Luxembourg Government, 2023–2028 Coalition Agreement*, p. 103, https://gouvernement.lu/fr/publications/accord-coalition/accord-de-coalition-2023-2028/accord-de-coalition-2023-2028.html.

Chapter 3. Sources of Medical Law

73. Luxembourg has a legal system essentially based on written norms, with a hierarchical organisation of norms by virtue of which higher norms take precedence over the lower norms within the legal order.

We will first present international sources of law, which are directly applicable and then take precedence over the national sources of medical law presented.

§1. International Sources of Medical Law

74. Luxembourg legal order recognises the supremacy of treaties and all other sources of international law, not only in relation to ordinary (infra-constitutional) law but also in relation to the Constitution itself.[85] The potential influence of international law sources is thus important. It exceeds the scope of this sub-chapter to present all relevant international sources. We will hereafter focus on two core issues.

I. Instruments Protecting Fundamental Human Rights

75. Luxembourg has signed and ratified an impressive list of international instruments recognising fundamental human rights and liberties. Some international human rights instruments explicitly recognise a right to (the highest attainable standard of) health. The fundamental rights to human dignity, the right to life, the prohibition of torture or degrading treatments, and the right to private life and non-discrimination are important human rights that are internationally protected and frequently invoked when it comes to health-related issues.

76. Amongst the many international instruments protecting such fundamental rights, the 'Universal Declaration of Human Rights' adopted on 10 December 1948 by the United Nations General Assembly must be mentioned first. It defines inalienable, indivisible, and universal fundamental human rights. Luxembourg is bound by sixteen of the eighteen treaties and protocols that form the United Nations (UN) human rights treaty system.[86] Amongst those, Article 12 of the International Covenant on Economic, Social and Cultural Rights of 16 December 1966 prominently recognises the right to health. Luxembourg has further approved the 'Convention against Torture and Other Cruel, Inhuman or Degrading Treatment or Punishment' (1984), as well as the optional protocol to that Convention (2002).[87]

---

85. Heuschling, L., *Les origines au XIXe siècle du rang supra-constitutionnel des traités en droit luxembourgeois: l'enjeu de la monarchie*, in: Riassetto, I., Heuschling, L. & Ravarani G. (dir.), *Liber amicorum Rusen Ergec*, Ed. Pasicrisie (2017), https://orbilu.uni.lu/handle/10993/29288.
86. https://www.ohchr.org/en/countries/luxembourg.
87. Loi du 11 avril 2010 (1) portant approbation du protocole facultatif se rapportant à la Convention contre la torture et autres peines ou traitements cruels, inhumains ou dégradants, adopté par l'Assemblée Générale de l'Organisation des Nations Unies à New York, le 18 décembre 2002 et (2) portant désignation du médiateur en tant que mécanisme national de prévention et fixant ses attributions, Mém. A – 56 du 16.04.2010, https://legilux.public.lu/eli/etat/leg/loi/2010/04/11/n1/jo.

77. UN instruments created to protect the human rights of particular groups must further be mentioned, specifically the 'Convention on the Rights of the Child' of 20 November 1989 and the 'Convention on the Rights of Persons with Disabilities' of 13 December 2006. Besides constituting important international sources of law that adapt basic human rights to specific contexts, these instruments have an important national impact through the UN mechanisms that support and monitor their national implementation.

78. Within the sphere of UN institutions, the World Health Organization (WHO) and its Constitution (1946) which states that the WHO's objective 'is the attainment by all people of the highest possible level of health' cannot be left unmentioned. As a specialised agency of the UN responsible for international public health, the WHO's scope of activities is broad. Amongst the legal instruments proven to be of utmost interest within the context of the COVID-19 pandemic appears the International Health Regulation. It aims to provide an overarching legal framework that defines countries' rights and obligations in handling public health events and emergencies that have the potential to cross borders. Within the large scope of activities of WHO, there is also a screening of existing national legislation, assistance to States, and the development of 'soft law' such as the 'Declaration on the Promotion of Patients' Rights in Europe', adopted by the Member States of the Regional Office for Europe of the WHO in 1994.

79. The Council of Europe (CoE) (1949) is the central actor promoting human rights and social rights at a European level. The European Convention for the Protection of Human Rights and Fundamental Freedoms of 4 November 1950 (ratified by Luxembourg in 1953)[88] constitutes its core instrument. From the procedures before the former European Commission on Human Rights and now the European Court of Human Rights (ECtHR), case law emanates, which can have a strong influence on national and international medical law practice.

80. Specifically concerning new technologies in the field of medicine, the Convention for the Protection of Human Rights and Dignity of the Human Being with regard to the Application of Biology and Medicine (Convention on Human Rights and Biomedicine), also called the 'Oviedo Convention', has become an important reference. The Convention was opened for signature on 4 April 1997 in Oviedo and was signed the same day by Luxembourg. Luxembourg was further amongst the first countries to sign its four additional protocols. The Grand Duchy has, however, not yet ratified it. In January 2006, a draft law aiming to ratify the Oviedo Convention, as well as the three additional protocols adopted until that date, was submitted to the Chamber of Deputies.[89] The National Ethics Commission (Commission

88. Loi du 29 août 1953 portant approbation de la Convention de sauvegarde des droits de l'homme et des libertés fondamentales, signée à Rome, le 4 novembre 1950, et du Protocole additionnel, signé à Paris, le 20 mars 1952, Mém. A – 53 du 29.08.1953, https://legilux.public.lu/eli/etat/leg/loi/1953/08/29/n1/jo.

89. Projet de loi 5528 portant approbation – de la Convention pour la protection des Droits de l'Homme et de la dignité de l'être humain à l'égard des applications de la biologie et de la médecine: Convention sur les Droits de l'Homme et la biomédecine, ouverte à la signature, à Oviedo, le 4 avril

Nationale d'Ethique (CNE)) issued a general opinion on the Oviedo Convention before the draft law was submitted to Parliament. The opinion of the Council of State dates from April 2006. The Council of State stresses that the draft Law foresees an *ad minima* transposition. Given the lack of a comprehensive national legal framework in many areas covered, the Council of State recommended a congruent regulation of key issues such as genetic testing and counselling, medically assisted procreation (MAP), or biomedical research. Concerning the issue of research on embryos and embryonic stem cells, a ban was foreseen by the draft law. The Council of State recalled in its opinion that the CNE was in favour of allowing research on supernumerary embryos and it formally opposed the wording of the proposed ban. As a result, the Government requested a further opinion from the C.N.E., which was available in 2011. In 2012, a draft framework for research on supernumerary embryos was elaborated. It was submitted and advised favourably by C.N.E. in 2013, however, not pursued.[90] Subsequent Governments declared being favourable to the ratification of the Oviedo Convention and its four additional protocols. At the same time, draft Law No. 5528 remains pending in Parliament without a major advancement since 2006. The same is true for draft Law No. 5552 on biomedical research,[91] also submitted to Parliament in 2006.

81. The CoE has further adopted numerous resolutions and recommendations on bioethical topics and health issues. It has successfully supported and promoted cooperation and exchange in specific public health domains, such as drug policy cooperation through the 'International Cooperation Group on Drugs and Addiction' (former 'Pompidou Group') or in the specific domain of standardisation, quality and safety of medicines and healthcare ('EDQM'). While not strictly binding, the work on these issues has a strong influence on national medical law and policy.

82. At EU level, the 'Charter of fundamental rights of the European Union' was elaborated in 1999–2000. It has been binding since the entry into force of the Lisbon Treaty on 1 December 2009. It reaffirms many of the political, social, and economic rights. Article 35 of the Charter specifically mentions the right to health as

---

1997 – du Protocole additionnel à la Convention pour la protection des Droits de l'Homme et de la dignité de l'être humain à l'égard des applications de la biologie et de la médecine, portant interdiction du clonage d'êtres humains, ouvert à la signature, à Paris, le 12 janvier 1998 – du Protocole additionnel à la Convention sur les Droits de l'Homme et la biomédecine relatif à la transplantation d'organes et de tissus d'origine humaine, ouvert à la signature, à Strasbourg, le 24 janvier 2002 – du Protocole additionnel à la Convention sur les Droits de l'Homme et la biomédecine, relatif à la recherche biomédicale, ouvert à la signature, à Strasbourg, le 25 janvier 2005 et modifiant la loi du 25 novembre 1982 réglant le prélèvement de substances d'origine humaine, https://www.chd.lu/fr/dossier/5528.

90. *La recherche sur les embryons surnuméraires au Luxembourg*, Avis No. 24, Commission consultative nationale d'éthique (2013), https://cne.public.lu/dam-assets/fr/publications/avis/Avis_24.pdf.; Schwebag, M. & Stoffel, D., *L'embryon humain en droit luxembourgeois,* RLDS, No. 3, pp. 21–23 (2020).

91. Projet de loi 5552 relatif à la recherche biomédicale, https://www.chd.lu/fr/techdossier/172.

follows: 'Everyone has the right of access to preventive health care and the right to benefit from medical treatment under the conditions established by national laws and practices. A high level of human health protection shall be ensured in the definition and implementation of all Union policies and activities.'

83. Further attention may finally be drawn to international declarations that are not of a legislative nature, but that merely have moral authority. Specifically, within the domain of medical law, one must mention the declarations of the World Medical Association, which have had a large impact (e.g., the Declaration of Helsinki concerning experiments on human beings).

II. European Union Law and Policy[92]

84. Historically, Luxembourg is a founding member of European Coal and Steel Community (ECSC) (1952) and European Economic Community (EEC) (1957), the predecessors of the EU. Luxembourg City hosted the ECSC and is one of the institutional seats of the EU. In 1952, Luxembourg was favourable to the creation of a European Health Community, a proposal that failed but has recently regained attention.[93]

85. Former Article 152 EC, currently Article 168 TUE, explicitly stresses that healthcare is an area of specific Member State competence, where the EU shall complete national policies. Traditionally, the EEC Treaty (1957) and its successor, the TUE (1992), are regarded as mainly economic ventures. At the same time, national health law is intensely influenced by EU law and policy.

The EU law corpus largely interferes in the health field through its internal market competencies. EU law sets through binding regulations and directives the basic framework for the free movement of goods and persons. This is why there is a significant influence of EU law on domains like medicines, medical devices, and blood, as well as when it comes to the free movement of patients and health professionals. In domains where EU regulations have been adopted, such as the recent EU clinical trials regulation, EU law applies directly, and complementary national legislation is limited to secondary issues such as the designation of the competent national authorities. In other domains where the EU has adopted directives, the national legislation must be transposed into national law, and there is generally a larger margin left at the national level. Luxembourg frequently refrains from making extensive use

92. Nys, H., *European Union Health Law*, in: Nys, H. (ed.), *IEL Medical Law*, Kluwer Law International (2023).

93. Davesne, A. & Guigner, S., *La Communauté européenne de la santé (1952–1954) – Une redécouverte intergouvernementaliste du projet fonctionnaliste de 'pool blanc'*, Politique européenne, No. 41, Ed. L'Harmattan (2013); Frischhut, M., *Eine Europäische Gesundheitsunion: Historische Ideen, aktuelle Pläne und Werte für einen resilienten Wiederaufbau*, Zeitschrift Für Öffentliches Recht, 78/2, pp. 177–201 (2023).

of national margins and typically limits itself as far as possible to a word-by-word transposition of EU directives in national law.

86. Besides written EU law, there has been a major impact of the ECJ case law on health law within EU Member States. Within the domain of cross-border healthcare, the 'Decker-Kohll' cases of the ECJ are a perfect illustration thereof.[94] Nicolas Decker, a Luxembourg lawyer, faced a refusal to reimburse a pair of glasses purchased in Belgium. The case was finally brought to the ECJ, which considered that the national reimbursement rules were a barrier to the free movement of goods not justified on grounds of public health (ECJ, 28 April 1998, *Decker v. CMEP*, C-120/95). In the case of Raymond Kohll, again a Luxembourg affiliate, prior authorisation to receive dental care in Trier (Germany) was refused for his minor daughter. The ECJ considered that the refusal was contrary to internal market rules and not justified on grounds of public health (ECJ, 28 April 1998, *Kohll v. UCM*, C-158/96). Following the rulings in 'Decker-Kohll', Luxembourg has been obliged to open its social security system early in comparison to other EU Member States. The case law of the ECJ extends, under certain conditions, the reimbursement of healthcare without prior authorisation. The impact on statutory and complementary healthcare systems cannot be denied.[95] Although the ECJ's reasoning is based on internal market principles, it resulted in extending patients' access to treatment and contributed to the adoption of directive 2011/24 on cross-border healthcare.[96]

87. Finally, according to Article 168(2) TUE, 'The Commission may, in close contact with the Member States, take any useful initiative to promote coordination, in particular initiatives aiming at the establishment of guidelines and indicators, the organisation of exchange of best practice, and the preparation of the necessary elements for periodic monitoring and evaluation. The European Parliament shall be kept fully informed.'

This paragraph formalises 'soft law' types of competencies at the level of the EU Commission. National health law and policy are de facto considerably influenced by EU coordination and action in the field of public health. This is particularly the case for non-communicable diseases.[97] Successful EU initiatives and financing have been allocated to areas such as rare diseases, cancer[98] and eHealth.

94. ECJ, *The judgements of 1998 in Kohll and Decker*, https://curia.europa.eu/jcms/jcms/p1_2018896/en/.
95. Jorens, Y., Coucheir, M. & Van Overmeiren, F., *Access to HealthCare in an Internal Market: Impact for Statutory and Complementary Systems*, BLQS, No. 18 (2005), https://www.aloss.lu/bulletin-luxembourgeois-des-questions-sociales/.
96. Directive 2011/24/EU of the European Parliament and of the Council of 9 Mar. 2011 on the application of patients' rights in cross-border healthcare, OJ L 88, 4.4.2011, pp. 45–65, http://data.europa.eu/eli/dir/2011/24/oj.
97. https://health.ec.europa.eu/non-communicable-diseases_en.
98. European Commission, *Europe's Beating Cancer Plan*, COM(2021) 44final, https://eur-lex.europa.eu/legal-content/en/TXT/?uri=COM:2021:44:FIN.

§2. National Sources

88. Luxembourg has a legal system essentially based on written norms, with a hierarchical organisation of norms by virtue of which higher norms take precedence over the lower norms within the legal order.

89. Laws, Grand-Ducal Regulations, Ministerial Regulations, and other norms are published in the official gazette of the Grand Duchy of Luxembourg, called 'Mémorial, Journal officiel du Grand-Duché de Luxembourg'. Current and past publications since 1839 are centrally available through the governmental website devoted to national legislation called 'Legilux' (www.legilux.lu).

A thematic compendium of consolidated texts applicable in the domain of health law, called 'Code de la Santé' (http://data.legilux.public.lu/eli/etat/leg/code/sante) comprises Laws and Grand-Ducal Regulations with a link to health matters. Texts applicable in the domain of social security are consolidated in the compendium called 'Code de la Sécurité Sociale, Lois et Règlements' (https://legilux.public.lu/eli/etat/leg/code/securite_sociale/). It comprises the CSS, a Law in the formal sense of the term, as well as linked Laws, Grand-Ducal Regulations, and other norms. Such consolidated texts are not authoritative.

I. Constitution

90. The 1815 Vienna Congress transformed Luxembourg into a Grand Duchy in personal union with the King of the Netherlands. The first Constitution was promulgated in 1841. A more liberal one followed in 1848, with the Constitution of 1856 restoring monarchical sovereignty. The current Constitution of the Grand Duchy of Luxembourg entered into force on 17 October 1868. It has since been amended many times. After the subdivision of a general constitutional revision proposal into four separate proposals, all four separate constitutional Laws entered into force together on 1 July 2023. The 2023 amendments proceed to a far-reaching revision regarded by some constitutionalists as forming a new Constitution. From a formal point of view, the Constitution has, however, not been repealed.

91. The 2013 amendments revise and reorganise Chapter II of the Constitution, dedicated to fundamental rights, public freedoms, and objectives of constitutional value.[99] Several articles of Chapter II, section 3, dedicated to 'Public freedoms' ('Des libertés publiques') are of particular interest to medical law.

Health is addressed by Article 34 of the revised Constitution. It reproduces in substance former Article 11, §5, and states that 'Social security, health protection and workers' rights are regulated by Law in their fundamentals.' The 2023 revision did not change its substantial content. Article 34 does not directly enshrine a right to

99. Proposition de révision du chapitre II de la Constitution, doc. parl. 7755, https://www.chd.lu/fr/dossier/7755.

health or formulate the substantial fundamental values of the health and social security system. The protection of health and social security remains formulated as a civil liberty and a constitutional objective to be regulated by Law.

Former Article 11, §1, of the Constitution, further specified that the State guarantees the 'natural rights of the human person and of the family'. In a 2004 decision, the Luxembourg Constitutional Court considered that such 'natural rights' concern 'existential questions of the human being, the respect of human dignity and freedom'.[100] The notion of 'natural rights' has not been reproduced in the revised Constitution. Inspired by the German Constitution and by international human rights instruments, Chapter 2 of the revised Constitution starts, however, with a new Article 12, according to which 'Human dignity is inviolable'. It remains to be seen how the Luxembourg Constitutional Court will in the coming years interpret this new article when faced with bioethical questions, potentially finding inspiration within the rich jurisprudence of the German 'Bundesverfassungsgericht', other Supreme Courts, and international fundamental rights bodies. Pursuant to the constitutional revision, the family life aspects are now guaranteed through Article 15, §4, which recognises the right to found a family, as well as the respect for family life. According to Article 15, §5, in all matters affecting the child, the child's best interests shall be a primary consideration. It further recognises the right of children to express their views freely in all matters affecting them and the right that their views be considered. It finally recognises the right to such protection, measures and care necessary for his or her well-being and development. The newly introduced Articles 13 and 14 of the Constitution further recognise the right to physical and mental integrity, the prohibition of torture or inhuman and degrading treatment or punishment, and the right to freedom of thought, conscience, and religion.

92. According to Article 35 (former §6 of Article 11), the freedom of liberal professions is guaranteed, save for the restrictions established by Law. The framework applicable to liberal professions, such as the medical profession, constitutes thus a domain reserved to the Law.

Former Article 11 of the Constitution provided that regarding the practice of the liberal professions, a formal Law may grant professional bodies with legal personality the power to make regulations. It further specified that such regulations must comply with Laws and Grand-Ducal Regulations and may be subject to approval, annulment, or suspension procedures without prejudice to the powers of the judicial or administrative courts. Article 129 of the revised Constitution reproduces, in substance, former Article 11, subparagraphs 2 and 3. A new limitation to the powers that may be delegated to a professional body has, however, been introduced. Article 129 adds that in matters reserved to formal Law by the Constitution, such regulatory powers may only be conferred by virtue of a specific formal legal provision that lays down the purpose of the measures and, where applicable, the detailed conditions to which they are subject. Within the domain of health law, such powers have

100. C. Const., 28 May 2004, Arrêt No. 20/04, https://legilux.public.lu/eli/etat/leg/acc/2004/05/28/n1/jo.

been attributed to the Medical College, as well as to the Superior Council of Certain Health Professions, with the mission to adopt a deontological code. It is uncertain whether the provisions attributing such powers currently suffice to the requirements of the revised Constitution.[101]

93. Section 3 of Chapter II of the revised Constitution ends with Article 37, setting out a so-called 'transversal clause' ('clause transversale') according to which 'Every limitation to these liberties must be provided for by a formal Law and respect the essential content of these rights. In accordance with the principle of proportionality, limitations may only be made if they are necessary in a democratic society and effectively meet objectives of general interest or the need to protect the rights and freedoms of others.' This wording is closely inspired by the international fundamental rights framework. Further, according to Article 45 of the Constitution, in matters reserved to the Law, the Grand Duke may only exercise regulatory powers by virtue of a specific legal provision which sets out the purpose of the implementing measures and, where applicable, the conditions to which they are subject.

Article 37, in combination with Article 45, means that it continues to require formal Laws when it comes to regulating matters related to the protection of health and social security, as well as for regulating questions related to a liberal profession, matters touching the inviolability of human dignity, etc. As a result, large domains of health law require formal laws, limiting accordingly the domain of Grand-Ducal Regulations to a strictly defined act.[102]

The general protection mechanism corresponds in substance to the constitutional review criteria already applied by the Constitutional Court in domains reserved to the Law, such as the protection of health or the freedom of liberal professions. However, the so-called transversal clause could lead to an increased scrutiny by the Constitutional Court, particularly with regard to the principles of necessity and proportionality.

II. Laws ('Lois')

94. The essential part of the health legislation is constituted by formal Laws voted by the Parliament. In the legislative system of the Grand Duchy, either the Parliament or the Government may make a legislative proposal. The right of initiative of the Government is exercised by submitting a 'draft law' ('projet de loi') to the Parliament. The initiative of the Chamber of Deputies is exercised by the presentation of a 'law proposal' ('proposition de loi'). The recent constitutional reform has further introduced a 'citizens legislative initiative procedure' ('proposition motivée aux fins de légiférer').[103]

---

101. *See:* para. 175 *infra.*
102. *See:* para. 101 *infra.*
103. Article 79 of the revised Constitution foresees that 125 voters must initially sign such a proposal. After a check of conformity, the proposal is open to signature for a period of four weeks. In case of support by at least 12.500 voters, Parliament must decide by a public vote on the continuation of the parliamentary process. In case of a positive vote, the proposal follows the standard legislative process.

All draft laws and all law proposals are published in the form of parliamentary documents ('documents parlementaires') which can be consulted through the website of the Parliament (www.chd.lu). Parliamentary documents further include all amendments, the opinion(s) of the Council of State, the reports of the competent parliamentary committee, and the opinions of professional bodies or other bodies consulted.

95. All legislative initiatives and all subsequent amendments are submitted to the Council of State. When giving his opinion, the Council of State proceeds to a legal assessment, which includes control of constitutionality and compatibility with international norms. The Council of State exercises its suspensive veto right called 'formal opposition' ('opposition formelle') in case the incompatibility with the Constitution or Luxembourg's international obligations is not addressed, thus playing an important role as a guardian of the Constitution and fundamental rights and freedoms.[104] Parliament may override a formal opposition through a second vote of the text after a reflection period of at least three months.

96. According to the Constitution, the Grand Duke must promulgate Laws within three months of their vote. Before the Grand Duke signs a Law, a responsible Member of the Government must countersign it. In 2008, Grand Duke Henri objected to signing the Law on euthanasia and assisted suicide voted by Parliament.[105] To overcome the institutional crises resulting thereof, the Constitution had to be amended. Since this revision, the Grand Duke signs but no longer promulgates laws. The Law on euthanasia and assisted suicide was finally promulgated just before the end of the three-month period on 16 March 2009 after having been voted by Parliament on 18 December 2008.

97. Judicial control of the constitutionality of the laws is performed *ex post* by the competent jurisdiction or by the Constitutional Court. When a question relating to the constitutionality of a Law arises before a judicial or administrative Court, the matter must be referred to the Constitutional Court for a preliminary ruling, unless the question is not vital for the solution of the case or if the constitutional question appears sufficiently clear to the jurisdiction.

III. Grand-Ducal Regulations ('Règlements Grand-Ducaux')

98. According to the Constitution, the Grand Duke shall make the necessary regulations to ensure the enforcement of the laws while being unable to derogate therefrom. In practice, the Member of the Government competent in the matter draws up the draft Grand-Ducal Regulation.

---

104. *Le Conseil d'Etat, gardien de la Constitution et des Droits et Libertés fondamentaux,* Ed. Conseil d'Etat (2007).

105. On this issue and the constitutional consequences: Heuschling, L., *Luxembourg: Grand Duke Henri's refusal, in 2008, to sign the bill legalizing euthanasia*, in: Hazell, R. & Morris, B., (eds), *The Role of Monarchy in Modern Democracy: European Monarchies Compared,* Hart Publishing (2020), https://orbilu.uni.lu/handle/10993/38953.

99. Within the Luxembourg constitutional separation of powers, the power to adopt Grand- Ducal Regulations is restricted to domains reserved to the Law by the Constitution. Such regulations can only be adopted under the conditions and following the modalities specified by a formal Law. The essential part of the normative framework must result from the Law, including the purposes, conditions, and modalities according to which the less essential elements may be regulated by the lower norm. As we have seen, the protection of health, social security, and the freedom of liberal professions are amongst such matters reserved to the law.[106] This significantly limits the regulatory power within the area of health law. In a recent judgment, the Constitutional Court has, however, held that the principles and essential elements are sufficiently circumscribed by referring to a higher European or international norm.[107]

100. The Council of State plays a consultative role in the regulatory procedure: its opinion is required for all draft Grand-Ducal Regulations, as well as any amendment, unless the Grand-Ducal Regulations is adopted under an emergency procedure. The draft proposal, as well as the amendments, are published together with the opinion of the Council of State and can be consulted through the website of the Council of State (https://conseil-etat.public.lu/fr/avis.html).

101. The administrative jurisdictions control the conformity of Grand-Ducal Regulations with the legal dispositions. For Grand-Ducal Regulations adopted under an emergency procedure, this control includes whether an objective or self-induced urgency existed.

IV. Further Sources

102. Ministerial Regulations or Regulations of the Government in Council may complete the normative framework without derogation from higher sources of law. The constitutionality of such regulations is generally subject to caution, specifically given that health and social security are matters reserved to formal Law by the Constitution.

103. A very limited number of Royal Grand-Ducal Decrees, validly taken before the entry into force of the current Constitution, remain applicable if not formally or implicitly abrogated. The fact that they concern matters later reserved by the Constitution to the Law does not invalidate them. One must distinguish between external (procedural) and internal (substantial) compatibility of such decrees with the current Constitution.[108]

---

106. *See*: paras 93–94 *supra*.
107. C. Const., 28 Nov. 2014, No. 114/14, http://data.legilux.public.lu/eli/etat/leg/acc/2014/11/28/n2/jo, the case concerned the determination of a VAT exoneration by a Grand-Ducal Regulation with reference to a corresponding EU Directive.
108. Conseil d'Etat (Comité du Contentieux), 29 May 1965, Pas. lux. XIX, pp. 528–535. The Council of State ruled that the King of the Netherlands and Grand Duke of Luxembourg was at the time (1841) vested with full legislative power and validly issued the Royal Grand-Ducal Decree of 12

104. The power to make regulations may be delegated by Law to the professional organs of a liberal profession. This is specifically the case for the professional orders of healthcare professionals. Law assigns such regulatory powers for their respective professions to the Medical College ('Collège médical') and the Superior Council of Certain Health Professions ('Conseil Supérieur de Certaines Professions de Santé'). The Codes of Professional Ethics ('Codes de déontologie') are of an infra-regulatory nature. They may thus not derogate to superior norms and must thus be in conformity with the Constitution, Laws, and Grand-Ducal Regulations.[109]

105. In the domain of social security, mandatory agreements with the most representative professional associations (unions) of the different types of healthcare providers determine the terms and conditions under which healthcare is covered by social security.[110] The statutes of CNS ('Statuts de la Caisse nationale de Santé') further regulate the rights and duties of the beneficiaries of the insurance.[111] These instruments are of an infra-regulatory nature and may not derogate from superior norms.[112]

106. To a certain extent, the sentences of courts and tribunals may be considered a national source of law, although these sentences may not be considered precedents. As a rule, judgments do not have any binding authority over similar cases arising afterwards and between different parties. In practice, however, the judgments of higher courts do enjoy considerable moral authority. Luxembourg jurisdictions frequently refer to the jurisprudence of the higher courts of the countries that inspired the relevant Luxembourgish legal norm, such as the jurisprudence of the French Court of Cassation in civil law matters.

107. Good practice rules accepted by a large majority within the medical profession, as formalised within guidelines, may further be considered a source of 'soft law'. While they are not strictly binding, deviation from good practice may potentially give rise to civil liability or deontological responsibility. In Luxembourg, the Health Scientific Council ('Conseil scientifique du domaine de la santé') has a general mission to develop and contribute to the implementation of standards of good medical practice.[113] Besides medical guidelines, the Health Scientific Council issued in 2017 a recommendation on patient information.

Oct. 1841 concerning the organisation of the medical service. This decree may thus continue to regulate matters reserved to the Law by the Constitution, such as the liberty of commerce of pharmacists.

109. *See:* para. 175 *infra*.

110. Article 61, Art. 75, CSS.

111. Article 45, CSS. Modifications of the statutes of CNS are published in the official gazette (Mémorial). A consolidated version is available on the CNS website (https://cns.public.lu/fr/legislations/textes-coordonnes/statuts-cns.html).

112. *See:* Part III., Ch. 4. Relations with Social Security *infra*.

113. Article 65bis, CSS.

Part I. The Medical Profession

Chapter 1. Access to the Medical Profession

§1. Medical Training

108. Founded in 2003, the University of Luxembourg is a relatively young university. Luxembourg lacked, until very recently, a medical school, and students from Luxembourg traditionally received their training abroad. GP training is available in Luxembourg since 2004. The University of Luxembourg more recently developed a Bachelor in medicine; the third year of the Bachelor took part in the academic year 2022/23. There are specific agreements with German, French and Belgian universities to allow students to complete their studies abroad. Since the academic year 2021/22, the University of Luxembourg has also offered three medical specialisations for students already holding a master's degree in medicine, general medicine, medical oncology and neurology.[114] No Master in medicine is currently offered; however, it is targeted after an evaluation of the first bachelor academic promotions. Enlarging the three medical specialisations already currently offered is further targeted, with a priority on adding psychiatry and paediatrics.[115]

Notwithstanding these efforts to develop a medical school and biomedical studies, most Luxembourg students continue to be trained abroad, mainly in Germany (+/– 48%) followed by France (+/– 26%) and to a lesser degree in Belgium and in Austria (8%–9% each).[116]

109. There is a legal[117] and deontological[118] requirement for physicians to keep up with the continuous development of medicine and good medical practice. The Directorate of Health has a legal mission to coordinate and promote continued medical education.[119] Subsequent Governments declared it favourable to introduce

114. Oncology and neurology have been major research priorities for several years.
115. *Luxembourg Government Coalition Agreement 2023–2028*, p. 134, https://gouvernement.lu/fr/publications/accord-coalition/accord-de-coalition-2023-2028/accord-de-coalition-2023-2028.html.
116. *Etat des lieux de la formation médicale au Luxembourg et des futurs médecins Luxembourgeois*, Association Luxembourgeoise des Etudiants en Médecine (2020), https://alem.lu/wp-content/uploads/2020/12/Etat-des-lieux-des-etudiants-en-medecine-ALEM-2020.pdf.
117. Article 6, §2, Law concerning the exercise of the medical profession.
118. Article 13, Code of Medical Ethics.
119. Article 1, Art. 4(4), Loi modifiée du 21 novembre 1980 portant organisation de la direction de la santé, Mém. A – 79 du 27.11.1980,http://data.legilux.public.lu/eli/etat/leg/loi/1980/11/21/n1.

mandatory continuous medical education with official certification. There is, however, currently no requirement for physicians to certify or document participation in continuous medical education.

In practice, local stakeholders and associations organise and promote continuous medical education. Hospital establishments have adhered to international accreditation programmes so that specific requirements may apply according to the accreditation.

§2. Freedom of Establishment, Recognition of Qualifications and Manpower Planning

110. There are no quantitative restrictions regarding the freedom of establishment for physicians. All practising physicians are registered with social security, as contracting with the social security system is compulsory.[120] There are further no geographical restrictions and physicians may freely choose where to establish their practice.

The effective exercise of specialist medical activities may de facto require contracting with a hospital establishment, particularly given the limited scope of ambulatory care that can be offered unless contractually linked to a hospital.[121]

111. Most practising physicians and non-medical healthcare professionals were trained abroad. The healthcare workforce is further dependent on high numbers of commuters residing in neighbouring countries. As a result, Luxembourg is strongly dependent on its neighbouring countries and their policies when it comes to the medical education of its healthcare professionals.

The Department of Health provides financial support to medical students at the University of Luxembourg, as well as to Luxembourg students studying abroad. There are also financial measures to stimulate the establishment of GP group practices.

Current policy aims to strengthen the resilience of the healthcare sector by raising the attractiveness of health professions amongst the resident population and by expanding the medical training opportunities within the country.

112. The recognition of a foreign diploma is governed by the amended Law of 28 October 2016 on the recognition of professional qualifications, hereafter 'Law on the recognition of professional qualifications'.[122] A formal recognition is not required if the foreign diploma in medicine was obtained in another EU Member State and corresponds to one of the diplomas listed within the relevant EU directives.[123]

120. *See:* para. 691 *infra*.
121. *See:* Part III., Ch. 3., §2. Private Healthcare Centres and Hospital Antennas *infra*.
122. Loi modifiée du 28 octobre 2016 relative à la reconnaissance des qualifications professionnelles, Mém. A231 – du 18.11.2016, http://data.legilux.public.lu/eli/etat/leg/loi/2016/10/28/n2/jo.
123. Annex V, point 5.1.1 of European Directive 2005/36/EC for basic training, point 5.1.4 of European Directive 2005/36/EC for general practitioners and Annex V, points 5.1.2 and 5.1.3 of European Directive 2005/36/EC for medical specialists.

Luxembourg generally does not assess third-country diplomas in medicine. If a diploma in medicine was obtained in a third country, the holder of the diploma is requested to apply for a full recognition of the diploma in another EU Member State. This prior recognition must entitle the holder to practise in the recognising EU Member country on an equal footing with the holders of a diploma specified in Annex V of Directive 2005/36/EC and in accordance with the conditions and criteria stipulated in Articles 24, 25 and 28 of the Law on the recognition of professional qualifications. By exception, third-country diplomas in a medical specialisation available at the University of Luxembourg (currently general medicine, medical oncology, and neurology) may be assessed.

§3. Authorisation to Practise Medicine and Temporary Service Provision

113. Practising medicine in Luxembourg is governed by the amended Law of 29 April 1983 concerning the exercise of the professions of physician, dental physician, and veterinary physician,[124] hereinafter 'Law concerning the exercise of the medical profession'. It submits the practice of the medical profession to an authorisation to practise delivered by the Minister of Health and Social Security. Practitioners already legally established in the EU, the EEA or Switzerland are entitled to temporarily provide services in Luxembourg, provided they file a specific declaration.

114. The simultaneous practice of pharmacy and the medical profession is forbidden, even in the case of persons holding diplomas authorising them to practise each of these professions. Persons with the necessary qualifications may exercise human medicine, veterinary medicine, or dentistry simultaneously.[125]

I. Standard Authorisation to Practise

115. The candidates applying for a standard authorisation to practise must fulfil the following general conditions:

- have Luxembourg citizenship, the citizenship of an EU member country, or that of an EEA country. Third-country nationals must have (or fulfil the conditions for) a Luxembourg residence permit or have been granted international protection;
- have a basic medical training qualification and hold the qualifications as a GP or a medical specialist, respectively as a dental practitioner or a specialist in dentistry, recognised or exempted from recognition in accordance with the Law on the recognition of professional qualifications;

124. Loi modifiée du 29 avril 1983 concernant l'exercice des professions de médecin, de médecin-dentiste et de médecin-vétérinaire, Mém. A – 31 du 10.05.1983, https://legilux.public.lu/eli/etat/leg/loi/1983/04/29/n1/jo.

125. Article 38, Law concerning the exercise of the medical profession; Art. 12, Loi du 31 juillet 1991 déterminant les conditions d'autorisation d'exercer la profession de pharmacien.

- meet the requirements of morality and good repute;
- meet the necessary physical and mental conditions to be able to exercise the medical profession;
- possess the necessary language skills for the exercise of the medical profession, either in German or in French, and understand the three official languages (Luxemburgish, German, and French) or acquire the necessary skills to understand them.

116. The authorisation to practise is granted as a GP ('médecin-généraliste') or for one of the officially recognised medical specialties ('médecin-spécialiste') listed by a Grand-Ducal Regulation,[126] which contains currently the following specialities: allergology; anaesthesia; anatomical pathology; biological haematology; cardiology; child psychiatry; clinical biology; clinical genetics; dental, oral and maxilla-facial surgery; dermatology; dermato-venereology; endocrinology; gastroenterology; gastrointestinal surgery; general haematology; geriatrics; gynaecology and obstetrics; general surgery; immunology; infectious diseases; internal medicine; labour medicine; maxilla-facial surgery; medical oncology; nephrology; neurology; neurophysiology; neurosurgery; neuropsychiatry; nuclear medicine; orthopaedics; ophthalmology; otorhinolaryngology; paediatrics; paediatric surgery; pharmacology; pneumology; physical medicine and revalidation; plastic surgery; psychiatry; public health and social medicine; radiology; radio-therapy; rheumatology; stomatology; traumatology and emergency medicine; tropical medicine; thoracic surgery; urology; vascular surgery; venereology; x-ray diagnosis.

117. In the field of dental medicine, the authorisation to practise is granted as a dental practitioner ('médecin-dentiste') or for the dental specialities of oral surgery ('médecin-dentiste spécialiste en chirugie buccale') or orthodontia ('médecin-dentiste spécialiste en orthodontie').

118. By derogation to the general regime, an authorisation to practise neuropathology may be granted based on a training title in the field of neuropathology, conferring the right to practise medicine as a specialist in neuropathology in the country in which the qualification was obtained, without the requirement to comply with the Law on the recognition of professional qualifications.[127]

119. The procedure to follow and the mandatory application form are specified by a Grand-Ducal regulation.[128] Applicants can apply online through the 'MyGuichet.lu' Government Web Portal or by submitting a mandatory application

126. Règlement grand-ducal modifié du 10 juillet 2011 fixant la liste des spécialités en médecine et médecine dentaire reconnues au Luxembourg, Mém. A – 139 du 19.07.2011, http://data.legilux.public.lu/eli/etat/leg/rgd/2011/07/10/n2/jo.
127. Article 1bis, Law concerning the exercise of the medical profession.
128. Règlement grand-ducal modifié du 14 janvier 2013 fixant la procédure à suivre pour obtenir l'autorisation d'exercer les professions de médecin, de médecin-dentiste, de médecin-vétérinaire et de pharmacien. Mém. A – 10 du 22.01.2013, https://legilux.public.lu/eli/etat/leg/rgd/2013/01/14/n1/jo.

form to the Ministry of Health. The applicant has to join relevant documents, notably: a recent (< three months) criminal record issued by the country of residence; a recent certificate of good mental and physical health; a copy of diplomas (basic medical training and specific training in general medicine or medical specialisation); a recent (< three months) certificate of good repute issued by the Order of Physicians of the country of the last establishment; as well as a curriculum vitae. The applicant finally must provide a proof of payment of the application fee (currently EUR 450).

If the applicant's mother tongue is not French, German, or Luxembourgish, a proof of the language skills is mandatory.

If the diplomas were obtained in a third country, a copy of the certification of recognition of the diplomas and of the licence to practise as a GP or specialist practitioner in another EU Member State is requested.

120. Once the application is complete, the Ministry of Health submits it to the Medical College for review. Based on the file and on an oral interview of the candidate, the Medical College issues a formal opinion to the Ministry.

121. The final decision by the Ministry of Health is subject to judicial review before the TA within one month of its notification.

II. Specific Temporary Authorisations

122. A medical trainee undergoing an internship ('médecin en voie de spécialisation') may apply for a temporary authorisation enabling him or her to practise under the authority of a physician authorised as a patron ('patron de stage'). This temporary authorisation may not exceed twelve months and is renewable.[129]

123. GP's in their final year of training may apply for an authorisation to replace a GP and physicians in their final year of specialisation may apply for replacement authorisation in their domain of specialisation. Such replacement authorisations are valid for a maximum period of six months. They may be renewed; the period of replacement may, however, not exceed eighteen months in total.[130] The conditions and procedure are further specified by a Grand-Ducal Regulation.[131]

124. Physicians licensed in a third country undergoing training in Luxembourg may apply for a six-month temporary authorisation.[132]

129. Article 2, §1, Law concerning the exercise of the medical profession.
130. Article 2, §2, Law concerning the exercise of the medical profession.
131. Règlement grand-ducal modifié du 30 mai 1996 fixant les modalités de remplacement en médecine et médecine dentaire ainsi que la procédure à suivre pour obtenir l'autorisation de remplacement, Mém. A – 90 du 21.12.1996, https://legilux.public.lu/eli/etat/leg/rgd/1996/05/30/n4/consolide/20030204.
132. Article 2, §3, Law concerning the exercise of the medical profession.

III. Duration and Lapsing

125. The standard authorisation to practise is not limited in time. It lapses, however, if the physician does not start practising his profession in Luxembourg within two years of the issue of the authorisation. The authorisation further lapses if a physician ceases his professional activity and leaves Luxembourg for more than two years.[133]

126. Once a professional activity has ceased for more than five years, the physician must inform the Ministry of Health of his intention to resume practising. Considering the specific nature of the discipline practised, the Minister of Health and Social Security may request a specific trainee period that may include a requirement to undergo specific training.[134]

127. Professionals registered who request to be struck off the professional register are omitted and do not have to pay the annual fee for the year to come. This request constitutes a waiver of their authorisation to practise their profession.[135]

IV. Suspension and Revocation

128. Two distinct procedures for suspending or revoking a physician's right to practise coexist: first, the ministerial procedure foreseen by the Law concerning the exercise of the medical profession and, second, the revocation or suspension by a disciplinary jurisdiction pursuant to the amended Law of 8 June 1999 relative to the Medical College.[136]

129. The Minister of Health and Social Security may decide a revocation or suspension if the legal requirements are no longer met,[137] in particular in case the requirements of morality and good repute are no longer met. According to jurisprudence, the requirement of morality and good repute imposes on the physician not to behave in a manner likely to damage the image and reputation of his profession or the health of his patients. A physician's behaviour outside the practice of his profession may be considered.[138]

A specific procedure allowing for a temporary suspension of an authorisation to practise if the necessary physical and mental conditions are no longer met is foreseen by the Law. This relatively cumbersome procedure demands an assessment by

133. Article 32bis, Law concerning the exercise of the medical profession.
134. Article 32ter, Law concerning the exercise of the medical profession.
135. Article 13, §4, Law relative to the Medical College.
136. *See:* Part I., Ch. 4., §1., V. Disciplinary Action *infra*.
137. Article 15, Law concerning the exercise of the medical profession.
138. CA, 25 May 2016, No. 37318C. The Court confirms a suspension of twelve months motivated by a bankruptcy judgment against a physician concerning a commercial activity without a link to his medical activity.

a group of three experts.[139] In case there is a risk that a continued professional practice would expose patients or third parties to serious harm, the Minister of Health and Social Security may order a suspension with immediate effect for a period of three months or submit continued practising to restrictions.[140] This procedure may be used in the event of problematic alcohol or drug abuse by a physician.

130. The jurisdictions consider that the principle of *'ne bis in idem'* does not preclude the coexistence of criminal and administrative sanctions, as each of these types of sanctions pursues different objectives. A physician convicted of criminal offences by a final decision of a criminal jurisdiction and disciplinary offences by a final decision of a disciplinary jurisdiction may, however, not be suspended for the same facts by ministerial decision. Such a third decision violates the *'ne bis in idem'* principle protected by Article 4 of Protocol No. 7, paragraph 1, of the European Convention on Human Rights (ECHR), mainly because two separate disciplinary sanctions may not coexist for the same facts.[141] A criminal jurisdiction may further pronounce a ban on practising as an accessory penalty.[142]

V. Judicial Review

131. Any decision to grant, refuse, suspend or withdraw an authorisation to practise is subject to judicial review before the administrative jurisdictions. Action against the granting of authorisation may exclusively be lodged by the Medical College in the case of physicians and dentists and by the Veterinary College in the case of veterinary medicine. Legal action must be lodged within one month of the notification of the decision. Administrative courts have full jurisdiction.[143]

VI. Temporary Service Provision

132. Nationals of an EU member country legally established in an EU member country other than Luxembourg may temporarily and occasionally practise medicine or dentistry in Luxembourg. Prior to the practice in Luxembourg, a formal declaration of temporary service provision must be submitted to the Ministry of Health. This declaration is valid for a renewable one-year period.[144]

133. Non-nationals of an EU member country legally established outside Luxembourg may temporarily and occasionally practise medicine or dentistry in Luxembourg as a consulting physician ('médecin consultant') assisting a physician or dentist authorised to practise in Luxembourg who has called them to assist him.[145]

139. Article 16, §1, Law concerning the exercise of the medical profession.
140. Article 16, §2, Law concerning the exercise of the medical profession.
141. CA, 15 Jan. 2015, No. 35052C.
142. Article 45, Art. 48, Law concerning the exercise of the medical profession.
143. Article 35, Law concerning the exercise of the medical profession.
144. Article 4, §1, Art. 11, §1, Law concerning the exercise of the medical profession.
145. Article 4, §2, Art. 11, §2, Law concerning the exercise of the medical profession.

134. A physician who has been suspended or banned from practising in Luxembourg may not provide such services if his suspension or ban is still in force in Luxembourg.

135. The physician must follow the rules of conduct directly related to the exercise of his profession, such as the definition of the profession, the use of titles and serious professional misconduct, and the disciplinary provisions applicable in Luxembourg. Although not registered on the Ordinal Register, the physician or dentist is subject to disciplinary action for his or her activities in Luxembourg.

Chapter 2. Practice of Medicine

§1. Legal Monopoly to Practise Medicine

136. The Law concerning the exercise of the medical profession regulates the practice of human, dental and veterinary medicine. Practising without being entitled to do so constitutes an illegal practice of medicine.[146] The Law establishes a legal monopoly for the practice of medicine. This monopoly has two characteristics: it is exclusive, which means that with the exclusion of all others, physicians are authorised to practise medicine, and it is all-embracing, which means that it covers every activity that must be considered to belong to medicine.

137. With respect to the exclusive character of the monopoly, the main exceptions concern other regulated healthcare professions. The exclusive character does not hinder the exercise of a recognised health profession within the limits of the powers under the laws and regulations governing the concerned profession.[147]

138. The all-embracing character of the monopoly to practise implies that every physician is legally competent to practise all activities that belong to medicine, from the simplest to the most sophisticated procedure. The all-embracing character of the monopoly is a legal fiction and is not absolute. Specific legal requirements may request a specific qualification or complementary certification. Prescribing certain medicines is reserved to specific specialists; similarly, the prescription of certain psychotropic substances, such as methadone or medicinal cannabis, is limited to the holders of a specific licence delivered by the Minister of Health and Social Security. More fundamentally, Article 5, §1, of the Law relative to patient rights and obligations, as well as medical deontology, obliges to abstain from treating a patient when the health issue transcends the physician's competence.

§2. Medical Practices

139. Physicians may freely decide where to establish. They must have a suitable installation, suitable premises, and sufficient technical resources in relation to the nature of the procedures carried out and the population cared for. This includes that the premises and equipment must allow that professional confidentiality can be respected, as well as that the hygiene, quality and safety procedures are followed.[148] The concrete standards to be met are, however, not subject to a specific norm or regulation.

140. Physicians and dentists were traditionally only allowed to be active in one medical practice. This limitation was abolished in 1995. If a physician or dentist

146. *See:* Part I., Ch. 3. Illegal Practice of Medicine *infra.*
147. *See:* Part III., Ch. 2. Relationship with other Professions *infra.*
148. Article 30, Code of Medical Ethics.

cannot meet his obligation of continuity of care due to the existence of several practices or places of establishment, the Minister of Health and Social Security may request him or her to limit the activity to one practice.[149] Exercise within associations or private healthcare centres is becoming more and more frequent.

See: Part III., Chapter 1., §2. Associations of Physicians *infra*; Part III., Chapter 3., §2. Private Healthcare Centres and Hospital Antennas *infra*.

§3. Professional Obligations and Rules of Conduct

I. Continuity of Care and Mandatory Duty Service

141. The Law concerning the exercise of the medical profession specifies that physicians must ensure continuity of care for the patients under their care. The same goes for the Code of Medical Ethics.

So-called medical houses (maisons médicales) ensure a replacement service for GPs to provide primary healthcare at night, on weekends and on public holidays when medical practices are closed. In the field of paediatric medicine, one centralised 'paediatric medical house' is run by a shift of paediatricians. Participation in these replacement services is mandatory for GPs and paediatricians. Article 6, §3, of the Law concerning the exercise of the medical profession foresees that a Grand-Ducal Regulation shall determine the modalities according to which the replacement service is organised. No such regulation has been adopted and this aspect remains regulated by an agreement of 14 December 2010 between the State and the Association of Physicians and Dentists (AMMD).

Physicians exercising within a hospital are obliged to participate in duty service shifts organised within their hospital. A compensation for duty services within the hospital sector was recently introduced.[150] Article 6, §3, of the Law concerning the exercise of the medical profession further foresees that in the event of a shortage of physicians attached to a hospital, specialists without a hospital activity may be required to participate in the duty service of a hospital under the conditions laid down by a Grand-Ducal Regulation. No such regulation has been adopted so far.

II. Insurance Coverage

142. Any person practising medicine in Luxembourg is required, under penalty of disciplinary sanctions, to dispose of insurance coverage of his or her civil liability for damages occurring in the course of his or her professional activity. Insurance

149. Article 6, §1, Law concerning the exercise of the medical profession.
150. Loi du 22 décembre 2023 portant modification de la loi modifiée du 8 mars 2018 relative aux établissements hospitaliers et à la planification hospitalière en vue d'autoriser l'Etat à participer au financement des gardes et astreintes des médecins hospitaliers dans les centres hospitaliers et les établissements hospitaliers spécialisés, Mém. A – 839 du 22 décembre 2023, http://data.legilux.public.lu/eli/etat/leg/loi/2023/12/22/a839/jo.

coverage may be personal or through group insurance. Physicians that are temporarily and occasionally practising medicine in Luxembourg are exempted if the service provision is covered by their home insurance or by an equivalent or substantially comparable specific regime. A Grand-Ducal Regulation may lay down the minimum conditions and modalities of mandatory insurance coverage.[151] No such regulation has been adopted so far.

III. Rules of Professional Conduct

143. The rules of professional conduct applicable to the medical profession are compulsory to all persons authorised to practise as a physician or dentist, to students doing a replacement, as well as to physicians or dentists established in another country who are temporarily and occasionally practising medicine in Luxembourg. Disciplinary liability concerns facts that occurred during the period of medical activity. Disciplinary action may be engaged in such acts even if a physician has meanwhile ceased his activity or after his deregistration. The violation is sanctioned by the disciplinary jurisdictions.[152]

§4. Use of Professional and Academic Titles

144. GPs are authorised to carry the professional title of 'doctor in medicine, general practitioner' ('docteur en médecine, médecin-généraliste') and specialist medical practitioners are authorised to carry the professional title of 'doctor in medicine, medical specialist in' followed by the concerned medical speciality ('docteur en médecine, médecin-spécialiste en … ').[153]

145. The academic title of 'Doctor' or 'Dr' is habitually used for physicians. Practitioners who have obtained a diploma abroad, entitling them to use an academic doctoral title after having defended a doctoral thesis, may only use their doctoral title in Luxembourg if their diploma has been recognised as the equivalent of level 8 in the Luxembourg Qualifications Framework ('Cadre luxembourgeois des qualifications – CLQ'). It is required to apply for registration of the foreign diploma in the register of higher education qualifications in order to be legally allowed to carry it. Applications can be made online through the Government web portal 'MyGuichet.lu' or by applying to the Ministry of Higher Education.

146. Besides the academic titles subject to recognition by the Ministry of Higher Education, a physician may be authorised by the Medical College to carry an academic function (such as Professor) or a title of training not recognised as a medical specialty.[154]

151. Article 33bis, Law concerning the exercise of the medical profession.
152. *See:* Part I., Ch. 4., §1., V. Disciplinary Action *infra.*
153. Article 5, §§ 1–2, Law concerning the exercise of the medical profession.
154. Article 5, §4, Law concerning the exercise of the medical profession.

§5. Compliance with Social Security Legislation

147. Contracting with social security is mandatory. Before taking up their practice, physicians are assigned an individual physician code by CNS after notifying their authorisation to practise and the address of their practice. All physicians exercising in Luxembourg are thus contracted with social security and must comply with social security requirements and fees.

See: Part III., Chapter 4. Relations with Social Security *infra*.

§6. Professional Freedom

148. Various legal norms affirm, directly or indirectly, professional independence, therapeutic freedom, and freedom to prescribe. Articles 7 to 9 of the Code of Medical Ethics are dedicated to professional independence and liberty to prescribe. According to Article 6, §2, CSS, the Convention between AMMD and CNS must take into account professional independence and liberty to prescribe. Furthermore, according to Article 33 of the Law on hospitals, the professional autonomy of a hospital physician regarding the diagnosis or treatment may not be questioned.[155] Furthermore, except in emergencies, medical coordinators may not intervene or take a decision relating to the medical treatment of a patient under the care of a physician hospitalised in a department he or she coordinates.[156] Professional freedom is, however, not absolute. Reasons of public health or other reasons of public interest may limit these freedoms.

155. *See:* para. 677 *infra*.
156. *See:* para. 681 *infra*.

Chapter 3. Illegal Practice of Medicine

149. The Law concerning the exercise of the medical profession creates a legal monopoly for the practice of medicine and protects this monopoly through the offence of illegal practice. It defines illegal practice of medicine,[157] of dentistry[158] as well as of veterinary medicine.[159] Limiting ourselves hereafter to human medicine and dentistry, we will distinguish illegal practice of medicine by a non-professional performing an act reserved to the medical profession (§1) and illegal practice by a healthcare professional (§2). We will finally see which sanctions are associated with the offence (§3).

§1. Illegal Practice by a Non-professional

150. Illegal practice of medicine is commonly understood as the practice of medicine by a non-professional. Article 7 of the Law concerning the exercise of the medical profession disposes under point a) that performs such illegal practice of medicine: *'any person who practices or takes part, even in the presence of a physician, in the diagnosis or treatment of pathological conditions, real or supposed, or in childbirth, by personal acts, verbal or written consultations or by any other means whatsoever, without being authorised to practise the profession of doctor of medicine, except in the case of a proven emergency'*. Article 14, point a) of the same Law states (in a tautological way) that performs illegal practice of dental medicine: *'any person who takes part, even in the presence of the dental practitioner, in the practice of dentistry without fulfilling the conditions of Article 8 [authorisation to practise] or Article 9 [temporary service provision] is practising dentistry illegally, except in cases of proven emergency'*. In substance, illegal practice of medicine is thus constituted when an unauthorised person performs an act reserved for the medical profession.

151. It results from the wording of Article 7a) cited above that establishing a diagnosis, treating a pathological condition (real or supposed), or practising childbirth are such acts of medicine reserved for physicians. Furthermore, Article 6bis of the same Law provides that the physician shall provide patients with the preventive, curative or palliative care required by their state of health in accordance with the scientific evidence and professional ethics. Besides diagnostic and curative acts, preventive and palliative care are thus considered acts of medicine. There exist, moreover, several specific legal dispositions preserving the carrying out of a certain act to physicians. The termination of a pregnancy has, for instance, to be carried out by a physician to be legal.[160] Another example is euthanasia and assisted suicide, which may only be practised by a physician.[161] The nomenclature of medical fees

157. Article 7, Law concerning the exercise of the medical profession.
158. Article 14, Law concerning the exercise of the medical profession.
159. Article 32, Law concerning the exercise of the medical profession.
160. *See:* Part II., Ch. 5., §4. Termination of Pregnancy *infra*.
161. *See:* Part II., Ch. 3., §3. Euthanasia and Assisted Suicide *infra*.

lists medical acts according to their speciality. Even though established for reimbursement purposes, the acts listed are, by nature, acts of medicine.

152. When it comes to dental medicine, Article 14 of the Law does not give further indications with regard to the acts concerned by the prohibition of illegal practice of dentistry. Article 13bis provides that dentists shall provide patients with the preventive, curative or palliative care required by their state of health. It surprises that the wording of Article 13bis repeats word-by-word Article 6bis of the same Law, including when it comes to palliative care. As specified by Article 34 of the Law on the recognition of professional qualifications, basic training as a dental practitioner provides the skills needed for preventive, diagnostic and treatment activities relating to anomalies and diseases of the teeth, mouth, jaws, and associated tissues. The profession of dental practitioner, oral surgery or orthodontia is supposed to focus on the teeth, gums, and mouth. The nature of dental medicine is, in our view, currently not sufficiently reflected in the current wording. Dentistry is not embracing human medicine. Both fields require separate authorisations, and the relevant EU legal framework precludes an interpretation of national legislation that would allow a dentist who does not possess evidence of basic medical training to practise acts of palliative care reserved to the profession of GP or medical specialist.[162]

153. The definition of illegal practice of medicine has its roots over two hundred years ago.[163] The jurisprudence of the Court of Cassation historically concerned mostly faith healers that promised to cure patients through prayer, use of unproven therapies and suggestive psychic action. On 11 November 1924 and 21 May 1926,[164] the Court of Cassation adopted a broad definition of illegal practice of medicine and held that the words used by the Law *'are general in scope and are to be understood as any acts tending to cure and alleviate a state of discomfort or disease'*. In 1937, in another case concerning faith healing, the Court of Cassation ruled that the fact of *'exposing sick people to a suggestive psychic action able to influence the morbid state of subjects with certain moral and psychic conditions constitutes a medical treatment within the meaning of Article 12 of the 1901 Act'*.[165] Contrary to Belgian and French law, Luxembourg law and jurisprudence consider that illegal practise does not need to be 'habitual'. Already in 1900, the Court of Appeal stressed that a single act is sufficient to constitute illegal exercise.[166] The Court of Cassation further confirmed in the three aforementioned faith healer cases that an isolated act might constitute illegal practice of medicine. There are no recent decisions of the Court of Cassation. There has, however, been no substantial change

162. In the same sense: CJEU, 19 Sep. 2013, *Conseil national de l'ordre des médecins*, C-492/12, https://eur-lex.europa.eu/legal-content/EN/TXT/HTML/?uri=CELEX:62012CJ0492&from=FR.
163. Nys, H. & Schwebag, M., *Illegal practice of medicine in the Benelux countries. A comparative study.*, RLDS, No. 13, pp. 18–25 (2022).
164. Cass., 11 Nov. 1924 and 21 May 1926, Pas. Lux., t. XII, 1930–1932, pp. 218–222.
165. Cass., 15 Jul. 1937, Pas. Lux., t. XII, 1936–1949, pp. 132–133.
166. Cour, 22 Jan. 1900, Pas. Lux. 1899–1901, I, pp. 227–229. The judgment stresses that the Act of 1818, which served as a model for the Law of 1841, had always been interpreted in this way before the Belgian interpretative law of 1853. It thus rejects that there need to be 'habitual' acts.

in the nature of the offence and it is reasonable to consider that the definition of illegal practice of medicine remains very broad and includes isolated acts.

154. When it comes to the question of which person has to be considered not being authorised to practise medicine, reference is made to §3 of the first chapter describing the regime of permanent or temporary authorisations. From this follows, *mutatis mutandis*, who is an unauthorised person.

The Law further specifies that illegal practice does not apply to medical students acting under the responsibility of a training supervisor or during an adaptation period, as well as to members of a health profession governed by the amended Law of 26 March 1992 on the practice and revalorisation of certain health professions, acting within the limits of their powers under the laws and regulations governing these professions (*See*: Part III., Chapter 2., §3. Law on the Practice and Revalorisation of Certain Health Professions). The Law concerning the exercise of the medical profession further specifies that cases of proven emergency are excepted. One may consider that such situations correspond to the 'state of necessity justification' foreseen in general criminal law.[167]

155. Besides the offence of illegal practice, Article 39bis of the Law concerning the exercise of the medical profession foresees a specific offence committed by anyone who incites an unlicensed person to commit illegal practice of medicine, dentistry, or veterinary medicine.

§2. Illegal Practice by a Healthcare Professional

156. The offence of illegal practice also applies to certain acts committed by persons having a qualification as a physician, dentist, or healthcare professional.

I. Physicians and Dentists Assisting in Illegal Practise

157. The Law specifies that any person who, in possession of a regular title, assists a person committing illegal practice for evading the legal requirements commits the offence of illegal practice. Although having a regular authorisation, a physician or dentist who is a partner in crime by assisting in committing illegal practice of medicine is considered to commit illegal practice.

Furthermore, the offence of incitement to illegal practice foreseen by Article 39bis of the Law concerning the exercise of the medical profession could apply according to the circumstances.

167. Concerning the state of necessity: Spielmann, D. & Spielmann, A., *Droit pénal général luxembourgeois*, pp. 283–294, Ed. Bruylant (2002).

II. Physicians Without a Regular Entitlement

158. The possession of a valid authorisation to practise allows its holder to exercise the medical profession in Luxembourg. A formal declaration of temporary service further allows a physician legally established within the EU or EEA to be assimilated for the purpose of temporarily and occasionally practising medicine in Luxembourg.

159. Performs illegal practice the physician who:

- practises while an authorisation has not (yet) been delivered;
- performs a service provision without fulfilling the notification condition laid down by the Law;
- performs a professional act during a sentence of suspension or prohibition from practising the profession;
- after not having practised for at least five years, takes up his practice without notifying the Minister of Health and Social Security or without having completed the additional training or adaptation course required by the Minister;
- a medical trainee who practises without being under the authority of a training patron.[168]

160. When a health professional exceeds the competence outlined by the rules of competence of the specific health profession, he or she commits illegal practice of medicine. This is, for instance, the case of a midwife running the private practice of a gynaecologist, performing medical gynaecological acts during his absence.[169]

§3. Non-conventional Practices and Professions Not Recognised

161. A Law of 14 July 2015 recognised the profession of psychotherapist as a regulated healthcare profession.[170] A Law of 21 August 2018 recognised osteopathy as a regulated healthcare profession.[171] The legislative recognition of non-conventional practices in medicine or other unregulated practices has, in general, been slow and limited and many activities remain unregulated. This is, for instance, the case for clinical psychologists (if not recognised as psychotherapists), homoeopaths, naturopaths, chiropractors, sophrologists, traditional Chinese medicine and many other professions. In theory, these non-regulated activities are subject to violating the legal monopoly of physicians. Given the broad definition of illegal practice of medicine, the exercise of such an activity by a person not recognised as a physician may be considered illicit. In practice, such activities are, however, exercised in a grey zone and no prosecution takes place. Hospitals and other recognised

168. Cour, 25 Jun. 2013, No. 342/2013 V.
169. Trib. Lux., 25 Feb. 2022, No. 824/2022, Comment. Ehrmann, M., RLDS, No. 16, pp. 22–26 (2023).
170. Mem. A – 136, 21.07.2015, https://legilux.public.lu/eli/etat/leg/loi/2015/07/14/n1/jo.
171. Mem. A – 777, 6.09.2018, https://legilux.public.lu/eli/etat/leg/loi/2018/08/21/a777/jo.

healthcare providers employ such professionals. The (illicit) activity is through this detour publicly funded, whereas no official tariff ensuring direct funding through social security is available when the exercise takes place in private practice.[172] We believe that regulating such activities would be in the interest of both patients and the concerned professionals.

§4. Sanctions

162. Article 39bis of the Law concerning the exercise of the medical profession provides for a fine of EUR 500 to EUR 20,000 for incitement of illegal practice of medicine. In the case of repetition within two years' time of a first sentence, the fine may be doubled.

Article 40 of the Law concerning the exercise of the medical profession provides for a fine of EUR 1,000 to EUR 50,000 for illegal practice of medicine. In the case of repetition within five years' time of a first sentence, a fine of EUR 2,000 to EUR 100,000 and/or a penalty of eight days to six months.

Article 41 of the Law concerning the exercise of the medical profession provides for a fine of EUR 5,000 to EUR 100,000 for illegal practice of medicine when the person has made undue use of a protected title. In the case of repetition within five years' time of a first sentence, a fine of EUR 10,000 to EUR 200,000 and/or a penalty of six months to one year.

172. Lair-Hillion, M.-L., *Etat des lieux des professions médicales et des professions de santé au Luxembourg: rapport final et recommandations*, pp. 535–563, Luxembourg (2019).

Chapter 4. Control over the Practice of Medicine

§1. Medical College and Rules of Professional Conduct

I. Introduction

163. The origins of the Medical College ('Collège médical') date back to the 'Medical Commission' ('commission médicale') created in the Grand Duchy of Luxembourg, as well as in the seventeen provinces of the United Kingdom of the Netherlands, pursuant to the Law of 12 March 1818 governing the practice of the different branches of the art of medicine. A Royal Grand-Ducal Decree of 12 October 1841 organising the medical service introduced the current designation 'Collège médical'. Notwithstanding necessary adaptations of its functioning and its missions, the auto-regulatory mission as the professional order of the medical profession has persisted over time.[173]

164. The Medical College is currently a public law institution governed by the amended Law of 8 June 1999 relative to the Medical College.[174] It functions as a common professional order for physicians, dentists, pharmacists, and psychotherapists. For all other recognised non-medical health professions, the function of professional order falls within the legal competencies of the Superior Council of Certain Health Professions ('Conseil Supérieur de Certaines Professions de Santé').[175]

II. Composition, Attributions and Functioning

165. The Medical College comprises fourteen regular members: eight physicians, two dentists, two pharmacists and two psychotherapists. The members are elected by their peers for a renewable mandate of six years. There are as many substitute members as regular members. The president, the vice-president and the secretary are elected by a secret vote amongst the elected members.

166. Article 2 of its organic law attributes four main missions to the Medical College:

(1) safeguarding the honour of the profession, maintaining and defending the principles of dignity, probity, delicacy and competence;
(2) ensuring compliance with the ethical standards;

---

173. Loutsch, H., *Aperçu historique sur les origines du Collège Médical*, in: *Le Collège médical 1818–1968*, Imprimerie Coopérative Luxembourgeoise, Esch-sur-Alzette (1970).
174. Loi du 8 juin 1999 relative au Collège médical, Mem. A – 84 du 29.06.1999, http://data.legilux.public.lu/eli/etat/leg/loi/1999/06/08/n8.
175. *See:* Part III., Ch. 2., §3. Law on the Practice and Revaluation of Certain Health Professions *infra*.

(3) studying all questions relating to the healing art and health issues referred to it by the minister in charge of health or which it deems useful or worth taking up;
(4) issuing a formal opinion on all draft laws and regulations concerning the professions of physician, dentist, pharmacist, psychotherapist, another healthcare profession, or the hospital sector.

167. The main mission of the Medical College is to auto-regulate, oversee and defend the interests of the professions represented. It formulates the general principles and rules of conduct within the Code of professional ethics. It ensures, if necessary, through disciplinary action, that the members of the professions observe the common rules of the profession.

168. As seen above, applications for an authorisation to practice medicine or dentistry are reviewed and candidates are interviewed by the Medical College. The opinion issued by the Medical College includes an assessment of the merits of the qualifications and other elements of the file, as well as on the language skills.[176]

169. The Medical College further settles disputes. The President of the Medical College, or a member delegated by the President, may offer his good offices to settle disputes that arise between physicians, dentists, pharmacists, and psychotherapists or between them and patients or clients in the practice of their profession.[177]

170. The meetings of the Medical College are not public and the discussions between the members are covered by secrecy. The functioning of the Medical College may further be specified by an internal regulation. The functioning is financed through State contributions and through an annual contribution that the professionals registered must pay.[178]

III. Registration on the Ordinal Register

171. According to Article 33(2) of the Law concerning the exercise of the medical profession, any physician or dentist authorised to practise is obliged to register in the month following his effective installation on the Ordinal Register maintained by the Medical College. Physicians or dentists entitled to temporarily provide medical services do not have to register. The information for the maintenance of the Ordinal Register is communicated to the Medical College by the Ministry of Health. The same goes for pharmacists[179] and psychotherapists.[180]

176. *See:* para. 120 *supra*.
177. Article 16, Law relative to the Medical College.
178. Articles 12–14, Law relative to the Medical College.
179. Article 5, amended Law of 31 Jul. 1991 concerning the conditions for exercise of the profession of pharmacist.
180. Article 7, §3, Law of 14 Jul. 2015 establishing the profession of psychotherapist.

172. Professionals registered who request to be struck off the professional register are omitted and do not have to pay the annual fee for the year to come. This request constitutes a waiver of their authorisation to practise their profession.[181]

IV. Rules of Professional Conduct

173. The rules of professional conduct applicable to the medical profession originate directly from the legislation applicable to the profession or from the Code of Medical Ethics ('Code de déontologie médicale'). The observance of these rules is compulsory to all persons authorised to practise as a physician or dentist, as well as to students, students doing a replacement and physicians or dentists who are entitled to temporarily provide medical services without being registered. The same goes for third-country nationals consulting upon request in Luxembourg.

A. *Legally Determined Rules of Professional Conduct*

174. The Law concerning the exercise of the medical profession contains certain obligations, the non-compliance of which has been made a disciplinary offence by the legislator. This is the case for the obligation to acquire the necessary language skills,[182] the obligation to register with the Medical College within a month following the installation,[183] as well as for the obligation to dispose of an insurance coverage.[184] Furthermore, failure to comply with the formal and procedural requirements of the Law on euthanasia is a disciplinary offence.[185]

B. *Code of Medical Ethics*

175. Pursuant to Article 18, §2, of the Law concerning the exercise of the medical profession, 'a code of ethics for the professions of physician and dentist is enacted by the medical college and approved by the minister of health. This code is published in the Mémorial'. Article 18, §2, assigns the regulatory power to adopt a deontological code to the Medical College and makes it subject to an approval procedure by the Minister of Health and Social Security. The current wording does not precisely describe the purpose of the norms to be established in such a Code. It may thus be considered insufficiently detailed with regards to the additional requirement foreseen by Article 129, §2, of the revised Constitution. This (potential) incompatibility concerns a newly introduced formal requirement. The current Code of Medical Ethics

181. Article 13, §4, Law relative to the Medical College.
182. Article 6, §2, Law relative to the Medical College.
183. Article 33, §1, Law relative to the Medical College.
184. Article 33bis, Law relative to the Medical College.
185. Article 8, Law on Euthanasia and Assisted Suicide.

remains, in our view, valid and enforceable. It is, however, not certain that the current wording allows to validly adopt new norms.[186]

176. A Code of Professional Ethics applicable to the medical profession called 'Code of Medical Ethics' ('Code de déontologie médicale') was adopted in 1991, as well as in 2005 and 2013. The Code of Medical Ethics currently applicable was approved by the Ministerial Order of 1 March 2013.[187] The preamble to the Code stresses that the Medical College felt it necessary to consider the increased role of patient autonomy, the adoption of the Law on euthanasia and assisted suicide (2009) and to anticipate the adoption of the Law on patient rights and obligations (adopted in 2014). The preamble further notes the changes in medical practice resulting from the increased use of ICT and the raise of new forms of collaborations between physicians.

The 123 articles of the Code of Medical Ethics are divided into twelve chapters:

- Chapters I, II and XII contain general provisions with regard to the contents, the scope and the compliance of the Code.
- Chapter III (Articles 3–37) is entitled 'General duties of physicians'. It includes the main principles of medical ethics in the form of duties, such as the duty of respect for life and the dignity of the person, the respect of professional secrecy and confidentiality, of free choice of the physician, the duty of non-discrimination of patients, the duty to assist persons in danger. It defines fundamental principles of professional practice: morality and integrity; professional independence; freedom to prescribe; the duty of training and to participate in education; the principle that medicine should not be practised in a purely commercial manner; the prohibition of dichotomy; the duty not to facilitate illegal practice; the prohibition of any behaviour that discredits the profession. It further contains operational professional rules concerning matters such as advertising, professional communication, internet sites and medical offices.
- Chapter IV (Articles 38–75) is entitled 'Patient Relationship'. It recalls the duty to respect patient autonomy, the patient's dignity, and his physical and psychological integrity, as well as the respect for family life. It further formulates the general rights of patients, such as informed consent, access to the patient file or the obligation to ensure the continuity of care. It contains specific obligations concerning minor patients or patients in end-of-life situations, etc. (*See:* Part II., Chapter 3. End-of-Life Care; Chapter 4., §1. Minor Patient). It further specifies professional duties such as the replacement duty and prohibits receiving undue benefits from patients.

186. The potential incompatibility with the revised Constitution is not of substantive nature and the wording of Art. 18, §2, validly attributed such powers before the revision of the Constitution. A validly adopted norm remains valid. In the same sense, concerning the deontological rules established by the Luxembourg Bar: Kinsch, P., *L'effet sur les règlements existants des nouvelles dispositions constitutionnelles réservant des matières à la loi*, JT, 2023/3, pp. 77–81 (2023).

187. Arrêté ministériel du 1er mars 2013 approuvant le Code de déontologie des professions de médecin et de médecin-dentiste édicté par le Collège médical, Mem. A – 47 du 13.03.2013, http://data.legilux.public.lu/eli/etat/leg/amin/2013/03/01/n1/jo.

- Chapter V (Articles 76–79) is dedicated to 'Research and experimentation on human beings' (*See:* Part II., Chapter 5., §8. Biomedical Research).
- Chapter VIII (Articles 89–95) entitled 'Control Medicine' and Chapter IX (Articles 96–104) 'Expert Medicine' formulates specific duties applicable to this activity.
- Chapter VI (Articles 80–83) concerns the duty of 'Good fellowship among physicians' (*See:* Part III., Chapter 1., §1. Professional Duties Towards Colleagues).
- Chapter VII (Articles 84–88) entitled 'Replacement' concerns the mandatory duty service (*See:* Part I., Chapter 2., §3., I. Continuity of Care and Mandatory Duty Services).
- Chapter X (Articles 105–114) is dedicated to 'Fees, professional collaboration between doctors and with other health professionals' and Chapter XI (Articles 115–118) concerns 'The practice of medicine in an institutional or community setting'.

V. Disciplinary Action

A. *Introduction*

177. A core mission of the Medical College is to ensure observance of the rules of professional conduct and the upholding of the reputation, standards of discretion, probity, and dignity of the medical profession, as well as of the professions of pharmacists and psychotherapists. Chapter 5 of the Law relative to the Medical College, entitled 'Discipline and procedure in disciplinary matters', determines disciplinary action, in particular the scope of disciplinary action, a specific prescription period and the procedural requirements to be followed, as well as the disciplinary sanctions.

While disciplinary action is an important assignment of the Medical College, bringing a case before the disciplinary jurisdiction is, in practice, a last resort. According to the annual report of the Medical College, while receiving 126 complaints of a different nature, 4 disciplinary actions were brought before the disciplinary jurisdiction in 2022.[188] Complaints for minor infringements are, in practice, mainly resolved by informal interventions or through a conciliation procedure.

B. *Scope and Nature of Disciplinary Action*

178. According to Article 19 of the Law relative to the Medical College, disciplinary action may be launched before the disciplinary jurisdictions for:

- violation of legal, regulatory and ethical requirements concerning the practice of the profession;
- serious professional misconduct and negligence;

188. *Rapport d'activité pour l'année 2022,* Collège médical (2023), http://www.collegemedical.lu/Fr/Documents/default.asp?Type=3.

– acts contrary to professional honour and dignity.

179. The scope of disciplinary action is broad and may thus overlap with other legal obligations. Disciplinary action is, however, distinct from criminal or other action. In disciplinary repression, only the interest of the concerned profession is considered. In this respect, Article 19 of the Law relative to the Medical College specifies that disciplinary action be without prejudice to action before judicial jurisdictions and without prejudice to the disciplinary action provided for by the statute of public servants or municipal servants for the same facts.

180. The rules of professional conduct generally formulate disciplinary incriminations with a certain margin of indeterminacy. In relation to disciplinary action, the Constitutional Court found, by interpreting (former) Article 14 of the Constitution relative to the legality of penalties, that this provision does not apply exclusively to criminal matters. At the same time, the Court decided that in disciplinary matters, a certain indeterminacy of incriminations does not infringe the principle of legality.[189] According to the Constitutional Court, in disciplinary matters, the conduct constituting the offence is predictable with sufficient certainty if the concretisation of the offence can reasonably be achieved by means of logical, technical and professional experience criteria, such as allowing the essential characteristics to be foreseen by a professional.[190]

C. Preparatory Phase of Disciplinary Action

181. The Law provides for a clear distinction between the Medical College and the disciplinary jurisdictions. The preparatory phase of disciplinary action is entirely in the hands of the Medical College, whereas disciplinary authority is exercised by the Disciplinary Jurisdictions.

The President of the Medical College, or a member delegated by the President, has the role to investigate cases referred to the Medical College or investigated ex officio.[191] This prior investigation must be made for and against the concerned professional. In a recent case, the Superior Disciplinary Council has found that although the President of the Medical College in charge of the disciplinary procedure is not formally subject to compliance with Article 6 of the ECHR, he remains bound to observe general principles of law, such as the principle of fair procedure, the principle of respect for the rights of the defence or the general principle of impartiality.[192] Besides the investigations directly carried out by the Medical College, the President (or his delegate) may contact the State Prosecutor to have judicial police officers carry out an investigation.[193]

189. Const., 14 Dec. 2007, Arrêts No. 41/07; 42/07; 43/07.
190. Const., 22 Mar. 2002, Arrêt No. 12/02.
191. Article 21, Law relative to the Medical College.
192. CSD, 15 Feb. 2017, Arrêt No. 03/17.
193. Article 22, Law relative to the Medical College.

182. Article 121 of the Code of Medical Ethics requires physicians to testify and reveal all the facts that are relevant to an investigation. Furthermore, Article 122 specifies that any deliberately inaccurate or incomplete statement made may result in disciplinary proceedings. This duty of transparency compensates for the limited means of investigation currently available to the Medical College during the preparatory phase of disciplinary action. The Superior Disciplinary Council has considered that a physician must thus be transparent, even in proceedings concerning himself. According to the Superior Disciplinary Council, a physician cannot invoke a right to silence under Article 6(2) and (3) of the ECHR in disciplinary matters.[194]

183. At the end of the investigation phase, the President (or his delegate) refers the case to the Disciplinary Council if he considers that the facts fall within the scope of disciplinary action. He must refer the case to the Disciplinary Council if the State Prosecutor initially seized the Medical College. Before referring a matter to the Disciplinary Council, the President of the Medical College draws up a report of the facts that gave rise to the investigation.

184. As a result, the President of the Medical College cumulates the functions of prosecution and investigation. The disciplinary jurisdictions consider that this is not incompatible with the jurisprudence of the ECtHR, as the control of a judicial body offering all the guarantees is given.[195]

D. Prescription Period and Interruption Thereof

185. Disciplinary action prescribes five years from the day on which the facts occurred.[196] The disciplinary jurisdictions have given a rigorous interpretation of the prescription period, according to which the acts carried out during the investigation of a compliant by the president of the Medical College are not interruptive of the five years prescription of disciplinary action. The same goes for a non-valid summons before the disciplinary jurisdiction. The only valid interruptive act is a valid act of disciplinary prosecution before the disciplinary jurisdiction.[197]

E. Disciplinary Jurisdictions

1. Disciplinary Council of the Medical College

186. The Disciplinary Council exercises the disciplinary authority. It is composed of the President of the District Court of Luxembourg City, or a delegated

194. CSD, 7 Dec. 2022, Arrêt No. 03/22, Comment. Mertz-Spet, A., RLDS, No. 14, pp. 20–26 (2023).
195. CSD, 16 Mar. 2022, Arrêt No. 02/22, RLDS issue 11–12, pp. 16–31 (2022).
196. Article 19, Law relative to the Medical College.
197. CSD, 3 Jul. 2013, Arrêt No. 04/13; Lauricella, P., *La prescription de l'action disciplinaire à l'encontre des professionnels inscrits au Collège médical*, RLDS, No. 1, pp. 38–44 (2019).

judge of the District Court, as well as sixteen assessors. The list of assessors comprises four physicians, four dentists, four pharmacists and four psychotherapists. The members must be of Luxembourg nationality. The elected or alternate members of the Medical College can neither intervene in the composition of nor sit on the disciplinary jurisdictions. The same goes for family members of the accused.[198] The chief registrar of the District Court of Luxembourg City, or a delegate, acts as the registrar of the Disciplinary Council.[199]

187. Two of the assessors of the profession of the accused professional are appointed to sit in each case. In disciplinary matters against a physician or dentist, there are thus two physicians and dentists, respectively. If the action is directed against members of two different professions, the Disciplinary Council includes one assessor from each profession concerned.[200] The procedure before the disciplinary jurisdictions is oral. The accused physician must appear in person and may be assisted by a lawyer. If he or she does not appear, the case will be decided in absentia.[201] At the opening of the disciplinary trial, the chairperson of the Disciplinary Council presents the case. The Council hears the accused and the President of the Medical College in his conclusions. Witnesses and experts appearing before the Board are heard under oath. The Disciplinary Council may order investigations and request expert reports. The meetings of the Disciplinary Council are public. However, they may be held on camera at the request of the person being prosecuted or if facts affecting the vital interests of third parties are to be raised in the proceedings.[202]

188. The decisions of the Disciplinary Council are taken by an absolute majority of votes and are signed by all members of the Council; they shall be motivated and read out in public session. The decisions of the Disciplinary Council may be appealed against within forty days, both by the person sanctioned and by the President of the Medical College. The appeal is brought before the Superior Disciplinary Council. The Appeal has a suspensive effect.

2. Superior Disciplinary Council of the Medical College

189. The Superior Disciplinary Council is composed of six judges of the Court of Appeal, as well as sixteen assessors. The list of assessors comprises four physicians, four dentists, four pharmacists and four psychotherapists. The members must be of Luxembourg nationality. Three of the judges and two assessors are appointed to sit in each case. The two assessors are of the profession of the accused professional. If the action is directed against members of two different professions, the Superior

198. Article 18, Law relative to the Medical College.
199. Article 34, Law relative to the Medical College.
200. Article 7, Law relative to the Medical College.
201. Article 23, Law relative to the Medical College.
202. Article 24, Law relative to the Medical College.

Disciplinary Council includes one assessor from each profession concerned.[203] The chief registrar of the Court of Appeal, or a delegate, acts as registrar of the Superior Disciplinary Council.[204] The Proceedings before the Superior Disciplinary Council correspond to the proceedings before the Disciplinary Council.

3. Cassation

190. The Court of Cassation considers that in the absence of a legal provision expressly providing for it, cassation is not available.[205] By contrast, by accepting a constitutional question issued by the Disciplinary Council, the Constitutional Court has (implicitly) considered that a constitutional issue may be brought before it by the disciplinary jurisdictions.[206]

F. Disciplinary Sanctions

191. The disciplinary sanctions that may be imposed[207] by the Disciplinary Council or, in the event of an appeal, the Superior Disciplinary Council are:

- a warning;
- a reprimand;
- a fine of EUR 125 to EUR 2,500;
- subordination of the exercise of the profession to certain conditions. A full or partial suspension of the sentence to a temporary suspension of the right to practise may be granted. This benefit is lost if the professional is subject to a new suspension sentence within five years;
- suspension of the right to practise the profession for a period which may not be less than fifteen days nor exceed five years;
- a lifetime ban on practising the profession.

A temporary suspension of the right to practise or a permanent ban automatically includes temporary or permanent deprivation of the right to vote and to stand for election of the Medical College.

The publication in the press or media may be ordered at the expense of the convicted professional. The fact that a professional is convicted/sentenced to a temporary suspension of the right to practise is further mentioned in the public directory of health professionals during the suspension period. A professional sentenced to a lifetime ban is omitted from the public directory.

203. Article 30, Law relative to the Medical College.
204. Article 34, Law relative to the Medical College.
205. Cass., 2 Apr. 2009, Arrêt No. 21/09.
206. Const., 23 Dec. 2005, Arrêt No. 28/05.
207. Article 20, Law relative to the Medical College.

192. A professional with an establishment abroad who has been convicted/sentenced to a temporary suspension of the right to practise or to a lifetime ban in Luxembourg loses the right to temporarily provide services in Luxembourg for the suspension period, respectively, for a lifetime.

193. Two distinct procedures for suspending or revocation of a physician's right to practise coexist. Besides the revocation or suspension pursuant to exercise of disciplinary powers, the Minister of Health and Social Security may suspend or revoke a valid authorisation in case the conditions for granting the authorisation are no longer fulfilled. Two separate decisions by the Minister and the disciplinary jurisdictions based on the same facts may, however, be in violation of the *'ne bis in idem'* principle (*See:* Part I., Chapter 1., §3., IV. Suspension and Revocation).

§2. Professional Liability

194. The expression 'professional liability' as used here connotes the responsibility of the physician in general in the exercise of his or her profession. This includes obligations imposed by civil law (I.) and criminal law (II.), as well as those resulting from disciplinary law (*See*: previous §1.) and liability resulting from a violation of social security legislation (*See:* Part III., Chapter 4. Relations with Social Security).

195. Physicians often fear legal consequences if something goes wrong; at the same time, patients are generally aware that healthcare is a risky activity.[208] The need for recognition of an incident and the altruistic need to prevent similar incidents from happening to another patient is often as important to patients as the prospect of financial compensation. In practice, recognition of incidents is unfortunately frequently unmet and open disclosure is not necessarily a given. Patients – by opposition to physicians – frequently do not expect that complaints are taken seriously and are dealt with impartiality.[209] To promote an open dialogue on complaints and favour out-of-court dispute resolution, the legislator has created the National Information and Mediation Service. Besides providing general information on patient's rights and obligations, it constitutes a sectorial mediation centre for any conflict between a patient and a healthcare provider. To facilitate out-of-court settlement of liability issues, insurance companies may be involved in the mediation process (*See:* Part II., Chapter 1., §14. Complaints and Mediation)

208. In a 2014 survey, 54% of respondents in Luxembourg answered 'likely' to the question (42% 'not likely') whether they think it is probable that patients will be harmed when receiving healthcare in a hospital. *See:* Special Eurobarometer 411, Patient Safety and Quality of Care, European Union (2014).
209. Friele, R., et al., *Complaint Handling in Healthcare: Expectation Gaps Between Physicians and the Public; Results of a Survey Study*, BMC Res Notes (2015).

I. Civil Liability[210]

A. *Introduction*

196. Civil liability claims remain the main field of medical law litigation; there is, however, no information available on the number and the type of patient liability claims. Insurance companies covering professional liability do not publish information on the number of patient claims and the nature of the cases settled. Court decisions are not easily accessible and official statistics do not specify such claims. Knowing that severe preventable incidents are not uncommon,[211] it is reasonable to assume that many potential claims do not result in financial compensation. Amongst many reasons, there is the fact that when the result of an intervention does not correspond to what was initially expected, commonly by both the patient and the physician, a further treatment usually follows. This leads to a form of 'redress in kind' financed through the social security system. No other compensation may further be needed or even possible if such supplementary healthcare resolves the health issue. In any case, an unsatisfactory outcome is not in itself evidence of a medical error, and it is often unclear whether a disappointing outcome was caused by a medical error or a medical hazard.

197. From a legal viewpoint, Luxembourg historically shares with France and Belgium the same Civil Code ('Code Napoleon'). The professional liability of physicians, hospitals and other healthcare providers has been developed by case law and doctrine from a limited number of articles in the Civil Code. Unlike in France, there is no distinction between private and public healthcare regarding the professional liability of healthcare providers. All claims fall under the jurisdiction of the ordinary courts. Luxembourg's jurisprudence in this area is largely based on French jurisprudence. However, there are some peculiarities, and it is becoming increasingly questionable to follow French jurisprudence. France has indeed taken legislative measures to address healthcare liability. Belgium and France have introduced no-fault compensation systems for medical accidents. The introduction of such a system in Luxembourg has been considered.[212] The Luxembourg legislator has so far never intervened to regulate civil liability or compensation for healthcare accidents.

---

210. Ravarani, G., *La responsabilité civile des personnes privées et publiques*, Pas. lux., 3. éd. (2014).
211. According to research, around one in twenty patients are exposed to preventable harm in medical care. Aproximately 12% of such preventable patient harm is considered severe or leads to death. *See:* De Vries, E.D., et al., *The Incidence and Nature of in-hospital Adverse Events: A Systematic Review*, 17 *BMJ Quality & Safety* 216–223 (2008); Panagioti, M., et al., *Prevalence, Severity, and Nature of Preventable Patient Harm Across Medical Care Settings: Systematic Review and Meta-Analysis*, *BMJ Clincal Research*, 366, l4185 (2019).
212. The creation of a no-fault system is a long-standing demand of the professional AMMD. The 2009 governmental coalition agreement foresaw to evaluate the introduction of such a system. Governments elected in 2013 and 2018 stated that a no-fault compensation fund would be introduced, considering the models existing in the neighbouring countries. The 2023 coalition agreement states, like in 2009, that this matter will be evaluated based on the models of the neighbouring countries.

B. Legal Nature of Medical Liability: Tort or Contract?

198. Civil liability arises when an obligation is not fulfilled. In general, liability may either be of a contractual nature or originate from tort. Luxembourg physicians predominantly practise as a liberal profession. The relationship between the physician and his patient is traditionally considered to be contractual in nature. However, several elements, such as the fact that the patient is free to withdraw consent, cannot be explained by a standard contractual approach. In specific situations, when the patient is unable to consent, liability is considered tortuous.[213] Some authors, however, do not exclude the formation of a quasi-contract in such circumstances. Liability is further tortuous when a damage is caused to third parties, such as a family member or a person accompanying or visiting a patient.

199. The contractual or tortious nature of liability further depends on the legal status of the physician practising in a hospital. In Luxembourg, hospital medicine is mainly practised under an 'open regime'. This means that the physician is a self-employed freelancer linked to the hospital by a contract of collaboration. Jurisprudence considers that in such an environment, the physician and his patient are contractually linked by a medical care contract, while the hospital is linked to the patient by a hospitalisation contract. In contrast, in a 'closed regime' setting, the physician is an employee of the hospital. The contract with the hospital covers both hospitalisation and medical care, and the hospital is contractually liable for any negligence on the part of the physician. There is an open debate as to whether the employed doctor is liable in tort, in addition to the liability of the hospital. So far, Luxembourg jurisprudence does not follow the jurisprudence of the French Court of Cassation, which immunises employed physicians.[214]

200. The tortious or contractual nature of liability does not have an impact on the assessment of the merits of a claim when it comes to deciding whether there is a fault or not. The same criteria are generally applied to qualify fault, whether contractual or in tort. The distinction may, however, be of processual importance. First, a plaintiff does not have the choice to act on a contractual or tortious ground; if there is a contract between the parties, the claim cannot be tortuous. Second, according to some case law, the legal ground of the liability must be mentioned in the original claim and cannot be amended later during the trial.[215]

213. Trib. Lux., 16 Jan. 1991, No. 21/91.

214. Cour, 24 Feb. 2010, No. 33.995, Pas. lux. 35, p. 161. This decision explicitly rejects the French 'Costedoat' jurisprudence (Cass. ass. plén., 25 février 2000, 'Costedoat', No. 97-17.378) for being in contradiction with Arts 1382 and 1383 of the Civil Code; in the same sense: Cour, 24 Jan. 2011, No. 24.259.

215. Ravarani, G., *supra* n. 210, para. 654. In practice, to avoid any pitfall, a claim usually indicates a principal contractual liability ground and, as a subsidiary ground, a tortious liability ground.

C. *Duties of the Physician*

1. Physicians Have a Duty to Care in Conformity with Best Practice

201. Luxembourg jurisdictions follow the landmark 'Mercier' decision of the French Court of Cassation, according to which the contract between the physician and his or her patient results in an obligation not to cure the patient but to offer him or her medical help conscientiously and diligently, in conformity with the advances of medical science. The main duty of a physician is to treat his patients. He or she must do everything reasonably possible to achieve healing by providing care and advice.[216] As a rule, a physician has an obligation of means ('obligations de moyens'). He does not have an obligation to achieve a specific result ('obligation de résultat') but must provide reasonable care and skill. Reasonable care and skill are subject to an *in abstracto* evaluation and undue deviation from the professional standard is considered a fault in the practice of medicine. Care may not lie below the care that would be shown in the same circumstances by a reasonable, careful physician of the same qualifications and experience. Physicians need, in general, to follow 'acquired' medical knowledge. It is a fault to have recourse to an outdated treatment. If a physician has a particular training or a specific experience, this element is considered and may lead to a stricter evaluation.[217]

202. It is up to the patient to prove a fault, the damage that occurred, and the causality between the fault and the alleged damage. In practice, it is often difficult to establish the existence of a fault, and the realisation of a purely therapeutic risk is not compensated. It may need expert advice to determine if the obligation of means has been fulfilled. The assessment of the fault considers the state of the art and known facts at the time of the events. Accordingly, an error in a diagnosis is not necessarily a fault and may be explained by the symptoms known when emitting a diagnosis. It is up to the patient to prove the fault committed that led to a diagnostic error.[218]

203. The physician further has a therapeutic freedom, which allows choosing amongst alternatives. The liberty to prescribe disappears if there is no alternative to a medicine; not to prescribe is then to be considered a fault.[219]

2. Physicians Have a Safety Obligation with Regard to Certain Risks

204. Luxembourg jurisdictions follow the French jurisprudence which admits an accessory obligation of safety with strict liability in certain areas, such as the functioning and quality of a medical device[220] or the correct functioning of equipment and

216. For an illustration: Cour, 22 Dec. 1996, 16.983, Pas. 29, p. 210.
217. Cour, 19 Dec. 2000, No. 382/00 V.
218. Cour, 7 May 2020, No. 42.846 – Concerning antenatal diagnostics; Trib. Lux., 30 Jan. 2019, No. 179.460 & No. 185.078, J.T.L. 2019, p. 120.
219. Trib. Lux., 10 Jul. 2019, No. 185.978, J.T.L., 2020, p. 52.
220. Cour, 1 Apr. 2009, No. 33.308.

material used to perform a medical procedure.[221] Concerning liability for nosocomial infections, after a first hesitation to follow the French jurisprudence, the Court of Cassation followed its French counterpart in 2013 and strict liability currently applies to nosocomial infections. The patient does thus not need to prove any fault; he or she has, however, to prove that the infection was acquired within healthcare.[222]

3. Liability for Failure to Inform

205. The physician has a duty to provide adequate information to the patient so that the patient can freely give well-informed consent. Informed consent is the only justification for a medical procedure, at least if the patient is capable of giving consent. Luxembourg jurisdictions have rapidly followed the ruling by the French Court of Cassation dated 25 February 1997, which obliged physicians to provide proof of the information given to patients.[223] The Law on the rights and obligations of the patient has confirmed this principle. The extend and the practical modalities governing the duty to inform are further detailed below (*See:* Part II., Chapter 1., §11. Informed Consent and Decision-Making Process).

206. The doctrine of loss of chance is applied in case of failure to duly inform. If there is no (proven) consent, the jurisdictions frequently scrutinise how far there is a loss of chance (not to consent) in the event the patient had been properly informed.[224] This means that no damages are granted if the jurisdiction considers that the well-informed patient would have given consent anyway. Damages may moreover be awarded for lack of preparedness to face an undisclosed risk, so-called unpreparedness damages (préjudice d'impréparation).[225]

4. Liability for Acts of Employees and Assistants

207. A person is liable for his or her own negligent acts or omissions. According to general liability rules, a physician who employs another person to help him or her perform his or her own duties will be liable for the wrongful acts or omissions of the person employed.

208. A hospital is, in general, responsible for the faults committed by its personnel; however, in open regime hospitals, the physician is considered the 'occasional

221. Cour, 1 Jan. 2001, No. 24.259.
222. Cass., 31 Jan. 2013, No. 08/13, Pas. Lux., 2014/1, Note Ancel, P.; Feltz, A., *Responsabilité médicale: Les infections nosocomiales: vers une responsabilité sans faute?*, JurisNews Droit des Assurances et de la Responsabilité (2013/1); Schwebag, M., *Responsabilité civile en matière d'infection nosocomiale et d'infection au nouveau coronavirus*, RLDS, No. 7, pp. 1–10 (2021).
223. Trib. Lux., 24 Nov. 1999, No. 1066/99; Cour, 14 Nov. 2002, No. 25.596.
224. For a critical viewpoint: Ravarani, G., *supra* n. 210, para. 1117.
225. Merz-Spet, A., *Perte de chance et préjudice d'impréparation: responsabilité civile en cas de manquement au devoir d'information*, RLDS, No. 7, pp. 20–25 (2021).

commander' of the hospital personnel while he has control over the acts of the hospital's personnel. This is, for instance, the case for nurses assisting a surgeon during an operation. As a result, the hospital or the physician may be liable for an act or omission, depending on who had the right to control the employee.

D. Liability of Hospitals

209. A hospitalisation contract governs the relationship between the hospital and the patient. The hospital provides mainly a room, nutrition, and comfort services (TV, Internet, etc.). In addition, the nurses and other healthcare professionals employed by the hospital provide accessory nursing and paramedical care. The professionals employed by the hospital dispense the medicine prescribed, supervise patients in their rooms, etc. According to the jurisprudence, the hospital is responsible for providing conscientious and attentive accessory care.[226] The hospital is, in general, responsible for any faults or omissions committed by its personnel. A physician may, however, be responsible, according to the factual situation, while he or she has control over the personnel of the hospital. The hospital is liable for an act that characterises a lack of organisation of a hospital service. The hospital is responsible for safety and supervision, depending on the patient's condition, and must have qualified and competent staff.[227] This security obligation is an obligation of means and it is up to the patient or third parties to establish the existence of a fault.

210. Strict liability is shared with self-employed physicians for nosocomial infections. In the case of blood products, it has been decided that the producer (i.e., the Luxembourg Red Cross) and the hospital are jointly responsible for contamination by the hepatitis C virus, even though this virus was not detectable at the time the blood was administered. The Court stressed that in an open regime hospital, the hospital is responsible for the supply and administration of blood with reference to the jurisprudence of the French Court of Cassation.[228]

E. Damage and Causation

211. Besides proving negligence or another cause of liability, the plaintiff patient must prove that this fact caused a damage he or she has sustained. A patient is only entitled to recover damages if he or she has suffered a damage. In principle, all the damage he or she suffered must be compensated, including *pretium doloris* and the different sorts of moral damage.

212. In Luxembourg, like in Belgium and France, according to the 'equivalence of conditions' theory, any factor that has necessarily contributed to the existence of

226. Trib. Lux., 27 mai 1981, Pas. 25, p. 31; Cour, 6 juillet 1989.
227. Trib. Lux., 15 juillet 1999.
228. Cour, 25 Novembre 2014, No. 38.586, 39.073 et 39.075.

damage has to be considered a *sine qua non* cause of this damage. The standard of proof is, however, high because the causal relation must be established with near certainty.

To alleviate the difficult burden of proof of the patient, the judge may use judicial presumptions. In applying the theory of equivalence, the judge has hypothetically to reconstruct the events leading to the damage and to imagine away the fault of the defendant. If the damage remains the same, the fault was not a necessary condition for the damage.

213. It may be hard to apply this reasoning in cases where it is uncertain what would have happened if a certain fault had not been committed. If a physician had applied the correct treatment, the patient still might not have recovered. Here, the courts found a way out by compensating the victim for the 'loss of a chance of recovery'. The 'loss of a chance' theory has long been established in Luxembourg, Belgian and French law, including in medical malpractice law. In simple terms, the loss of chance may be qualified as a loss of a possible more favourable outcome. The 'loss of a chance' theory is frequently used by jurisdictions as an instrument to compensate patients if a causal link between fault and physical damage cannot be clearly established. A prominent Luxembourg author stresses that this use is partly questionable. According to G. Ravarani, the loss of chance theory should not be used to introduce a partial causality in the event of a 'negative' loss of chance. As the author stresses: 'Once the damage has occurred, the victim has always been deprived of the entire chance to avoid it' (...) 'It seems that one must reason in terms of causality, either the medical fault or omission is causally related to the damage or risk, or it is not. To say that a fault or omission deprived the victim of a loss of chance of survival or of avoiding aggravation is to mitigate the causality between the medical fault and the part due to chance or the unknown.' The author adds that 'if a damage is caused by a combination of events, one of which is medical malpractice, the culprit of the malpractice may be held liable for the entire damage.'[229] Given the current orientation of the French and Belgian Supreme Courts, it seems nonetheless probable that the loss of chance theory will continue to be extensively applied in medical malpractice cases in Luxembourg, including as a palliative to causality.

F. Prescription Period

214. The Luxembourg legislator has so far not intervened to regulate the prescription of healthcare liability. As there is no specific delay, the general prescription of thirty years foreseen by Article 2262 of the Civil Code applies to healthcare liability. Unlike in Belgian law, civil and criminal prescriptions are not linked. The prescription period is thirty years, even if a fault may qualify as a criminal act. In our view, the thirty-year liability period is excessively long and should be reduced.

229. Ravarani, G., *supra* n. 210, paras 1112–1118.

II. Criminal Liability[230]

215. The Criminal Code of Luxembourg ('Code Pénal') dates from 1879 and has been largely inspired by the Belgian Criminal Code of 1867. It defines general penalties that apply to any person who commits an offence. Criminal liability of legal persons was introduced in 2010.

216. Acts of physicians are, by nature, likely to cause physical or psychological harm to a patient. If a fault of a physician causes harm to the patient, it may be qualified as a criminal act. According to jurisprudence, a fault in the sense of the Criminal Code and a civil fault are identical. Thus, the criterion of the reasonable, careful physician is valid both to judge the civil and criminal liability of a physician. Any deviation, also a minor one, of the professional standard that causes bodily harm to the patient is punishable as a criminal offence.[231]

217. The same act may give rise to both civil and criminal liability, so the question of the influence of criminal proceedings on civil liability issues is of practical importance.

The victim of a criminal act has the choice to act before a criminal or a civil jurisdiction. Once a claim has been brought before a civil jurisdiction, the victim is, however, no longer allowed to act before a criminal jurisdiction ('*una via electa*' principle).

Luxembourg jurisprudence traditionally followed the principle that criminal and civil faults are identical ('principe d'unicité des fautes'). To avoid contradictory decisions, if a criminal jurisdiction is investigating the same facts, the civil case is put on hold ('le pénal tient le civil en état'). In 2017, the legislator specified in Article 3, §6, of the Criminal Code that 'The absence of criminal fault for lack of foresight or precaution within the meaning of articles 418 to 422 of the Criminal Code and the special laws punishing homicide or involuntary bodily harm does not prevent an action being brought before the civil courts to obtain compensation for the damage in accordance with the rules of civil law'. Currently, the absence of a criminal fault does thus no longer imply the absence of a civil fault.

Acting before a criminal jurisdiction has the advantage that the public prosecutor is searching for evidence and paying for experts. The patient (or third party) is also, under certain circumstances, allowed to testify in his own favour. There are further generally fewer costs associated with a criminal court case. At the same time, any claim before a criminal jurisdiction must be based on fault and the claim is subject to positive proof of a personal fault of the accused.

230. Hennau-Hublet, Chr., *L'activité médicale et le droit pénal,* in: Fondation bibliothèque du droit luxembourgeois (ed.), *La responsabilité médicale en droit luxembourgeois*, ed. Bruylant (1992).

231. Cour, 24 Mar. 2010, No. 151/10 X. The case concerned a male nurse with a drug addiction, who had injected himself parts of the narcotics intended for patients, thereby contaminating the syringe administered to patients with the hepatitis C virus. Besides the nurse, the management of the hospital was sentenced for not having transferred, immediately when getting to know of the suspicion, the nurse from the sensitive area of the operational block to prevent access to narcotics. Two anaesthesiologists, who had requested management to act, were further sentenced for having continued to work with the already highly suspected nurse.

218. Criminal proceedings are for most part based on the following criminal offences: Articles 398 et seq. of the Criminal Code (voluntary homicide and voluntary injury); Articles 418 et seq. of the Criminal Code (involuntary homicide and involuntary injury); Article 410-1 and 410-2 of the Criminal Code (abstention to intervene). Abusing of the weakness induced by a vulnerability due to age, illness, infirmity, or physical or mental disability of a patient may further be qualified as abuse of weakness in the sense of Article 493 of the Criminal Code. The breach of medical secrecy is a crime punishable under Article 458 of the Criminal Code (*See:* Part II., Chapter 2., §2. Protection of Professional Secrecy under Article 458 of the Criminal Code).

In addition to general criminal law, the legal framework governing a medical activity may provide for specific grounds for criminal liability. This is, for instance, the case for performance of an abortion in violation of the conditions provided for by the modified Law of 15 November 1978 on sexual information, the prevention of clandestine abortion and the regulation of termination of pregnancy (*See:* Part II., Chapter 5., §4. Termination of Pregnancy).

§3. Quality Assurance

219. According to Article 4, §1, of the Law on patient rights and obligations, every patient shall have equal access to the healthcare required by his health condition. Healthcare must be provided in an effective manner, in accordance with scientific evidence, and legally prescribed standards of quality and safety (*See:* Part II., Chapter 1., §9. Equal Access to Quality Care). Furthermore, at the patient's request, the information to be provided prior to consenting to healthcare must include information on the quality and safety of healthcare, including the number of procedures performed by the provider and the complication rate.[232] In practice, such information is rarely requested and available.

220. Each hospital must set up structures and mechanisms for risk management, the evaluation and promotion of quality, and the prevention, reporting and control of adverse events, including the prevention and control of nosocomial infections. These structures report to the national interhospital management committee.[233] One of the several missions of this Committee is to define quality assurance systems for hospital services, to ensure national coordination of policy to promote quality in hospitals, and to draw up an annual report.[234] One of the core missions of the medical coordinator is to contribute to quality of care in the hospital.[235] Hospitals generally apply the European Foundation for Quality Management (EFQM) quality

232. Article 8, §4, subpara. 5, Law on patient rights and obligations.
233. Article 25, Law on hospitals.
234. Article 28, Law on hospitals.
235. *See:* para. 681 *infra.*

management model. Under the CNS-FHL agreement for the hospital sector,[236] hospitals may participate in a 'quality program', which sets quality and performance criteria for the payment of a financial incentive. Under this framework, accreditation efforts are financially honoured. Hospitals may either choose 'Joint Commission International (JCI)' or 'Accréditation Canada International (ACI)' accreditation. Hospitals have all engaged in such accreditation processes at different levels. There are further specific accreditation efforts at the level of specific hospital services or units, such as accreditation according to 'OkoZert' of the German Cancer Society. Accreditation efforts are completed by indicators relative to patient safety, organisation of hospital activities and management of hospital resources. These indicators are fixed annually under the CNS-FHL agreement for the hospital sector and may concern quality of documentation of care, process quality indicators and outcome measurements.

221. There is currently no publicly available outcome measurement of the medical activity. The creation of an independent 'centre for medical excellence' is foreseen by the coalition agreement. It would be mandated to put up a nationwide database with structured data on the results of patient treatment, set minimum quality standards, and make recommendations on new treatments and diagnostic tests based on scientific and medical literature.[237]

§4. Medical Ethics Committees

222. In line with international bioethical recommendations, ethics committees have been set up in Luxembourg since the 1980s. The 1998 Law on hospitals[238] introduced local hospital committees by introducing an obligation to establish an ethics committee in every hospital. The same Law further established a single National Research Ethics Committee (CNER). More recently, with the development of such activities, new structures have been set up in the domain of biomedical research. At the time of writing, newly introduced Ethics Committees are being put in place in Long-Term Care.

I. National Ethics Commission (Commission Nationale d'Ethique)

223. In 1988, the Government set up the National Ethics Commission for the Life and Health Sciences. It is currently called the 'National Ethics Commission'

236. Convention entre la Caisse nationale de santé et la Fédération des Hôpitaux Luxembourgeois, conclue en exécution de l'article 75 et suivants du Code de la sécurité sociale, https://cns.public.lu/fr/legislations/fhl/cns-fhl-convention.html.
237. *Luxembourg Government, 2023–2028 Coalition Agreement*, p. 100, https://gouvernement.lu/fr/publications/accord-coalition/accord-de-coalition-2023-2028/accord-de-coalition-2023-2028.html.
238. Loi du 28 août 1998 sur les établissements hospitaliers, Mém. A – 78 du 19.08.1998, http://data.legilux.public.lu/eli/etat/leg/loi/1998/08/28/n1/jo.

('Commission Nationale d'Ethique'). It is governed by a modified Regulation of the Government in Council of 28 November 2014.[239]

224. The CNE is an advisory body to the Government responsible for studying, either on its own initiative or at the request of the Government, ethical, social, scientific, and medical issues and their possible implications for individuals and society, arising in particular from life and health sciences.

The CNE prepares opinions and recommendations on policy and legislative measures, promotes discussion in society, and cooperates with national ethics bodies and international institutions. The opinions may reflect in annex a minority position supported by at least three of its members. All opinions and recommendations are sent to the Government and made public on the website of the Commission.[240] To promote an open public debate and dissemination of its work, the Commission organises public debates and public conferences.

225. The CNE is composed of fifteen members, including a chairperson and a vice-chairperson, appointed by the Government in Council on the proposal of the Minister of Higher Education. The members are chosen for their qualifications and give a personal independent opinion. Members are appointed for a five-year term, renewable once.

II. Ethics Committees in Hospitals

226. In 1998, hospital legislation introduced an obligation to establish an ethics committee in every hospital. The current Law on hospitals requires every hospital to dispose of a hospital ethics committee, either alone or in association with one or more other hospital(s). It is set up by the hospital's managing body or, in the case of a committee responsible for more than one hospital, by a joint decision of the concerned managing bodies. It must be composed to ensure a diversity of expertise in the medical field and with regard to ethical, social and legal issues. The committee may include both members from outside the hospital and members attached to the hospital. There is no formal requirement to include a patient representative. As a first mission, the hospital ethics committee assumes a supportive task regarding ethical aspects of decision-making in difficult end-of-life situations. In the absence of an end-of-life provision or advance directive, whenever a plurality of approaches can be envisaged from the medical point of view and the choice between them gives rise to ethical dilemmas, it may give decision-making assistance to the patient or his relatives, if the patient is no longer able to express himself, as well as to the physician. This individual decision-making assistance is given in the form of an independent, confidential, and non-binding opinion. The Ethics Committee is entitled to

239. Règlement du Gouvernement en Conseil modifié du 28 novembre 2014 portant création d'une Commission consultative nationale d'éthique indépendante, abrogeant le règlement du Gouvernement en Conseil du 9 septembre 1988 portant création d'une Commission consultative nationale d'éthique pour les sciences de la vie et de la santé, Mém. A – 251 du 23.12.2014, https://legilux.public.lu/eli/etat/leg/rgc/2014/11/28/n1/jo.

240. https://cne.public.lu/fr/publications.html.

obtain communication of the medical and other elements of the file of the patient concerned that it needs. As useful as this first mission may be, the scope and formulation do not formally include other clinical decisions that may give rise to ethical dilemmas. As a second mission, the committee may prepare guidelines on ethical issues in general. Any physician or member of the hospital staff may suggest the establishment of an internal ethical guideline on a specific issue. Besides these two missions, most ethics committees further organise conferences or other events to promote reflection on ethical issues (Law on hospitals, Article 26)

III. Ethics Committees for Long-Term Care

227. Every accommodation facility for the elderly, day care centre for the elderly and domestic nursing care service for the elderly must dispose of an ethics committee, either alone or in association with one or more other such services. The ethics committee must be composed such as to ensure a diversity of expertise in the medical and nursing care domain and regarding ethical, social, and legal issues. The committee may include both members from outside and members linked to the long-term care provider. There is no formal requirement to include a patient representative. The ethics committee may, at the request of a person taken care of or at the request of a legal representative, provide assistance in deciding on an ethical issue or answer questions relating to respect for the fundamental rights of residents. On request, it assists and advises the management and senior staff on ethical issues or issues relating to respect for the fundamental rights of residents. Such advice is formulated in the form of a confidential and non-binding opinion. The Ethics Committee is entitled to obtain communication of the medical and other elements of the file of the patient concerned that it needs. The Committee may further provide general internal guidance on ethical issues or issues relating to respect for residents' fundamental rights.[241]

IV. Research Ethics Boards

A. *National Research Ethics Committee (Comité National d'Ethique de Recherche)*

228. According to Article 27 of the Law on hospitals, 'no trial, no study or clinical experiment may be carried out on human beings with a view to developing biological or medical knowledge without prior authorisation from the Minister, the opinions of the Health Directorate and the CNER having been sought beforehand'. A Grand-Ducal Regulation of 26 June 2019 further specifies the organisation and functioning, as well as the fees for submission of a research project.[242]

241. Article 7, Law of 23 Aug. 2023 on the quality of services for the elderly.
242. Règlement grand-ducal du 26 juin 2019 relatif: – à l'organisation et au fonctionnement du Comité national d'éthique de recherche; – à la fixation des taxes à percevoir pour un projet de recherche;

Even though the Law on hospitals focuses on hospital care, Article 27 and the Grand-Ducal Regulation are considered to apply to both hospital and out-of-hospital research activities. There is thus one common procedure and one common research ethics board for all research carried out on human beings.

229. The fifteen members of the CNER are appointed for a term of four years that may be renewed three times. The CNER must comprise six medical specialists, one pharmacist, two members with expertise in the field of basic research in biological or biomedical sciences, one member with competences in the psychosocial field, a lay person, a representative of the non-medical healthcare professions, a specialist in the field of life sciences, social and behavioural sciences, cultural anthropologist, philosopher, psychologist or specialist in the sociology of medicine, and a biostatistician. It may invite external experts.

230. The CNER issues its opinions in complete independence and potential conflicts of interest must be declared.[243]

B. University of Luxembourg Bodies

231. The University of Luxembourg has established several bodies for handling questions in the field of research ethics. An internal Ethics Review Panel evaluates the ethical aspects of research projects carried out at the University to ensure that ethical considerations are met and good scientific practices are followed. The University requests prior submission of any research involving human participants, human biological material, personal data, or potentially harmful and/or irreversible changes to the environment. An Ethics Advisory Committee provides advice on ethical issues involved in the activities of the university community, addresses complaints, and conducts investigations regarding alleged discrimination at the University. A specific Animal Experimentation Ethics Committee ensures that care and use of animals for research and teaching are conducted in compliance with animal protection requirements. A Biosafety Committee further ensures compliance with the biosafety policies and measures at the University.[244]

C. Luxembourg Agency for Research Integrity

232. The Luxembourg Agency for Research Integrity (LARI) was formally created by the National Research Fund (FNR), the University of Luxembourg, as well

et modifiant le règlement grand-ducal modifié du 30 mai 2005 relatif à l'application de bonnes pratiques cliniques dans la conduite d'essais cliniques de médicaments à usage humain, Mém A-453 du 02.07.2019, http://data.legilux.public.lu/eli/etat/leg/rgd/2019/06/26/a453/jo.

243. *See:* Part II., Ch. 5., §8. Biomedical Research *infra.*

244. University of Luxembourg website, https://lari.lu/.

as the main research centres (LISER; LIST and LIH) in 2016 in the form of a non-profit association.[245] LARI may be called upon by any person or organisation which has knowledge of suspected scientific misconduct occurring in LARI member organisations. It may also investigate cases of suspected scientific misconduct on its own initiative. Handling of alleged cases of research misconduct is investigated by an internal Commission for Research Integrity.

§5. Social Security Jurisdictions

233. *See* Part III., Chapter 4., §4. Social Security Litigation.

245. LARI website, https://lari.lu/.

Part II. The Physician-Patient Relationship

Chapter 1. General Rights and Obligations of the Patient

§1. Introduction

234. Medical Ethics has traditionally formulated fundamental principles of medicine based on the Hippocratic Oath. First, do no harm; respect for human life; medical secrecy and other prescripts have always been an essential part of professional ethics. These prescripts to physicians mirror corresponding patient rights. They have evolved over time, with the evolution of the medical profession and its role and status in society. Considering this evolution, the Code of Medical Ethics of 2005 already took into account a large range of duties of physicians and corresponding patient rights. The Code of Medical Ethics adopted in 2013 anticipated the entry into force of the 2014 Law on patient rights and duties (*See:* Part I., Chapter 4., §1., IV. Rules of Professional Conduct).

235. The first catalogue of patient rights, applicable to hospital care, was enacted as a separate chapter of the 1998 Law on hospitals. The adoption of the Law of 24 July 2014 relating to the rights and obligations of the patient[246] marks a further milestone in a gradual shift from a mainly provider-oriented approach, formulating duties of physicians, towards a patient-oriented approach, transposing the obligations of physicians into formal rights of the patient. The 2014 legislator consolidated and modernised the disparate pre-existing legal framework. Luxembourg legislation was significantly inspired by the Belgian Law on the rights of the patient of 22 August 2002, as well as by the French Law of 4 March 2002 on the same matter. It further took into account directive 2011/24/EU on patients' rights in cross-border healthcare.[247]

236. The amended Law of 24 July 2014 relating to the rights and obligations of the patient, hereinafter 'Law on patient rights and obligations', constitutes the main

246. Loi modifiée du 24 juillet 2014 relative aux droits et obligations du patient, portant création d'un service national d'information et de médiation dans le domaine de la santé et modifiant: – la loi modifiée du 28 août 1998 sur les établissements hospitaliers; – la loi modifiée du 2 août 2002 relative à la protection des personnes à l'égard du traitement des données à caractère personnel; – le Code civil, doc. parl. 6469, Mém. A – 140 du 31 juillet 2014, https://legilux.public.lu/eli/etat/leg/loi/2014/07/24/n2/jo.

247. Schwebag, M., 'Implementation of the Cross-border Care Directive in EU Member States: Luxembourg', *EJHL issue* 21(1) (2014).

source for the 'core' of patient rights. It covers a wide range of individual patient rights. These rights are sometimes further addressed by additional legal instruments, principally by social security legislation and by medical deontology. Dedicated Laws, Grand-Ducal Regulations or other legal instruments further cover specific aspects and activities. Where this is the case, the 2014 Law on patient rights and obligations plays a subsidiary role, governing, for instance, access to the patient file commonly not specifically regulated within such specific legislation. This is notably the case for end-of-life issues, most aspects being governed by two Laws dated 16 March 2009. From a legislative viewpoint, it might have been coherent to consolidate the specific rights applicable in end-of-life situations within the Law on patient rights and obligations. The legislator of the time preferred, however, not to reopen the discussions around end-of-life issues that had led to a political divide in 2009 (*See:* Part II., Chapter 3. End-of-Life Care). Other specific interventions or activities, such as abortion, are also governed by ad hoc legislation (*See:* Part II., Chapter 5. Specific Activities and Issues).

§2. Scope of the Law on the Rights and Obligations of the Patient

237. The Law on patient rights and obligations is applicable whenever a patient seeks to receive or receives healthcare in Luxembourg. It further applies to cross-border provision of telemedicine services provided by a physician established in Luxembourg (Article 1, §1).

238. Article 2b) defines the term 'patient' as 'any individual seeking or receiving healthcare services'. The terms 'healthcare', 'health professional' and 'healthcare provider' are defined by Article 2c), d) and e) and delimit the scope of the Law on patient rights and obligations. It results from the combination of Article 1 with these definitions that both the status of the service provider, as well as the nature of the care, delineate the scope of the Law:

(a) 'Healthcare provider': the care must be provided by: (i) a member of a recognised health profession, or (ii) a hospital establishment, or (iii) another provider legally performing his/her profession outside of the hospital sector and referred to by subparagraph 2 of Article 61 CSS.
The medical profession is, of course, a recognised health profession covered by point (i) above. The same is true for dentists, pharmacists, and psychotherapists, as well as for recognised non-medical healthcare professions (*See:* Part III., Chapter 2., §3. Law on the Practice and Revalorisation of Certain Health Professions). Hospital establishments (ii) are those defined by the Law on hospitals.[248]
It results from point (iii) that services provided by professionals not recognised as a healthcare profession fall within the scope of the law if referred to by Article 61, §2, of the CSS. This is notably the case for opticians, suppliers of orthopaedic prostheses, and professional providers of patient transportation.

248. *See:* definition in para. 674 *infra*.

Considering the nature of the service, providers of patient transportation do generally not qualify, as the service provided is not 'healthcare'.

(b) 'Healthcare' is defined as 'assessing, maintaining or restoring health, including prescriptions, the delivery and supply of medicinal products and of medical devices'.
This definition is broad and covers occupational health, medical expertise, and prevention, as these activities imply assessing the patient's health and/or aiming to maintain it. Medical experiments carried out on patients generally assess their health status and experimental treatments generally aim to maintain or restore health. They are, thus, in our view, medical acts that constitute healthcare in the sense of the Law on patient rights and obligations.
In the silence of the law, the performance of purely aesthetic acts, the removal of an organ from a donor, the termination of a pregnancy, and the performance of euthanasia are medical acts that do not constitute healthcare in a strict interpretation of the Law on patient rights and obligations.

239. Long-term care is partly excluded from the scope of the Law. Even if provided by a recognised healthcare profession, such care is not considered healthcare if the main purpose is to support people in need of assistance with the performance of common daily tasks (Article 1, §4). It is, however, considered healthcare if the main purpose is to assess, maintain or restore health. This distinction appears in line with the exclusion of such care from directive 2011/24/UE and the definition of healthcare by other relevant EU secondary legislation, as well as the interpretation given by the jurisprudence of the ECJ in case law.[249]

§3. Privacy, Dignity and Respect of Religious and Philosophical Values (Article 3, §1)

240. Healthcare is about healing and caring for a human being. The doctor-patient relationship is, by its nature, an intimate one, potentially affecting the physical and psychological integrity of the patient. Accordingly, healthcare has a strong ethical dimension and must take into account fundamental rights and values. Chapter 2 of the Law on patient rights and obligations, entitled 'Rights and obligations of the patient', starts with Article 3, §1, recalling such fundamental values: 'The patient has the right to privacy, confidentiality, dignity, and respect for his or her religious and philosophical convictions.'

241. The necessity to respect the privacy and the dignity of the patient and his or her values has been a deontological obligation long before being enshrined within

249. *See:* ECJ, 11 Jul. 2013, *Femarbel,* Case C 57-12: concerning the scope of the exclusion of healthcare from the services directive (directive 2006/123/UE) a similar definition is given by the ECJ with regards to day care centres and night-care centres providing assistance and care to elderly persons.

the Law on patient rights and obligations. The current Code of Medical Ethics provides that 'The physician, in the service of the individual and of public health, carries out his or her mission with respect for the person and his or her dignity. Respect for human dignity is necessary even after death.' (Article 3) and that 'The physician's primary duty is not to harm the person with whom the therapeutic relationship is established, to respect the autonomy of his or her will (care contract), his or her dignity, and his or her bodily and psychological integrity' (Article 38).

242. Article 12 of the recently amended Luxembourg Constitution grants fundamental protection to human dignity, setting out that 'Human dignity is inviolable.'[250]

243. A Law of 11 August 1982 on the protection of privacy further establishes a general protection of privacy. According to Article 1, 'Everyone has the right to privacy. Judges may, without prejudice to compensation for damage suffered, prescribe any measures, such as sequestration, seizure, and others, to prevent or stop a violation of privacy; such measures may, if urgent, be ordered in summary proceedings.'

244. Notwithstanding the patient's right to respect his or her religious values, the legislator introduced in 2018 a specific offence of concealing one's face in certain public places, which is also applicable on hospital premises.[251]

245. Confidentiality is further addressed in Chapter 2 *infra*.

§4. Patient Obligations

246. The title of the Law on patient rights and obligations stresses that patients have not only rights but also obligations. According to the first subparagraph of Article 3, §2, 'By providing information relevant to his or her care in accordance with his or her capacity, and by adhering and collaborating in his or her care, the patient participates in the optimal provision of healthcare.'

247. The patient's duty to cooperate in optimal healthcare delivery by adequately informing the healthcare provider is a cornerstone of the therapeutic relationship. It is in line with the shared decision-making model favoured by Article 8 of the Law on patient rights and obligations.[252] Accurate information is crucial to enable optimal provision of healthcare. It is thus not surprising that Article 3, §2, specifically mentions the patient's obligation to provide information relevant to

250. *See:* para. 91 *supra*.
251. Law of 23 May 2018 amending Art. 563 of the Criminal Code by creating an offence of concealing one's face in certain public places, Mém. A – 413 du 28.05.2018, https://legilux.public.lu/eli/etat/leg/loi/2018/05/23/a413/jo.
252. *See:* para. 293 *infra*.

healthcare delivery. At the same time, the obligation to disclose information is limited to relevant information. The Article further stresses that the patient informs in accordance with his capacity to do so. These limitations reflect in our view the complexity of patient duties. First, a patient may have a legitimate privacy interest in not disclosing all information and limit the information shared to relevant information. At the same time, it is difficult for patients to judge what information might be relevant, as there is generally a knowledge asymmetry. A patient may thus, in good faith, ignore that certain information is relevant to healthcare or may become so. Second, information currently not particularly relevant may become relevant at a later stage of healthcare delivery. Third, a patient may give false information because the medical facts were not understood. Finally, a patient cannot always be expected to be able to answer a medically relevant question correctly. In fact, a patient may not be able to give any information, or to give it adequately. For example, a patient cannot be expected to give an adequate answer if he or she is still under the influence of a recent shock or trauma. Neurodegenerative diseases also undermine the ability of elderly patients to provide reliable information, etc. In substance, it results thereof that a healthcare professional cannot expect that information provided by his patient is always complete and accurate.

248. Does the obligation to adhere and collaborate in the optimal provision of healthcare according to Article 3 imply an obligation to engage in a collaborative shared decision-making process? In discussing this interrogation, it is important to consider that Article 9 of the Law also establishes a general right not to know. Respecting the patient's choice not to know means that the patient can choose a passive role in healthcare. Furthermore, a patient has a general right to refuse care and may change his decision at any time.[253] The duty to enable 'optimal provision of health care' can thus not mean an obligation to accept what the physician considers 'optimal provision of healthcare'. Considering the contrary would reintroduce a paternalistic healthcare model. Article 3, §2, has, in our view, to be understood as a general obligation to collaborate in good faith to the dispensation of a treatment negotiated within a shared decision-making process or simply accepted by the patient. There can, however, be no obligation to stick to a planned treatment, as a patient remains free to withdraw consent. However, we believe that a patient has a duty to communicate his decision not to follow a previously accepted treatment as part of his general duty of loyal cooperation.

249. The second subparagraph of Article 3, §2, finally formulates a general duty to respect the rights of the healthcare provider and those of other patients. This duty is quite straightforward and might be resumed with the well-known quote: 'Your right to swing your arms ends just where the other man's nose begins' (Zechariah Chafee Jr.). It concretely means that patients may not deliberately act in a way that compromises other patients' safety or the safety of healthcare professionals, for instance, through violent behaviour. At the same time, such behaviour towards other patients or towards healthcare professionals may be uncontrollable to the patient

253. *See:* para. 295 *infra.*

and triggered by his or her health condition (e.g. acute psychiatric patients). In relation to other patients, the duty to respect their rights can also be seen as a duty to respect their privacy during hospitalisation. It may mean waiting for one's turn for non-urgent care, facilitating optimal provision and equal access to healthcare, and so on.

250. It is not possible to draw up an exhaustive list of patient obligations. Often, conflicting rights and interests must be weighed up. The authors are not aware of any case law explicitly applying patient obligations to illustrate the concrete meaning of patient duties. To sum it up, in our view, Article 3, §2 establishes a general obligation to a loyal collaboration within the limits of the patients' concrete abilities to do so. It includes an obligation to respect the rights of others. However, weighing the colliding rights may be necessary. The personal self-determination of the patient generally prevails over the physician's professional duties.

251. Finally, notwithstanding the fact that the Law on patient rights and obligations does not enumerate this obligation, a physician has a right to a fee or remuneration for the medical services provided. The patient has, accordingly, a duty to pay for the service received, even if this obligation is partly concealed by third-party payment.

252. The Law on patient rights and obligations does not further specify what the consequences may be if patient duties are not fulfilled. A practical legal meaning would be that a healthcare professional who is sued by a patient seeks a defence by invoking a patient's duty. By giving an incorrect answer to a question posed by the physician, the patient may commit a fault by which the damage he or she suffered would not have occurred in the same way. However, as seen above, a patient cannot always be expected to be able to answer a medically relevant question correctly. Negligence or fault needs *a priori* to be proven. A physician may, in our view, refuse care if a loyal collaboration is not possible within the limits of the concrete abilities of the patient. In such circumstances, continuity of care must, however, be ensured. Urgent care cannot be refused.

§5. Free Choice of Provider and Second Opinion

I. General Right to Free Choice

253. Interpersonal aspects and the personal qualities of the physician characterise the patient-physician relationship. The free choice of the healthcare professional and the healthcare institution in primary and secondary care, including direct access to specialists, is an important characteristic and value of the Luxembourg health system.

254. Article 5 of the Law on patient rights and obligations reaffirms that the patient has the right to freely choose the healthcare provider by whom he or she wishes to be treated and that this choice may be changed at any time. Even when a patient has chosen a reference doctor, this physician currently has guidance but no gatekeeping function.

II. Second Opinion

255. Although not specified, the right to freely choose and change the healthcare provider implies the right to consult a physician for a second opinion.

III. Limitations

256. Article 5 specifies that for all medical acts provided within a hospital establishment, the choice is limited to the physicians and healthcare professionals approved by that establishment. This limitation of choice corresponds to the physician's obligation to dispose of a contractual link with the hospital.[254]

257. Other legal limitations not mirrored in Article 5 exist. A psychiatric patient has, for instance, no choice whether and where he is hospitalised, if the conditions of the Law of 10 December 2009 on hospitalisation without the consent of persons with mental disorders are fulfilled (*See:* Chapter 4., §4. Psychiatric Patients and Hospitalisation without Consent). The choice of the hospital is further determined by the regulating centre of the emergency medical service in case urgent medical aid is called.[255] Given the country's size, specialised care may further be available in one single hospital unit ('national service') to ensure quality of care.

258. Furthermore, long-term care institutions limit the choice of physicians to those contractually linked to the institution (*See:* Part III., Chapter 3., §3. Long-Term Care Institutions).

259. Access limitations further result from the limitation of coverage by social security (*See:* Part III., Chapter 4., §3. Medical Fees and Nomenclature of Fees).

§6. Refusal of Care by the Physician

260. The interpersonal nature of the patient-physician relation and the liberal nature of the medical profession imply that physicians generally do not have to accept a patient. Article 6 regulates refusal of care by the physician, stressing that healthcare providers may generally refuse to treat a patient for personal or professional reasons. The corollary of this freedom is that once a physician has agreed to respond to a request, he or she generally undertakes to provide *personal care* to his

254. *See:* para. 679 *infra.*
255. Law of 27 Mar. 2018 on the organisation of civil security.

patient.[256] Article 6 specifies that care must be refused if the professional cannot usefully provide the required care. The latter means that a physician must refrain from accepting to provide a treatment when he or she does not have the necessary competence to do so.

261. The right to refuse care is not without limits. First, a distinction must be made between care that can be postponed and urgent care. Article 6 stresses that urgent first aid and continuity of care must always be ensured. Failure to ensure urgent first aid could further be regarded as a breach of the duty to help. Second, Article 6, §2 stresses that such refusal of care cannot be linked to discriminatory considerations. Where there are factual elements that lead to presume that there might be discrimination, the physician must justify his decision to refuse care on objective, non-discriminatory grounds. Finally, at the patient's request, the physician must assist the patient in finding a healthcare provider qualified to offer the required treatment and any useful information must be transmitted to the successor.

§7. Patient Companion

262. Many patients need the support of an accompanying person. They may need help because of language barriers, have limited mobility or simply feel safer with the support of a relative. Even before the legal status of patient companions was clarified, in practice, relatives or others have accompanied patients during healthcare.

263. Article 7 confers a patient's right to be assisted in healthcare procedures and decision-making by a third person, called a 'patient companion' ('accompagnateur'). The accompanying person is freely chosen by the patient. It may be a health professional or not. The role of the accompanying person is to assist the patient to the extent required by the patient. There is no formalism, and Article 7 allows for an informal process of implicit patient consent in the presence of the person chosen by the patient. The accompanying person's credentials may be requested and documented in the patient file. The accompanying person chosen by the patient must be allowed, as far as possible and to the extent desired by the patient, to participate in healthcare delivery. Medical secrecy is waived in the presence of the patient. However, the physician may at any time request an exchange without the presence of the companion.

264. The mere fact of being a habitual companion of a patient does not confer access to the patient file or imply any other specific right. A patient wishing to confer his or her companion direct access to his patient file must confer a written mandate.[257] The patient may designate his companion as his person of trust, but there is no automatism.

256. Article 39, Code of Medical Ethics.
257. *See:* para. 308 *infra.*

§8. Person of Trust

265. According to Article 12, any patient who has reached the age of majority and can give consent may appoint a representative called a 'person of trust' ('personne de confiance'). This person of trust may be any natural person, whether or not a health professional. The appointment must be made in writing, dated, and signed by the patient. If the patient is physically incapable of writing and signing, a third person may draft the document. Two witnesses must certify that the designation is in accordance with the free will of the patient.

266. The mission of the person of trust is to act in the interests of a patient who is temporarily or permanently incapable of exercising his rights. The person of trust has access to the patient file and exercises patient rights. If a patient is temporarily or permanently incapable of exercising his rights, the healthcare provider must establish the presumed patient will. To that end, the physician must consult the person of trust.[258] The person of trust thus co-decides with the physician, bearing in mind that his or her role is to be a witness to the patient's will. In principle, the person of trust remains responsible for exercising patient rights notwithstanding the opening of a tutelage measure.[259]

267. Both the Law on palliative care and the Law on euthanasia and assisted suicide provide for the possibility of designating a person of trust. The mechanism foreseen is similar, although there are minor differences. To prevent patients from having to designate their person of trust more than once, Article 12, §5 stipulates that the designation of a person of trust in accordance with the Law on patient rights and obligations constitutes a valid designation within the meaning of the Law on palliative care and within the meaning of the Law on euthanasia and assisted suicide. Similarly, if a patient has already appointed a person of trust under one of these two laws, that person of trust may also act under the Law on patient rights and obligations. However, it is possible to split responsibilities and appoint different persons of trust, for example, to appoint a different person of trust to witness the request for euthanasia expressed in an end-of-life provision.

§9. Equal Access to Quality Care

268. Patient safety and quality are fundamental to healthcare delivery. Equal access to quality healthcare has both an individual and a collective systemic component. The latter component concerns financial and organisational matters related to the social security and healthcare system. The scope of the Law on patient rights and obligations is limited to the individual relation of the patient and his healthcare provider, so such matters are not addressed here. Both levels are interdependent and

258. Article 11, §1, Law on patient rights and obligations.
259. *See:* para. 467 *infra.*

applying general principles to concrete individual decisions may be ethically difficult, specifically in a context of limited available resources.[260]

269. According to Article 4, §1, every patient shall have equal access to the healthcare required by his or her health condition. Healthcare must be provided in an effective manner, in accordance with scientific evidence and legally prescribed standards of quality and safety.

On an individual level, equal access to quality care means first non-discriminatory access to such healthcare objectively required by the patients' individual health condition and according to the patient's therapeutic options. Physicians have diagnostic and therapeutic freedom in determining the means recommended to the patient. The physician shall exercise this freedom by orienting himself in relation to the state of acquired medical knowledge. He must 'limit his prescriptions and actions to what is necessary for the quality, safety and effectiveness of care'.[261]

As stressed by the second phrase of Article 4, §1, quality in healthcare services also includes a technical (clinical) aspect, focussing on the skills, accuracy of procedures and medical diagnosis. Although there are minor differences in wording, the Law concerning the exercise of the medical profession requires likewise to provide 'the patients under his care with the preventive, curative or palliative care required by their state of health, in accordance with scientific knowledge and professional ethics'.[262] In other words, it is mandatory for a physician to act as a *'bonus medicus'*.

270. Quality of healthcare is frequently addressed in jurisprudence through the prism of liability without a clear reference to Article 4. Physicians need, in general, to follow 'acquired' medical knowledge and to observe at least legal safety prescripts. When deciding whether a physician acted as a *bonus medicus*, advice of a medical expert is habitually sought. Medical experts and jurisdictions refer to standards and norms issued by a medical-professional organisation or other competent bodies when verifying whether a physician has acted carefully. In Luxembourg, the Health Scientific Council issues recommendations for good medical practice. In the absence of a clear national recommendation or consensus, reference is frequently made to standards/norms issued by distinguished foreign medical-professional organisations. Courts remain, however, free not to follow such elements, according to the case.

271. According to Article 4, §2, healthcare shall be organised in such a way as to ensure continuity of care in all circumstances. This paragraph recalls the general

260. The Covid-19 pandemic has prominently shown the ethical dilemmas. On this issue, *see*: *Position statement of the C.N.E. on the essential ethical benchmarks when guiding patients in a context of limited available therapeutic resources due to the pandemic crisis of COVID-19*, CNE (31 Mar. 2020), https://cne.public.lu/dam-assets/fr/publications/avis/Position-statement-COVID-19.pdf.

261. Article 9 of the Code of Medical Ethics.

262. Articles 6bis and 13bis, Law concerning the exercise of the medical profession.

obligation not to discontinue a course of treatment unless all necessary arrangements have been made for it to be continued by another practitioner. The wording of Article 4, §2, corresponds to Article 66 of the Code of medical ethics.

§10. Right to Information about the State of Health

I. General Right to Information

272. According to Article 8, §1, every patient has the right to receive all relevant information concerning his or her state of health and his or her prognosis. This general right to know exists even when no treatment exists or is being considered. The right to know concerns not only information already available but also information not yet available, which may be brought to light by appropriate diagnostic methods or other indicated means.

273. In our view, the general right to know about one's state of health entitles the patient to request and receive information about an incident that has affected or is likely to affect the patient's health condition. In 2016, the National Health Information and Mediation Service adopted a recommendation encouraging the adoption and implementation of open disclosure policies.[263] While some hospitals have adopted open disclosure policies, there is no general legal framework that requires them to be proactively informed of a healthcare incident.

II. How to Inform

274. Information is given orally in one of the three official languages, namely Luxembourgish, French and German. Communication with the patient must take place in a clear and comprehensive language adapted to each individual patient. The information may, where appropriate, be supplemented by written information.[264] Written information is of medico-legal interest when it comes to proving adequate information prior to consent (*See:* §11. Informed Consent and Decision-Making Process). However, there is no legal obligation to provide written information, even if the patient requests it.

275. There is no obligation to provide information in the patient's mother tongue.[265] The patient can be informed with the help of an accompanying person

---

263. *Rapport d'activité 2015–2016*, SNIMS (2016), https://mediateursante.public.lu/fr/publications.html.
264. Article 8, §4, Law on patient rights and obligations.
265. The ECtHR noted that the possibility for a patient to be treated by staff who speak his or her language, even where it is an official language of the State, is not an established ingredient of the right enshrined in Art. 3 ECHR, or in any other Convention provision, particularly with regard to the provision of appropriate care to individuals who have been deprived of their liberty (ECtHR, Grand Chamber, 31 Jan. 2019, *Rooman v. Belgium*, No. 1805/11).

who translates under the responsibility of the patient.[266] In practice, hospitals have identified internal resources that can be called to translate. It is also possible to use intercultural interpreting services by the Luxembourg Red Cross in more than forty-five languages and dialects. However, this service is not free of charge, which limits access to it.[267]

276. Every health professional shall provide information, on the one hand, in relation to the services for which he or she is responsible and, on the other hand, in relation to his or her participation in the care delivered and within the limits of his or her competences and in compliance with the professional rules.[268] As the provision of information to the patient is a fundamental part of medical practice, it cannot be delegated per se by the physician to a nurse or another health profession. However, nurses and other healthcare profession have a personal duty to inform of the activities that they are legally entitled to perform.

277. In view of the shared need to provide patients with adequate information when several health professionals collaborate, they keep each other informed, unless the patient objects.[269] The jurisprudence accepts that information already given previously, in the context of a first intervention or by a referring physician, may be considered when deciding whether the patient was adequately informed.

III. Right Not to Know about One's State of Health

278. According to Article 9, a patient's choice not to be informed of a diagnosis, a prognosis, or any information concerning his or her condition or its probable course must be respected. Such a patient request must be documented in the patient file. If the patient exercises his or her right not to know, then the physician and all professionals involved are prohibited from providing such information.

279. Despite the patient's explicit request, it is permissible to provide information if failure to do so would clearly cause serious harm to the patient's health or the health of third parties. For example, it is permissible to disclose HIV infection even if the patient has asked not to be informed of a possible infection. It should be emphasised that the law permits the disclosure of known information. However, it does not allow a diagnostic measure, such as a blood test, to be taken without the patient's consent or against the patient's will.[270]

280. Even before the right not to know was recognised, it was accepted that the patient has a right to relinquish his or her right to information. To be legally valid,

266. Article 8, §2, Law on patient rights and obligations.
267. Luxembourg Red Cross, https://www.croix-rouge.lu/en/service/intercultural-interpreting/.
268. Article 8, §2, Law on patient rights and obligations.
269. *Ibid.*
270. Lux., 18 Apr. 2012, No. 105/12.

this relinquishing must take place voluntarily and it must be certain. If the patient relinquishes his or her right to information, then the physician is no longer required to inform the patient.

IV. Therapeutic Exception

281. In exceptional cases, the treating physician may decide to withhold information about the patient's state of health, if disclosure risks causing serious harm to the patient. Not informing the patient under these circumstances is referred to as the therapeutic exception. Article 10 ensures that the therapeutic exception is applied with restraint. The treating physician must seek the opinion of a second physician. The therapeutic exception is intended to be a temporary measure; as soon as there is no longer a risk of causing serious harm, the treating physician must lift the therapeutic exception. Article 10 further specifies that any physician may have access to the concerned information and lift the exception if he or she considers that the measure is no longer justified in light of the patient's state of health. The physician who lifts the exception must provide the information in a manner appropriate to the patient or ensure that the patient receives such information from a colleague as soon as possible.

V. Announcement Consultation

282. A prior announcement consultation may be requested by the attending physician or by the professional who has discovered sensitive information, if he or she considers that direct disclosure may endanger the patient's health condition. In this case, disclosure must be made in the presence of a competent health professional.[271] The purpose of this disposition is not to prevent rapid disclosure but to ensure that appropriate counselling is available when a patient learns of a critical diagnosis or other distressing information.

§11. Informed Consent and Decision-Making Process

I. Informed Consent: A Precondition to Healthcare Provision

283. Healthcare may only be provided to a patient who has the necessary capacity with his or her free and informed consent, given after adequate prior information.[272] Health professionals are required to make sure, before providing healthcare, that the patient has received timely advance information and freely consents.[273]

271. Article 16, §5, Law on patient rights and obligations.
272. Article 8, §4, subpara. 1, Law on patient rights and obligations.
273. Article 8, §6, Law on patient rights and obligations.

Healthcare professionals therefore have a common duty to guarantee informed consent and are well advised to make clear arrangements to ensure that informed consent is given.

284. As the jurisprudence emphasises, the physician's obligation to provide information is different from that of other professionals in that the patient's consent to the physician's intervention is essential. Prior information is an essential condition for informed consent. Medical acts performed without prior consent are unlawful and punishable under Article 392 of the Penal Code (general provision incriminating intentional bodily harm, assault, and battery).[274]

During an intervention, when the patient is no longer able to give consent, a new unforeseen element may be discovered. Any reasonably foreseeable discovery must be discussed in advance before consent to an intervention is given. If a reasonably unforeseeable circumstance requires an adaptation of the healthcare originally envisaged, the Law foresees two situations in which the procedure initiated may be continued and extended despite the impossibility of obtaining the patient's additional consent. First, a medical intervention may always be extended in case the procedure is urgent and medically necessary. Second, even if not urgent, the procedure can be extended if the patient is not exposed to significant additional risk.[275]

II. Content of Adequate Prior Information

285. The aim of adequate information is to enable the patient to consent, refuse consent or choose between alternatives on the basis of fair, unbiased information.[276] Subparagraphs 2 to 5 of Article 8, §4, determine in detail the content of the information to be provided. A distinction is made between mandatory information that must always be provided (subparagraphs 2 and 3) and information that must only be provided on request (subparagraphs 4 and 5).

286. Adequate prior information must include the essential characteristics of the recommended healthcare.[277] It must include the scope and the foreseeable consequences of the proposed treatment, its benefit and possible urgency, the risks and common adverse effects, possible alternative treatment options and foreseeable consequences of a refusal of treatment. According to the last phase of the second subparagraph, the risks specifically linked to the known health condition of the patient must be evaluated and specifically addressed. The third subparagraph stipulates that the obligation to inform the patient of commonly known risks of an intervention may be given by means of a standardised document.

274. Trib. Lux., 4 Jul. 2002, No. 205/2002.
275. Article 8, §6, subpara. 2, Law on patient rights and obligations.
276. Article. 44, Code of Medical Ethics.
277. Article. 8, §4, subpara. 2, Law on patient rights and obligations.

287. According to Article 8, §4, subparagraph 4, the patient must be provided with an assessment of the foreseeable costs if he or she so requests. Regarding providing patients with prior information on the cost of a treatment, Article 45 of the Code of Medical Ethics stipulates that a patient must always be informed of the amount of his or her personal financial contribution. In addition, Article 106 of the Code of Medical Ethics states that for procedures not included in the nomenclature, the physician must draw up a cost estimate covering all foreseeable fees and charges of the treatment. This estimate must be countersigned by the patient.

The deontological rules go thus go beyond the obligation laid down in Article 8. In a recent case, the Superior Disciplinary Council of the Medical College has confirmed that patients must always be informed of financial aspects. In this case, the physician invoked Article 8, §4, and the absence of any request from the patient to receive specific cost information. The physician further stressed that he had put up a poster on the wall of his medical practice with general information on costs. The disciplinary jurisdiction took the view that general information on a poster is insufficient and that the physician had to specifically inform his patient about financial matters when offering healthcare services not foreseen by the nomenclature.[278]

288. The physician must further provide information on request about the availability (waiting times), quality and safety (including the number of procedures performed to date and the complication rate), authorisation or registration status and insurance coverage.[279]

289. Finally, Article 8 entrusts the Health Scientific Council with the task of elaborating a general guideline on patient information, as well as specific guidelines on specific health issues. A general guideline on patient information was adopted in 2017 and was recently renewed.[280]

III. Expression and Proof of Informed Consent

290. While informed consent is a prerequisite for the provision of healthcare, the legislator has taken into account that information is frequently given in a dynamic process. Consent or refusal must be given explicitly. At the same time, the healthcare professional may reasonably infer consent from the patient's behaviour after having provided the patient with adequate information. Consent may be given, for example, by holding up an arm for an injection after having received the necessary information. The health professional seeking the patient's decision shall ensure he or she has understood the information provided when making his or her decision.[281]

278. CSD, 7 décembre 2022, Arrêt No. 03/22, Mertz-Spet, A., RLDS, No. 14, pp. 20–26 (2023).
279. Article 8, §4, subpara. 5, Law on patient rights and obligations.
280. https://conseil-scientifique.public.lu/fr/publications/information-patients/info-patients.html.
281. Article 8, §8, Law on patient rights and obligations.

291. The burden of proof of the information provided and of the patient's consent lies with the healthcare provider under whose responsibility the care was provided or offered. Such proof may be provided by any means. The elements recorded in or added to the patient file benefit from a presumption of being correct.[282]

In other words, physicians need to provide adequate information and consent. They are well advised to document the decision-making process adequately. The legal presumption is rebuttable; patients can prove that the inscription in the patient file is incorrect.

Standardised informed consent forms are becoming common. Even when used, prior information must nevertheless always be tailored to the individual patient and cannot rely solely on a standardised consent form. Furthermore, risks specifically linked to the known health condition of the patient must be evaluated and specifically discussed.

292. For certain activities, legislation requires that prior informed consent is given in writing, often with additional requirements regarding the content of prior information and/or a specific procedure to be followed. This is particularly the case for minor women requesting voluntary termination of pregnancy,[283] for patients requesting euthanasia or assisted suicide,[284] as well as for removal of organs,[285] tissues, and cells.[286] Furthermore, prescription of genetic testing needs prior written consent to be reimbursed by health insurance.[287]

IV. Shared Decision-Making

293. According to Article 8, §3, it is up to the patient to make decisions about his or her health together with health professionals, considering the information relevant to his or her care that he or she has provided to the physician (or to the healthcare professional) and the information and advice provided to the patient. This disposition confers a right to active participation in a collaborative decision-making process ('shared decision making').[288] It does not only enshrine a right to co-decide but also further recalls the obligation of the patient to provide information relevant to provision of healthcare.[289]

Does this mean that patients must proactively participate in shared decision-making? In our view, it results from the general spirit of the law that the legislator aimed to 'empower' patients to take an active role but not to impose on them an obligation to engage actively in shared decision-making.

282. Article 8, §9, Law on patient rights and obligations.
283. *See:* para. 538 *infra.*
284. *See:* paras 415 and 424 *infra.*
285. *See:* para. 556 *infra.*
286. *See:* para. 575 *infra.*
287. *See:* para. 518 *infra.*
288. The wording has been inspired by, but is not identical to, the definition given in French health law (Art. L 1111-4 Code de la Santé Publique).
289. *See:* para. 248 *supra.*

V. Presumed Consent in Cases of Emergency

294. In a medical emergency, when a patient is not able to make decisions about his or her health and his or her will is not established, any urgent measures required may immediately be taken in the patient's best interest.[290] This provision presumes consent if the patient's will is not known. However, a physician may not disregard a known and well-considered refusal of treatment.

§12. REFUSAL OR WITHDRAWAL OF CONSENT[291]

I. General Right to Refuse Care

295. Patients have the right to refuse or withdraw their consent at any time, without such a decision entailing the extinction of the right to quality healthcare in accordance with the accepted therapeutic options.[292] In other words, refusal by itself does not terminate the legal relations between the patient and the physician.

II. Advance Refusal for Future Care

296. If a patient is temporarily or permanently unable to express his or her wishes, the healthcare provider must seek to establish his or her presumed will.[293]

The Law on patient rights and obligations does not explicitly specify the status of so-called advance refusals. However, the 2009 law on palliative care specifically foresees the possibility to refuse or limit care in advance. An advance refusal generally has the same legal effect as a currently expressed refusal: a clear will of the patient refusing care must be respected. For an advance refusal to be binding, there must be no doubt that the refusal comes from the person involved, the meaning must be clear and there must be no element to support a change of the patient's will since the advance refusal was documented.[294]

III. Mandatory Care Imposed by Law

297. Although legislation recognises a large degree of autonomy for patients, this autonomy is limited for the sake of protecting patients who are considered vulnerable. In case of a serious danger to life or health, the law allows to override the refusal of care of a minor patient, of a patient under tutelage, or of his or her representative(s).[295]

---

290. Article 11, §2, Law on patient rights and obligations.
291. Schwebag, M., *Regard juridique sur le droit du patient de refuser des soins de santé*, RLDS, No. 1, pp. 11–18 (2019).
292. Article 8, §5, Law on patient rights and obligations.
293. Article 11, Law on patient rights and obligations.
294. *See:* paras 399–406 *infra*.
295. Article 13, §3; Art. 14, §3, Law on patient rights and obligations.

298. A person suffering from a serious mental disorder who constitutes a danger to himself or to others may further be hospitalised against his or her will.[296] There are further exceptions of mandatory treatment foreseen by Law: the 1973 Law on combating drug addiction allows, under certain circumstances, to propose or order drug users to undergo a detoxification cure.[297] Despite his or her refusal, a contagious patient can be hospitalised and receive mandatory care under an ad hoc procedure involving authorisation by a judge.[298] There is no mandatory vaccination regime since compulsory vaccination against smallpox was abolished in 1977.

§13. Patient File

299. The term 'patient file' is used as a generic term for all types of patient records kept by a healthcare provider. Article 2f) of the Law on patient rights and obligations gives the following broad definition of the patient file ('dossier patient'): 'all documents containing data, assessments and information of any kind concerning a patient's health status and its evolution during treatment, regardless of their medium'.

I. Right to a Carefully Kept Patient File

300. According to Article 15, §1, every patient has a right to a carefully maintained patient file. This patient file must document chronologically and accurately the patient's health status and its evolution during treatment and record all information relevant to the safety and further evolution of the patient's condition. The objective of this obligation to carefully keep a patient file is to ensure quality and safety, as the patient file is an important tool for communication, coordination, and information between healthcare professionals and, incidentally, their patients. The patient file further ensures the traceability of healthcare and the evolution of the health status.

301. Depending on his or her responsibilities, every health professional involved in healthcare is responsible for ensuring the documentation of his or her instructions, prescriptions and services, as well as any other information relevant to the safety and development of the patient's condition. If a third party records such elements, it is up to the physician or responsible health professional to validate them. The health professional who provided the healthcare must be identified. The date and, where appropriate, the time must be specified to situate the service chronologically in the pathway of the patient.[299]

---

296. *See:* Part II., Ch. 4., §4. Psychiatric Patients and Hospitalisation without Consent.
297. Articles 23–27, Loi du 19 février 1973 concernant la vente de substances médicamenteuses et la lutte contre la toxicomanie.
298. Article 11, Loi modifiée du 11 novembre 1980 portant organisation de la direction de la santé.
299. Article 15, §2, Law on patient rights and obligations.

302. It is possible to share a common file between health professionals. When several health professionals, whether physicians or not, are involved in the care of the same patient and use a shared patient record, they are exempted from maintaining their own patient record. After the end of their service, they retain access to the elements of the shared record related to their part in healthcare delivery.[300]

303. Neither the physician nor the patient may remove items relevant to the maintenance of the patient record before the expiry of the retention period. The correction of an inaccurate or incomplete entry may be carried out under the responsibility of the physician who provided the service. It must be reversible and documented.[301]

304. A Grand-Ducal Regulation may regulate in detail the minimal content and fix the norms to which the patient files kept by the different categories of health professionals must comply. So far, no such regulation has been adopted, except for the content of the patient file kept within hospital establishments (*See:* V. Patient File in Hospital below).

II. Access Rights and Right to a Copy of the Patient File

305. The patient has a right of access to his patient file and to all information relating to his health held in any capacity by a healthcare professional or hospital establishment.[302] Based on this right, the patient can exercise control over the personal data included in the patient file, thus protecting his or her privacy. Although the patient's information needs are primarily addressed by the right to information about one's state of health, access to the patient file supports the patient's self-determination and capacity to take an active role.

306. As it may be difficult to read and understand the contents of the patient file (medical language used; abbreviations, etc.), the Law on patient rights and obligation grants a right to request the presence of a qualified professional who is able to (re-)explain the contents of the patient file.

307. A patient can exercise his or her right of access by consulting the patient file or by requesting access to the data relating to his or her health. The patient's accompanying person may assist the patient. The patient may further mandate a third person to access the patient file.[303] A written mandate is not necessary in case access is requested by a health professional to ensure continuity of care or to determine the best course of treatment.[304]

300. Article 15, §3, Law on patient rights and obligations.
301. Article 15, §4, Law on patient rights and obligations.
302. Article 16, §1, Law on patient rights and obligations.
303. Article 16, §2, Law on patient rights and obligations.
304. Article 18, §2, Law on patient rights and obligations.

308. In addition, the patient has the right to obtain a copy of the entire patient file or parts of it. He or she may request that the copies be communicated to the healthcare provider of his or her choice. Copies shall be made on paper or on an electronic medium, allowing later consultation at the patient's choice and within the limits of technical possibilities.[305] The patient may be charged a contribution, which may not exceed the cost of copying and, where applicable, postage.[306] Requesting payment to obtain a first copy would be contrary to Article 15.3 of the General Data Protection Regulation (GDPR), which only allows a reasonable payment to be required for additional copies.[307]

309. Except where the patient's state of health requires more urgent access, requests shall be acted upon within a maximum of fifteen working days from receipt of the request.[308]

III. Conservation of Patient Files

310. The custodian of a patient file is obliged to keep it for at least ten years from the date of the end of the treatment[309] and may keep it t for a longer period, up until the end of the time limit for medical liability claims that is thirty years. According to Article 65 of the Code of Medical Ethics, when a medical practice is transferred to another physician, this physician becomes the custodian of the patient file and must provide any patient who so requests with his or her file or pass it on to the physician chosen by the patient. Furthermore, physicians who stop practising must notify patients by appropriate means and keep the files at the disposal of patients who wish to collect them for a period of at least three months. In the event of the physician's death, the patient file in his possession must be made available to patients. In practice, patients are frequently notified through a simple publication in newspapers, and it may happen that patient files are not recoverable after cessation of activity of a physician.

311. If the depositary of a patient file is unable to produce the documents of which he or she is deemed to be the depositary, the patient is entitled to request reimbursement of the costs incurred without prejudice to the right of the health insurance to recover the costs it has incurred.[310]

---

305. Article 16, §3, Law on patient rights and obligations.
306. *Ibid.*
307. CJEU, 26 Oct. 2023, *FT v. DW*, (C-307/22), https://curia.europa.eu/juris/liste.jsf?language=en&td=ALL&num=C-307/22; Schwebag, M., *L'encadrement national du droit d'accès au dossier patient au regard des dispositions du RGPD,* RLDS, No. 18, pp. 13–18 (2024).
308. Article 16, §4, Law on patient rights and obligations.
309. Article 15, §4, Law on patient rights and obligations.
310. Article 60bis, CSS.

IV. Access by Next of Kin after the Death of a Patient

312. After the death of an adult patient, a relatively large group of next of kin may request access to the patient file. The law grants access to the person of trust, the spouse, the patient's children of full age, other dependants of the patient, the patient's legal partner, as well as any person who, at the time of death, lived in the community with the patient. The above-mentioned persons may also request a copy of the patient file. Access requests must be reasoned; however, the law grants large grounds to do so. Access may be requested to understand the causes of death, defend the patient's memory or assert a legitimate right of the requesting person. Unless a request is not reasoned, rejecting a request needs to be particularly well measured as the notion of 'legitimate right' is not further defined by the law.[311]

The main reason to refuse access appears to be a previously expressed opposition of the patient to such access. The patient will must be respected. The Belgian Court of Cassation has considered that the Belgian Law of 2002 on patient rights grants a relatively large margin of appreciation to physicians for considering the facts and interests at stake (C. Cass., 14 mars 2016, C.15.0069F). However, this reasoning cannot necessarily be transposed; the Belgian Law requires an objection to have been expressed 'specifically' ('expressément'), while the Luxembourg Law on patient rights and obligations requests such an opposition to have been expressed in writing ('par écrit').

313. For patients who deceased before majority, Article 19, §2, provides for a general access right to the parents or any person with parental authority over the minor. Such a request does not need to be reasoned. During his lifetime, a minor patient with the necessary capacity of discernment to make a reasonable assessment of his or her interests may decide to oppose such a consultation in writing. In such a case, access must be refused.

V. Patient File in Hospital

314. In a hospital, an 'individual hospital file' provides for a chronological and accurate history of the patient's health status and its evolution during the course of treatment. It covers medical, nursing, and administrative aspects and contains all information relevant to the safety and development of the patient's health status.[312] A Grand-Ducal Regulation of 13 January 2019 regulates the minimal content of the patient files and of the discharge summary.[313] According to the Law on hospitals,

---

311. Article 19, §1, Law on patient rights and obligations.
312. Article 37, §1, Law on hospitals.
313. Règlement grand-ducal du 13 janvier 2019 déterminant le contenu minimal du dossier individuel du patient hospitalier et du résumé clinique de sortie, Mem. A – 48 du 31.01.2019, http://data.legilux.public.lu/eli/etat/leg/rgd/2019/01/13/a48.

the general director of the hospital must ensure that the legal requirements are complied with, take the organisational measures required to prevent any illicit access and ensure that patients' rights are respected in accordance with the Law on patient rights and obligations.[314]

§14. Complaints and Mediation

315. There is no specific right to complain directly recognised as a patient right by the Law on patient rights and obligations. Under the hospital legislation, every hospital establishment must, however, dispose of a mechanism allowing patients to submit their complaints.[315] The functioning of the complaint mechanism is not regulated in detail and differs amongst hospitals. Patients may further lodge a complaint before the competent deontological order for physicians, the Medical College.[316]

316. Chapter 3 of the 2014 Law on patient rights and obligations introduces a national information and mediation service for healthcare ('Service national d'information et de médiation dans le domaine de la santé') called 'service' hereafter.[317] The service is headed by the 'mediator for health' ('médiateur de la santé') and is nominated by a decision of the Council of Ministers for a renewable period of five years.

317. Any person (physicians, healthcare providers, patients or simply citizens) can request general information on the patient's rights and obligations, the functioning of the health system, its operation, and its main actors. The information mission includes information for patients hospitalised without consent. The service has also been designated as a national contact point for cross-border healthcare in cooperation with CNS.[318]

318. The service operates a sectorial mediation centre open to patients and healthcare professionals.[319] Mediation is understood as a voluntary and open process based on the responsibility and autonomy of the participants. It is thus not mandatory. The mediator for health and the mediators charged with a request intervene as a neutral, independent, and omni-partite person. The mediators assist the parties in finding a consensual solution without having any decision-making power. The confidentiality of the mediation is guaranteed. Article 458 of the Criminal Code is applicable in case of a violation of professional secrecy. The mediators working for

314. Article 37, §2; Art. 37 §4, Law on hospitals.
315. The 1998 Law on hospitals introduced this obligation. It was repealed by the 2018 Law on hospitals and hospital planning, which contains a similar obligation in Art. 40.
316. *See:* Part I., Ch. 4., §1. Medical College and Rules of Professional Conduct.
317. Official website: www.mediateursante.lu.
318. Pursuant to directive 2011/24/EU of the European Parliament and of the Council of 9 Mar. 2011 on the application of patients' rights in cross-border healthcare.
319. Schwebag, M., *Médiation dans le domaine de la santé au Luxembourg,* Lettre des Médiations, No. 8 (2019), https://www.observatoiredesmediations.org/Asset/Source/refBibliography_ID-134_No-01.pdf.

the service are trained in mediation theory and practice and have been approved by the Minister of Justice as mediators in civil and commercial matters.[320] In case compensation for damages is requested by a patient, the professional liability insurer of the healthcare provider may be associated with the mediation process. Parties in mediation may be assisted by a person of their choice, including a legal counsel.

320. Loi du 24 février 2012 portant introduction de la médiation en matière civile et commerciale dans le Nouveau Code de procédure civile.

Chapter 2. Medical Secrecy, Confidentiality and Data Protection

§1. Introduction

319. 'Whatever I see or hear in the lives of my patients, whether in connection with my professional practice or not, which ought not to be spoken of outside, I will keep secret, as considering all such things to be private' (Hippocratic Oath).[321]

Patients have a right to the protection of their privacy. Secrecy is an important pillar of the relationship of trust between the physician and his patient. Quality healthcare needs open communication in a secured environment. Medical secrecy aims to protect the patient and his or her interests. It protects against revelations to third parties and allows the patient to confide safely, with the guarantee that his or her intimacy and privacy are respected. Even a patient in an irregular or marginal situation who needs care must be able to confide without fear of disclosure. Any breach of confidentiality could indeed deter patients from consulting healthcare professionals or from openly communicating with them. Beyond the individual relationship towards the physician, medical secrecy thus further protects public health in general.

320. The confidentiality of information concerning a patient is protected by multiple national and international norms. The main national protection of the duty of secrecy lies in Article 458 of the Luxembourg Criminal Code that protects professional secrecy in general (§2.). A breach of secrecy might further be in violation of a professional or a contractual obligation (§3.). We will finally provide an overview of the protection of patient data and the obligations of physicians resulting from the GDPR (§4.). It is generally considered that these legal protections apply in a complementary manner, without one derogating from the other.

§2. Protection of Professional Secrecy under Article 458 of the Criminal Code[322]

I. Scope of Article 458 of the Criminal Code

321. Modelled on the Belgian Criminal Code, Article 458 of the Luxembourg Criminal Code protects professional secrecy in identical terms: 'Physicians, surgeons, health officers, pharmacists, midwives and all other persons having knowledge, by their state or by profession, of secrets entrusted to them, who, except in cases where they are called upon to testify in Court and except where the law obliges them to make these secrets known, will be punished by imprisonment for a period of between eight days and six months and a fine of between 500 euros and 5.000 euros.'

321. National Library of Medicine, https://www.nlm.nih.gov/hmd/greek/greek_oath.html.
322. Schiltz, P., *Le secret professionnel des médecins et autres professionnels de la santé*, RLDS, No. 16, pp. 1–20 (2023).

A. Persons Covered by the Duty of Secrecy

322. Concerning the persons covered by the duty of secrecy, physicians, surgeons, health officers, pharmacists and midwives are specifically enumerated by Article 458 of the Criminal Code. Article 458 further enumerates 'health officers'; this term is, however, not currently used.

323. Recalling the importance of professional secrecy, the legislation explicitly submits health professionals to Article 458. This is the case for physicians and dentists,[323] psychotherapists,[324] and pharmacists,[325] as well as for all recognised non-medical healthcare professions governed by the amended Law of 26 March 1992.[326]

324. Article 458 further imposes a duty of professional secrecy on 'all other persons having knowledge, by their state or by profession, of secrets entrusted to them'. Professional secrecy may thus apply to everyone who, during his or her professional practice, gets necessary knowledge of confidential information. There is some fluctuation in case law regarding the scope of Article 458 with regard to non-specifically covered professions. Luxembourg jurisprudence has considered that Article 458 applies to employees of the national health insurance (CNS) concerning the personal information of patients to which they have professional access.[327] It is considered that a medical secretary is to be considered a necessary auxiliary bound by medical secrecy, by opposition to other staff such as a cleaner, gardener, dog walker or housekeeper.[328] Experts are subject to professional secrecy;[329] a decision has, however, excluded sworn interprets and translators.[330]

B. Professional Knowledge

325. Professional secrecy applies, in general, in a professional context. Article 458 thus, in general, does not cover information that a physician (or any other professional) gets to know in a private context. However, Article 18, §1, of the Law on patient rights and obligations specifies that Article 458 applies to the person accompanying the patient and to the person of trust. Although not acting as professionals, both the patient companion and the person of trust are thus bound to the duty of

323. Article 6, §2, Art. 13, §2, amended Law of 29 Apr. 1983 concerning the practice of the professions of physician, dentist, and veterinary surgeon.
324. Article 8, Law of 14 Jul. 2015 creating the profession of psychotherapist.
325. Article 11, §4, amended Law of 31 Jul. 1991 determining the conditions for authorisation to practice the profession of pharmacist.
326. Article 15, amended Law of 26 Mar. 1992 on the practice and revalorisation of certain health professions.
327. Trib. Lux., 19 Jan. 2017, No. 201/2017.
328. Trib. Lux., 22 Jan. 2008, No. 244/2008, JUDOC: 99864554.
329. Cour, 17 Dec. 1955, Pas. lux., 16, p. 408.
330. Trib. Lux., 8 Jul. 2021, No. 553/2021: Acquittal of an interpreter assisting the Police during a preliminary investigation on the grounds that Art. 458 is not applicable to sworn interpreters.

secrecy regarding the confidential information they may acquire while assisting a patient or acting in the interests of a patient.

C. *Personal and Secret Information*

326. Even though Article 458 speaks of secrets that have been 'entrusted', the jurisprudence considers that the obligation of secrecy 'must not be restricted to the facts that have literally been entrusted to the doctor, but extends to everything that he may have observed or deduced, even without the knowledge of the person who has sought his care'[331] and that 'in particular, a doctor's professional secrecy covers everything that he has seen, known, learned, observed, discovered or even surprised in the exercise of his profession'.[332]

327. To be protected, the information needs to be secret information. Secrets are facts not known to the public, where there is a legitimate interest in keeping them hidden.[333] If a patient has already made a fact public, confirmation by a physician does, in general, not constitute a breach of secrecy. However, the confirmation by a physician may transform what has been subject to controversy into an established and certain fact, in which case there is a breach of secrecy, giving rise to criminal liability.[334]

328. According to the jurisprudence, the information further needs to be personal information. An indiscretion relating to a professional matter not linked to the confidence of a patient is not a breach of medical secrecy. Article 458 presupposes the existence of a secret entrusted by a private individual to a necessary confidant.[335]

II. Shared Professional Secrecy

329. Article 458 of the Criminal Code has a large field of application in that it not only applies to physicians but also to non-medical healthcare professionals. Because all the members of a medical team are obliged to respect the confidentiality of the patient's information, it has been generally accepted that information may circulate within the team. The Law on patient rights and obligations has formally recognised this so-called shared professional secrecy rule. According to

331. Cass., 20 Jan. 1893, No. 4/1983, Pas. lux., 3, p. 20.
332. Cour, 3 Nov. 1976, Pas. lux., 23, p. 469.
333. Cour, 27 Jun. 2012, No. 341/12X; Cour, 9 Jan. 2018, No. 12/18V.
334. Cour, 15 Dec. 1970, Pas. lux., 21, p. 421.
335. Cour, 19 Jun. 1967, No. 154/67, JUDOC: 96707928; Trib. Lux., 18 Jan. 2018, No. 239/2018, RLDS, No. 16, pp. 21–31: acquittal of a nurse who disclosed a rumour from the corridor about an incident within a day care centre that led to the hospitalisation of a child. The name or personal data of the child was not revealed. The name of the day care centre had been revealed to the mother of another child, who posted the rumour on Facebook.

Article 18, §2, of the Law on patient rights and obligations, two or more health professionals may exchange information relating to the same patient under their care in order to ensure continuity of care or to determine the best course of treatment. Furthermore, when a patient is being cared for by a care team in a hospital or another entity providing healthcare, the information is deemed to be entrusted by the patient to the entire healthcare team. Nevertheless, according to Article 18, §2, the duly informed patient may refuse at any time to have information communicated to one or more health professionals. A patient may thus decide to limit the circulation of his data. The health professional who provides healthcare to the patient always maintains access to the elements of the patient file relating to his or her service.

III. Consent of the Patient or Waiver of Medical Secrecy

330. Medical secrecy protects both the private interest of the person (patient) concerned by any violation thereof and protects public (health) interest in general. The jurisprudence traditionally considers professional secrecy to be of a general and absolute nature. Medical secrecy was thus considered to protect a general interest, which the consent of the beneficiary cannot make disappear.[336] Recent jurisprudence tends, however, to privilege the patient's informational autonomy, considering that medical secrecy mainly protects the interest of the patient and that the patient is the master of his secrecy. The jurisprudence has considered on such grounds that the patient has the right to relieve, even in advance, his or her physician from the secrecy with regards to his life insurer. Based on a waiver of secrecy, the insurer may thus require medical data for the purposes of concluding a life insurance contract or request information – such as the causes and circumstances of death – for the purposes of the execution of the contract.[337]

331. In the same sense, Article 16, §2, of the Law on patient rights and obligations provides for the possibility to authorise in writing access to the medical record to a third party. A patient may thus, in writing, validly waive medical secrecy and authorise a third party to consult his patient file.

332. Physicians are sometimes requested to make a public statement. In our view, as the patient is the master of his secrecy, a physician may accept making a public statement about the health condition of his patient if authorised to do so by his patient. However, a patient can't oblige a physician to do so.

IV. Accompanying Person, Person of Trust, and Relatives

333. It may be in the interest of a patient to share medical secrecy with the next of kin, keeping in mind that the patient remains the master of his secrecy.

336. Cour, 16 May 1988, No. 54/88, JUDOC: 98811505.

337. Cour, 10 Dec. 2003, No. 27.057; Cour, 4 Apr. 2003, No. 26786, Pas. lux., 2002–2004/1b, pp. 272–279.

334. If a patient can express wishes, his consent is always required to lift medical confidentiality and involve a relative. Confidentiality thus precludes communication to the next of kin without the patient's knowledge.[338]

335. A patient has the right to choose a companion and medical secrecy is implicitly waived for the accompanying person. The accompanying person may only participate in the exchange with healthcare professionals to the extent desired by the patient. The physician or the patient can request an exchange without the presence of the accompanying person.[339] Although not acting as a professional, the patient companion is bound to secrecy with regard to the information he gets to know.[340]

336. If a patient is no longer able to decide himself and has designated a person of trust, the professional secrecy is lifted with regard to the person of trust who acts in the interest of the patient.[341] This waiver is a necessity to enable the person of trust to exercise his or her role. The person of trust further has access to the patient file. Although not acting as a professional, the person of trust is bound to secrecy with regard to the information he or she gets to know.[342]

337. In the event of a serious diagnosis or prognosis, consent is not required towards a next of kin when the patient is incapable of expressing his or her wishes and has not previously objected to the lifting of medical confidentiality.[343] This legal exception pursues the aim of enabling the association of the next of kin in a critical situation. A next of kin not designated as a person of trust is not submitted to Article 458 of the Criminal Code.

V. Testimony

338. If called as a witness about facts covered by professional secrecy, a physician must accept to appear before the judge.[344] A physician may agree to speak or testify or refuse to do so. Even if authorised by his or her patient or requested to speak by a judge, a physician is not obliged to testify and may prefer to remain silent on the basis of his or her secrecy if he or she believes in good conscience to be obliged to maintain secrecy. The decision to testify or not to disclose secret information rests upon the physician, having regard to the interests of the patient.[345]

338. Article 18, §1, Law on patient rights and obligations.
339. Article 7, §2, Law on patient rights and obligations.
340. Article 18, §1, Law on patient rights and obligations.
341. Article 12, Law on patient rights and obligations.
342. Article 18, §1, Law on patient rights and obligations.
343. *Ibid.*
344. Article 77, Code d'Instruction Criminelle.
345. Cour, 6 juin 1960, Pas. lux., 18, p. 351.

VI. Reporting to Judicial or Police Authorities

339. If a physician learns or suspects during his or her work that a patient is the perpetrator of a criminal offence, he or she may generally not report information to the judicial or police authorities as this would be in breach of the duty of medical secrecy. Article 458 Criminal Code is, however, not absolute. Statutory obligations and general principles of criminal law may, under certain circumstances, allow or request to report.

340. Article 140 of the Luxembourg Criminal Code requires, in the interests of the protection of minors, that any crime against a minor be reported to the judicial authorities when it is still possible to prevent it or limit its effects or when the perpetrator is likely to commit a new crime that could be prevented. A physician must thus, if necessary to prevent a recurrence, report child abuse.

Physicians are furthermore obliged to report information about a minor patient who may be at risk to the Youth Court or the Public Prosecutor's Office.[346]

341. The Belgian Cour de Cassation considers that Article 458 of the Criminal Code intends to protect the interests of the patient. According to the jurisprudence, the prohibition to divulge information may therefore not be extended to facts of which the patient has become a victim.[347] There is so far no Luxembourg jurisprudence known to the authors; however, this reasoning could be followed. A physician would thus be allowed to report a crime against his patient, but he should, however, always bear in mind the interest of the patient. He may prefer to remain silent, according to the circumstances.

342. Under general criminal Law, the so-called state of necessity ('état de nécessité') is a general ground of justification that may make an act lawful otherwise punishable by criminal law. State of necessity concerns a situation in which a person is faced with the threat of serious, present, imminent, and real harm that can only be avoided by violating a criminal statute. It is generally accepted that if breaking medical secrecy is the only manner to avoid a greater evil, medical secrecy can be outweighed by higher values and interests.[348] It must not be possible to safeguard the greater or equal value in any other way than by a breach of confidentiality.

343. Pursuant to Article 410-1 of the Criminal Code, anyone who, without serious danger to himself or to others, voluntarily refrains from coming to the aid of, or providing assistance to, a person exposed to serious danger is punishable by imprisonment from eight days to five years and/or a fine from EUR 251 to EUR 10,000.

---

346. Article 7, Loi du 10 août 1992 relative à la protection de la jeunesse.
347. Cour de Cassation, 9 Feb. 1988, *Arr. Cass.*, 1988, 720–721; Cour de Cassation, 26 Mar. 2021, *T. Gez.*, 2021–2022, 41–42.
348. Concerning the state of necessity: Spielmann, D., Spielmannm A., *Droit pénal général luxembourgeois*, pp. 283–294, Ed. Bruylant (2002).

A physician having knowledge of a serious danger to a person's integrity risks such charges. If necessary to avoid bodily injury, a physician may be compelled to act and breach the medical secrecy to avoid such charges of not rescuing a person in danger ('non-assistance à personne en danger').

VII. Statutory Obligations to Disclose

344. The protection of medical secrecy is further waived where communication is legally required. There is, for instance, an obligation for physicians to:

- declare a birth in the absence of a declaration by the parents[349] and declare deaths and causes of death;[350]
- declare cases of notifiable diseases;[351]
- provide the CMSS, upon request, with information on the patient's state of health;[352]
- respond to a magistrate's summons,[353] requesting, for instance, a certificate of fitness for imprisonment, a certificate in view of a measure of legal protection, or a certificate in view of hospitalisation without consent;
- provide all the facts that are relevant to an investigation of the Medical College.[354]

345. The duty of medical secrecy cannot be invoked in the event of an investigation by the Director of Health pursuant to a complaint alleging a general failure or defective operation of a hospital service.[355] Duly authorised by the patient or the person representing the patient, information may further be requested by the national health information and mediation service.[356]

VIII. Consequences of an Infringement

346. According to Article 458 of the Criminal Code, infringement of the secrecy exposes the physician to imprisonment for a period of between eight days and six months and a fine from EUR 500 to EUR 5,000.

349. Article 56, Code civil.
350. *See:* paras 638–640 *infra.*
351. Loi modifiée du 1 août 2018 sur la déclaration obligatoire de certaines maladies dans le cadre de la protection de la santé publique, http://data.legilux.public.lu/eli/etat/leg/loi/2018/08/01/a705.
352. Article 421, CSS.
353. Article 36, Loi modifiée du 29 avril 1983 concernant l'exercice des professions de médecin, de médecin-dentiste et de médecin-vétérinaire.
354. Article 121, of the Code of Medical Ethics; *See:* Part I., Ch. 4., §1., V. Disciplinary Action.
355. Article 41, Law on hospitals.
356. Article 21, Loi modifiée du 24 juillet 2014 relative aux droits et obligations du patient.

§3. Complementary Protection of Confidentiality

347. We will briefly address hereinafter complementary protection of confidentiality, the scope of which may apply even if an act is not subject to a criminal sanction under Article 458 of the Criminal Code. A violation of medical secrecy or of a secrecy obligation may further give rise to civil liability claims for compensation of the material and moral damages resulting thereof by the patient or a damaged third party.

348. The duty of secrecy is a deontological obligation of physicians. Any violation of medical secrecy by a physician is, at the same time, a violation of the Code of Medical Ethics (Articles 4–6) that may give rise to disciplinary action.[357]

349. For physicians employed in the public sector, a breach of confidentiality may be in violation of the statutory confidentiality obligation imposed on all public agents. It can thus give rise to disciplinary sanctions, including suspension and loss of employment. The scope of the secrecy obligation imposed on public servants covers information not protected by Article 458 of the Criminal Code.

For physicians employed in the private sector, a breach of confidentiality may give rise to a penalty by the employer, including termination of the employment contract. Finally, a violation of secrecy by a physician admitted as a self-employed liberal professional in an 'open regime' hospital may give rise to cancellation of the collaboration contract.

Contractual arrangements, in service or employment contracts, may impose a secrecy obligation beyond the general scope or on persons not covered by Article 458 of the Criminal Code. A confidentiality clause does not allow an extension of the scope of Article 458, so that infringements do solely give rise to civil liability for violation of a contractual obligation.

§4. General Data Protection Regulation

I. Introduction

350. Since 1979, Luxembourg has had a general legislation protecting the individual with regard to processing of personal data in IT data processing.[358] In 1987, Luxembourg ratified Convention No. 108 of the Council of Europe of 28 January 1981.[359] A Grand-Ducal Regulation of 2 October 1992 contained specific rules as to

357. *See:* Part I., Ch. 4., §1., V. Disciplinary Action.
358. Loi du 31 mars 1979 réglementant l'utilisation des données nominatives dans les traitements informatiques, Mém. A – 29 du 11.04.1979, https://legilux.public.lu/eli/etat/leg/loi/1979/03/31/n1/jo.
359. Loi du 19 novembre 1987 portant (a) approbation de la Convention pour la protection des personnes à l'égard du traitement automatisé des données à caractère personnel, faite à Strasbourg, le 28 janvier 1981; (b) modification de la loi du 31 mars 1979 réglementant l'utilisation des données nominatives dans les traitements informatiques, Mém. A – 94 du 27.11.1987, https://legilux.public.lu/eli/etat/leg/loi/1987/11/19/n1/jo.

the protection of personal health-related data.[360] In 2002, a Law of 2 August 2002 on the protection of individuals with regard to the processing of personal data repealed the Law of 1979 in order to comply with Directive 95/46, leaving the Grand-Ducal Regulation of 1992 into force.

351. These rules have been replaced by the GDPR from 25 May 2018 onwards.[361] A Law of 1 August 2018 on the organisation of the National Data Protection Commission and the general data protection framework complements the GDPR.[362] A law amending the Law of 7 December 2015 on the insurance sector specifically addressing the processing of health-related data in insurance and reinsurance is currently pending in Parliament.[363]

352. In this part, we deal with the protection of the patient's health and genetic data and the obligation of the physician to respect the patient's privacy and to protect these data, as laid down by the GDPR, considering the specific national aspects.[364]

II. General Rule for Processing of Personal Health Data and Genetic Data

353. GDPR protects the fundamental rights and freedoms of natural persons and, in particular, their right to the protection of personal data (Article 1.2. GDPR). GDPR does not apply to the personal data of deceased persons (Preamble, Recital 27 GDPR).

Personal data means any information relating to an identified or identifiable natural person ('data subject'); an identifiable natural person is one who can be identified,

360. Règlement grand-ducal du 2 octobre 1992 réglementant l'utilisation des données nominatives médicales dans les traitements informatiques, Mém. A – 74 du 06.10.1992, https://legilux.public.lu/eli/etat/leg/rgd/1992/10/02/n2/jo.
361. Regulation (EU) 2016/679 of the European Parliament and of the Council of 27 Apr. 2016 on the protection of natural persons with regard to the processing of personal data and on the free movement of such data, and repealing Directive 95/46/EC, OJEU, https://eur-lex.europaeu/eli/reg/2016/679/oj.
362. Loi du 1er août 2018 portant organisation de la Commission nationale pour la protection des données et mise en œuvre du règlement (UE) 2016/679 du Parlement européen et du Conseil du 27 avril 2016 relatif à la protection des personnes physiques à l'égard du traitement des données à caractère personnel et à la libre circulation de ces données, et abrogeant la directive 95/46/CE (règlement général sur la protection des données), portant modification du Code du travail et de la loi modifiée du 25 mars 2015 fixant le régime des traitements et les conditions et modalités d'avancement des fonctionnaires de l'État, Mém. A – 686 du 16.08.2018, https://legilux.public.lu/eli/etat/leg/loi/2018/08/01/a686/jo.
363. Projet de loi 5711 relative au traitement de données concernant la santé en matière d'assurance et de réassurance et portant modification de la loi modifiée du 7 décembre 2015 sur le secteur des assurances, https://www.chd.lu/fr/dossier/7511.
364. Bock H., *La conformité RGPD des médecins exerçant sous statut libéral et quelques réflexions sur des traitements de données liés au covid-19*, RLDS, No. 4, pp. 3–9 (2020).

directly or indirectly, in particular by reference to an identifier such as a name, an identification number, location data, an online identifier or to one or more factors specific to the physical, physiological, genetic, mental, economic, cultural or social identity of that natural person (Article 1(1) GDPR).

Processing means any operation or set of operations which is performed on personal data or on sets of personal data, whether or not by automated means, such as collection, recording, organisation, structuring, storage, adaptation or alteration, retrieval, consultation, use, disclosure by transmission, dissemination or otherwise making available, alignment or combination, restriction, erasure or destruction (Article 1(2) GDPR).

354. The processing of 'special categories of personal data' is prohibited by Article 9.1. GDPR. Recital 10 in the Preamble refers to such data as 'sensitive data'.[365] The special categories of personal data are, among others, genetic data and data concerning health (Article 9.1. GDPR).

Data concerning health or health data means personal data related to the physical or psychiatric health of a natural person, including the provision of healthcare services, which reveal information about his or her health status (Article 4(15)). According to Recital 35 in the Preamble, this information relates to the past, current or future physical or psychiatric health status of the data subject and includes information about the natural person collected in the course of the registration for, or the provision of, healthcare services to that natural person; a number, symbol or particular assigned to a natural person to uniquely identify the natural person for health purposes; information derived from the testing or examination of a body part or bodily substance, including from genetic data and biological samples; and any information on, for example, a disease, disability, disease risk, medical history, clinical treatment or the physiological or biomedical state of the data subject independent of its source, for example, from a physician or other healthcare professional, a hospital, a medical device or an in vitro diagnostic test.

Genetic data means personal data relating to the inherited or acquired genetic characteristics of a natural person which give unique information about the physiology or the health of that natural person and which result, in particular, from an analysis of a biological sample from the natural person in question (Article 4(13)), [in particular chromosomal, deoxyribonucleic acid (DNA) or ribonucleic acid (RNA) analysis, or from the analysis of another element enabling equivalent information to be obtained] (*see* Recital 34 in the Preamble).

365. Paragraph 3 of the European Parliament Resolution of 14 Mar. 2017 on fundamental rights implications of big data: privacy, data protection, non-discrimination, security and law enforcement (2016/2225(INI)) points out that sensitive information about persons can be inferred from non-sensitive data, which blurs the line between sensitive and non-sensitive data.

III. Derogation from the Prohibition on Processing of Data Regarding Health and Genetic Data

A. Compliance with the Principles Relating to Processing of Personal Data

355. When processing personal data, the following principles always have to be respected: the principles of lawfulness, fairness and transparency (Article 5.1a); the principle of purpose limitation (Article 5.1b); the principle of data minimisation (Article 5.1c); the principle of accuracy (Article 5.1d); the principle of storage limitation (Article 5.1e); and the principle of integrity and confidentiality (Article 5.1f).

356. Moreover, the controller is responsible for and able to demonstrate compliance with these principles (principle of accountability, Article 5.2). Controller means the natural or legal person, public authority, agency, or other body which, alone or jointly with others, determines the purposes and means of the processing of personal data (Article 4(7)).

357. With regard to the patient file in hospitals, Article 37 of the Law on hospitals confers to the general director the obligation to ensure that the legal requirements are complied with and to take the organisational measures required to prevent any illicit access. In our view, he or she must therefore be regarded as the data controller of the hospital file in the sense of the GDPR. At the same time, physicians are to be considered co-controllers of the data of their respective patients.

B. One of the Following Justifications Applies

1. The Data Subject Has Given Explicit Consent

358. Data regarding health or genetic data may be processed for one or more specified purposes if the data subject has given explicit consent, except where EU law or Member State law provides that the prohibition to process such data may not be lifted by the data subject (Article 9.2a). The GDPR does not define 'explicit' consent, nor is it explained in the Preamble. An oral consent can also be considered explicit consent.

359. Article 7 of GDPR defines the conditions for consent. The controller must be able to demonstrate that the data subject has consented to process his or her data (Article 7.1). If the data subject's consent is given in the context of a written declaration which also concerns other matters, the request for consent must be presented in a manner which is clearly distinguishable from the other matters, in an intelligible and easily accessible form, using clear and plain language. Any part of such a declaration which constitutes an infringement of the GDPR is not binding (Article 7.2).

360. The data subject has the right to withdraw his or her consent at any time. The withdrawal of consent does not affect the lawfulness of processing based on consent before its withdrawal. Prior to giving consent, the data subject must be informed thereof. It must be as easy to withdraw as to give consent (Article 7.3).

2. Necessity to Protect the Vital Interests of the Data Subject or of Another Natural Person

361. Health data or genetic data may be processed in order to protect the vital interests of the data subject or of another natural person where the data subject is physically or legally incapable of giving consent (Article 9.2c). According to Recital 46 in the Preamble, a vital interest is an interest 'which is essential for the life'. Processing of personal data based on the vital interest of another natural person should, in principle, take place only where the processing cannot be manifestly based on another legal basis (*See:* Recital 46 in the Preamble).[366]

3. Necessary for Reasons of Substantial Public Interest

362. Health data or genetic data may be processed when this is necessary for reasons of substantial public interest, on the basis of Union or Member State law, which has to be proportionate to the aim pursued, respect the essence of the right to data protection and provide for suitable and specific measures to safeguard the fundamental rights and the interests of the data subject (Article 9.2g). According to Recital 52 in the Preamble, one of the reasons for the substantial public interest is health security, monitoring and alert purposes, and the prevention or control of communicable diseases and other serious threats to health. And the recital continues: 'Such a derogation may be made for health purposes, including public health and the management of healthcare services, especially in order to ensure the quality and cost-effectiveness of the procedures used for settling claims for benefits and services in the health insurance system.'

4. Necessary for Health-Related Purposes

363. Health data or genetic data may be processed when this is necessary for the purposes of preventive or occupational medicine, for the assessment of the working capacity of the employee, for medical diagnosis, the provision of health or social care or treatment or for the management of health or social care systems and services on the basis of Union or Member State law or pursuant to a contract with a

366. The concept of 'vital interest' was already present in the text of Directive 95/46/EC. The Art. 29 Data Protection Working Party has provided clarifications on the concept of 'vital interests' in its Opinion No. 06/2014 on the notion of legitimate interests of the data controller (WP 217). The national data protection authorities are as of May 2018 responsible for monitoring and enforcing the provisions of the GDPR. Questions regarding the application of the 'vital interest' legal basis in a specific case should in the first place addressed to them according to the answer given by Ms Jourova on behalf of the Commission on 11 Jan. 2018 to the Parliamentary question E-006389-2017.

healthcare professional and subject to the conditions and safeguards referred to in Article 9.3 (Article 9.2h). Recital 53 in the Preamble calls this the processing for health-related purposes. This recital specifies 'that such processing should be necessary to achieve those purposes for the benefit of natural persons and society as a whole, in particular in the context of the management of health or social care services and systems, including processing by the management and central national health authorities of such data for the purpose of quality control, management information and the general national and local supervision of the health or social care system, and ensuring continuity of health or social care and cross-border healthcare or health security, monitoring and alert purposes (…) based on Union or Member State law which has to meet an objective of public interest (…)'.

Article 9.3 requires that the data are processed by or under the responsibility of a professional subject to the obligation of professional secrecy under Union or Member State law or rules established by national competent bodies or by another person also subject to an obligation of secrecy under Union or Member State law or rules established by national competent bodies.

5. Necessary for Reasons of Public Interest in the Area of Public Health

364. Health data or genetic data may be processed if it is necessary for reasons of public interest in the area of public health, such as protecting against serious cross-border threats to health or ensuring high standards of quality and safety of healthcare and medicinal products or medical devices, on the basis of Union or Member State law which provides for suitable and specific measures to safeguard the rights and freedoms of the data subject, in particular professional secrecy (Article 9.2i). Recital 54 in the Preamble emphasises that in such a case, the processing is possible without the consent of the data subject. This is remarkable because this is also the case in the situation mentioned under subheadings b, c, and d above. Public health should be interpreted as defined in Regulation (EC) No. 1338/2008 of the European Parliament and of the Council on Community Statistics on public health and health and safety at work,[367] : all elements related to health, namely health status, including morbidity and disability, the determinants having an effect on that health status, healthcare needs, resources allocated to healthcare, the provision of, and universal access to, healthcare as well as healthcare expenditure and financing, and the causes of mortality (Recital 54 in the Preamble).

Such processing of data concerning health for reasons of public interest should not result in personal data being processed for other purposes by third parties such as employers or insurance and banking companies (*see* Recital 54 in the Preamble).

There seems to exist an overlap between Article 9.2g and Article 9.2i in regard to the explanations given in the Recitals accompanying both provisions. Obviously, the difference is between substantial public interest (Article 9.2g) and substantial interest (Article 9.2i), but where to draw the line and what the consequences are remains vague.

367. OJEU, L 354, 31.12.2008, pp. 70–81, http://data.europa.eu/eli/reg/2008/1338/oj.

C. Comply with Member States Further Conditions

365. Member States may maintain or introduce further conditions, including limitations, with regard to the processing of genetic data or health data (Article 9.4). However, this should not hamper the free flow of personal data within the Union when those conditions apply to the cross-border processing of such data (*see* Recital 53 in the Preamble). With regards to genetic data, Luxembourg prohibits processing of genetic data for the purposes of exercising the data controller's rights in terms of employment law and insurance.[368]

IV. Rights of the Data Subject

A. The Right to the Protection of Personal Data

366. The GDPR protects the fundamental rights and freedoms of natural persons and, in particular, their right to the protection of personal data (Article 1.2). The right to the protection of personal data concerning him or her is also provided for in Article 8.1 of the Charter of Fundamental Rights of the EU.

B. Information to Be Provided Where Personal Data Are Collected from the Data Subject

367. Where personal data relating to a data subject are collected from the data subject, the controller has, at the time when personal data are obtained, to provide the data subject with all of the following information: the identity and the contact details of the controller and, where applicable, of the controller's representative; the contact details of the data protection officer, where applicable; the purposes of the processing for which the personal data are intended as well as the legal basis for the processing; the recipients or categories of recipients of the personal data, if any (Article 13.1a, b, c, and e).

368. In addition to this information, the controller has, at the time when personal data are obtained, to provide the data subject with the following further information necessary to ensure fair and transparent processing: the period for which the personal data will be stored, or if that is not possible, the criteria used to determine that period; the existence of the right to request from the controller access to and rectification or erasure of personal data or restriction of processing concerning the data subject or to object to processing as well as the right to data portability; where the processing is based on Article 9.2a, the existence of the right to withdraw consent at any time, without affecting the lawfulness of processing based on consent

---

368. Article 66, Loi du 1er août 2018 portant organisation de la Commission nationale pour la protection des données et du régime général sur la protection des données.

before its withdrawal; the right to lodge a complaint with a supervisory authority; whether the provision of personal data is a statutory or contractual requirement, or a requirement necessary to enter into a contract, as well as whether the data subject is obliged to provide the personal data and of the possible consequences of failure to provide such data; the existence of automated decision-making, including profiling, referred to in Article 22(1) and (4) and, at least in those cases, meaningful information about the logic involved, as well as the significance and the envisaged consequences of such processing for the data subject (Article 13.2).

369. Where the controller intends to further process the personal data for a purpose other than that for which the personal data were collected, the controller has to provide the data subject prior to that further processing with information on that other purpose and with any further relevant information as referred to in Article 13.2 (Article 13.3).

370. Article 13.1, 2, and 3 do not apply where and insofar as the data subject already has the information (Article 13.4).

C. The Right of Access by the Data Subject

371. The data subject has the right to obtain confirmation from the controller as to whether or not personal data concerning him or her are being processed and, where that is the case, access to the personal data (Article 15.1). The controller provides a copy of the personal data undergoing processing. For any further copies requested by the data subject, the controller may charge a reasonable fee based on administrative costs (*see also* Article 12.5). Where the data subject makes the request by electronic means, and unless otherwise requested by the data subject, the information is provided in a commonly used electronic form (Article 15.3). The right to obtain a copy referred to in Article 15.3 should not adversely affect the rights and freedoms of others (Article 15.4).

A data subject has the right to access personal data which has been collected concerning him or her and to exercise that right easily and at reasonable intervals in order to be aware of and verify the lawfulness of the processing. According to Recital 63 in the Preamble, this right includes the right for data subjects to have access to data concerning their health, for example, the data in their medical records containing information such as diagnoses, examination results, assessments by treating physicians and any treatment or interventions provided.

The ECJ has clarified that in the context of a doctor/patient relationship, the right to obtain a copy of personal data undergoing processing implies that the patient must be provided with a faithful and intelligible reproduction of all such data. This right implies the right to obtain a full copy of the documents in the patient file, such as diagnoses, test results, opinions of treating doctors and any treatment or intervention administered. The physician is obliged to provide the patient with an initial copy free of charge and national legislation may not permit to charge the costs of the initial copy to patients.[369]

D. Right to Rectification

372. The data subject has the right to obtain from the controller without undue delay the rectification of inaccurate personal data concerning him or her. Taking into account the purposes of the processing, the data subject has the right to have incomplete personal data completed, including by means of providing a supplementary statement (Article 16). The controller must communicate any rectification to each recipient to whom the personal data have been disclosed unless this proves impossible or involves disproportionate effort. The controller must inform the data subject about those recipients if the data subject requests it (Article 19). Concerning the right to rectification, national law provides that the rectification of an inaccurate or incomplete entry may be made under the responsibility of the healthcare professional who provided the care. The rectification must be reversible and documented (Law on patient rights and obligations, second phrase of Article 15, §5).

E. Restricted Right to Erasure of Personal Health Data or Genetic Data ('Right to Be Forgotten')

373. The data subject has the right to obtain from the controller the erasure of personal data concerning him or her without undue delay, and the controller has an obligation to erase personal data without undue delay where one of the following grounds applies:[370]

(a) the personal data are no longer necessary in relation to the purposes for which they were collected or otherwise processed;
(b) the data subject withdraws consent on which the processing is based according to Article 9.2a and where there is no other legal ground for the processing;
(c) the data subject objects to the processing pursuant to Article 21.1, and there are no overriding legitimate grounds for the processing or the data subject objects to the processing pursuant to Article 21.2;
(d) the personal data have been unlawfully processed;
(e) the personal data have to be erased for compliance with a legal obligation in Union or Member State law to which the controller is subject;
(f) the personal data have been collected in relation to the offer of information society services referred to in Article 8(1).

369. CJEU, 26 Oct. 2023, *FT v. DW*, (C-307/22), https://curia.europa.eu/juris/liste.jsf?language=en&td=ALL&num=C-307/22; Schwebag, M., *L'encadrement national du droit d'accès au dossier patient au regard des dispositions du RGPD,* RLDS, No. 18, pp. 13–18 (2024).
370. H. Nys, 'Towards a Human Right "to Be Forgotten Online"?', 18 *Eur. J. Health L.*, pp. 469–475 (2011).

374. However, the right to erasure does not apply to the extent that processing of health data and genetic data is necessary for reasons of public health in accordance with Article 9.2h (processing is necessary for health-related purposes), with Article 9.2i (processing is necessary for reasons of public interest in the area of public health) as well as Article 9.3 (processing under the responsibility of a professional subject to the obligation of professional secrecy) (Article 17.3c).

More in general, the right to erasure is not applicable, also with regard to health data and genetic data, to the extent that their processing is necessary for exercising the right of freedom of expression and information and for the establishment, exercise, or defence of legal claims (Article 17.3a and e). However, the right to erasure is applicable if health data or genetic data have been processed with the explicit consent of the data subject based on Article 9.2a. The controller has to communicate any erasure of personal data to each recipient to whom the personal data have been disclosed unless this proves impossible or involves disproportionate effort. The controller has to inform the data subject about those recipients if the data subject requests it (Article 19).

Concerning the right to erasure, national law provides that no element relevant to the keeping of the patient file may be removed thereof before the expiry of the mandatory ten years retention period.[371]

F. Right to Restriction of Processing

375. Restriction of processing means the marking of stored personal data with the aim of limiting their processing in the future (Article 4(3)). The data subject has the right to obtain from the controller restriction of processing where one of the following applies:

(a) the accuracy of the personal data is contested by the data subject for a period, enabling the controller to verify the accuracy of the personal data;
(b) the processing is unlawful, and the data subject opposes the erasure of the personal data and requests the restriction of their use instead;
(c) the controller no longer needs the personal data for the purposes of the processing, but they are required by the data subject for the establishment, exercise or defence of legal claims;
(d) the data subject has objected to processing pursuant to Article 21.1 pending the verification of whether the legitimate grounds of the controller override those of the data subject (Article 18.1).

376. Where processing has been restricted, the personal data should, with the exception of storage, only be processed with the data subject's consent or for the establishment, exercise or defence of legal claims or for the protection of the rights of another natural or legal person or for reasons of important public interest of the Union or of a Member State (Article 18.2). A data subject who has obtained a

371. Article 15, §5, Law on patient rights and obligations.

restriction of processing has to be informed by the controller before the restriction of processing is lifted (Article 18.3). The controller has to communicate any restriction of processing to each recipient to whom the personal data have been disclosed unless this proves impossible or involves disproportionate effort. The controller has to inform the data subject about those recipients if the data subject requests it (Article 19). Methods by which to restrict the processing of personal data could include, *inter alia*, temporarily moving the selected data to another processing system, making the selected personal data unavailable to users, or temporarily removing published data from a website. In automated filing systems, the restriction of processing should, in principle, be ensured by technical means in such a manner that the personal data are not subject to further processing operations and cannot be changed. The fact that the processing of personal data is restricted should be clearly indicated in the system (*see* Recital 67 in the Preamble).

G. Restricted Right to Portability of Health Data or Genetic Data

377. The data subject has the right to receive the personal data concerning him or her, which he or she has provided to a controller, in a structured, commonly used and machine-readable format and has the right to transmit those data to another controller without hindrance from the controller to which the personal data have been provided when the processing is carried out by automated means. When it concerns health data or genetic data, this so-called right to portability only applies when these data have been processed upon explicit consent (*see* Article 9.2a) (Article 20.1) and not in the other situations mentioned in Article 9.2a (*see also* Recital 68 in the Preamble: 'It should not apply where processing is based on a legal ground other than consent'). In exercising his or her right to data portability, the data subject has the right to have the personal data transmitted directly from one controller to another, where technically feasible (Article 20.2). The right to portability of data may not adversely affect the rights and freedoms of others (Article 20.4).

H. Right Not to Be Subject to Automated Individual Decision-Making, Including Profiling

378. The data subject has the right not to be subject to a decision based solely on automated processing, including profiling, which produces legal effects concerning him or her or similarly significantly affects him or her (Article 22.1).[372] Profiling means any form of automated processing of personal data consisting of the use of personal data to evaluate certain personal aspects relating to a natural person, in particular, to analyse or predict aspects concerning that natural person's performance at work, economic situation, health, personal preferences, interests, reliability, behaviour, location or movements (Article 4(4)). However, the data subject may be subject to such a decision when it is based on, *inter alia*, the data subject's

372. *See:* Art. 29 Data Protection Working Party, *Guidelines on automated individual decision-making and profiling for the purposes of Regulation 2016/679,* 3 Oct. 2017, WP251. Rev.01.

explicit consent (Article 22.2). However, health data and genetic data are excluded from this possibility unless the decision is based on such health data or genetic data processed after the explicit consent of the data subject (*see* Article 9.2a) or the processing of which is necessary for reasons of substantial public interest (*see* Article 9.2g) (Article 22.3).

I. Right to Transparent Information and Communication Concerning Rights of the Data Subject

379. The controller takes appropriate measures to provide any information referred to in Articles 13 and 14 and any communication under Articles 15–22 and 34 relating to processing the data subject in a concise, transparent, intelligible, and easily accessible form, using clear and plain language, in particular for any information addressed specifically to a child. The information is provided in writing or by other means, including, where appropriate, electronic means. When requested by the data subject, the information may be provided orally, provided that the identity of the data subject is proven by other means (Article 12.1). The controller facilitates the exercise of the data subject rights under Articles 15–22 (Article 12.2). The controller provides information on action taken on a request under Articles 15–22 to the data subject without undue delay and, in any event, within one month of receipt of the request. That period may be extended by two further months where necessary, taking into account the complexity and number of the requests. The controller informs the data subject of any such extension within one month of receipt of the request, together with the reasons for the delay. Where the data subject makes the request by electronic form means, the information has to be provided by electronic means where possible, unless otherwise requested by the data subject (Article 12.3). If the controller does not take action on the request of the data subject, he has to inform the data subject without delay and, at the latest, within one month of receipt of the request of the reasons for not taking action and the possibility of lodging a complaint with a supervisory authority and seeking a judicial remedy (Article 12.4).

Pursuant to the entry into force of GDPR, the Medical College has published a model patient information sheet concerning the use of patient data.[373]

J. Right to Lodge a Complaint and to an Effective Judicial Remedy

380. Without prejudice to any other administrative or judicial remedy, every data subject has the right to lodge a complaint with a supervisory authority, in particular in the Member State of his or her habitual residence, place of work or place of the alleged infringement if the data subject considers that the processing of personal data relating to him or her infringes the GDPR. The supervisory authority with which the complaint has been lodged has to inform the complainant of the progress

373. *Fiche d'information à l'attention du patient concernant la protection de ses données de santé*, Collège médical (2018), http://www.collegemedical.lu/Fr/Recommandation/.

and the outcome of the complaint, including the possibility of a judicial remedy pursuant to Article 78 (Article 77). Without prejudice to any other administrative or non-judicial remedy, each data subject has the right to an effective judicial remedy where the supervisory authority, which is competent, does not handle a complaint or does not inform the data subject within three months of the progress or outcome of the complaint lodged pursuant to Article 77. Proceedings against a supervisory authority are to be brought before the courts of the Member State where the supervisory authority is established (Article 78.2 and 3).

The National Commission for Data Protection (*Commission nationale pour la protection des données* (CNPD)) supervises the processing of personal data carried out in Luxembourg.[374]

381. Without prejudice to any available administrative or non-judicial remedy, including the right to lodge a complaint with a supervisory authority pursuant to Article 77, each data subject has the right to an effective judicial remedy against a controller or a processor where he or she considers that his or her rights under the GDPR have been infringed as a result of the processing of his or her personal data in non-compliance with the GDPR. Such proceedings are to be brought before the courts of the Member State where the controller or processor has an establishment. Alternatively, such proceedings may be brought before the courts of the Member State where the data subject has his or her habitual residence unless the controller or processor is a public authority of a Member State acting in the exercise of its public powers (Article 79).

K. Right to Be Represented

382. The data subject has the right to mandate a not-for-profit body, organisation or association which has been properly constituted in accordance with the law of a Member State, has statutory objectives which are in the public interest, and is active in the field of the protection of data subjects' rights and freedoms with regard to the protection of their personal data to lodge the complaint on his or her behalf, to exercise the rights referred to in Articles 77, 78, and 79 on his or her behalf, and to exercise the right to receive compensation referred to in Article 82 on his or her behalf were provided by Member State law (Article 80.1).

L. Right to Compensation and Liability

383. Any person who has suffered material or non-material damage as a result of an infringement of the GDPR has the right to receive compensation from the controller or processor for the damage suffered. Any controller involved in processing is liable for the damage caused by processing which infringes on the GDPR. A processor is liable for the damage caused by processing only where it has not complied

374. Official website: www.cnpd.lu.

with obligations of the GDPR specifically directed to processors or where it has acted outside or contrary to lawful instructions of the controller. A controller or processor is exempt from liability if it proves that it is not in any way responsible for the event giving rise to the damage. Where more than one controller or processor, or both a controller and a processor, are involved in the same processing and where they are responsible for any damage caused by processing, each controller or processor is held liable for the entire damage in order to ensure effective compensation of the data subject (Article 82.1–82.4).

V. Modalities for the Exercise of the Rights of the Data Subject

384. Information provided under Articles 13 and 14 and any communication and any actions taken under Articles 15–22 and 34 are provided free of charge (*see also* Article 15.3, above paragraph 346). Where requests from a data subject are manifestly unfounded or excessive, in particular because of their repetitive character, the controller may either: charge a reasonable fee taking into account the administrative costs of providing the information or communication or taking the action requested, or refuse to act on the request. The controller bears the burden of demonstrating the manifestly unfounded or excessive character of the request (Article 12.5). Where the controller has reasonable doubts concerning the identity of the natural person making the request referred to in Articles 15–21, the controller may request the provision of additional information necessary to confirm the identity of the data subject (Article 12.6). The information to be provided to data subjects pursuant to Articles 13 and 14 may be provided in combination with standardised icons in order to give in an easily visible, intelligible and clearly legible manner a meaningful overview of the intended processing. Where the icons are presented electronically, they have to be machine-readable (Article 12.7). The Commission is empowered to adopt delegated acts in accordance with Article 92 for the purpose of determining the information to be presented by the icons and the procedures for providing standardised icons (Article 12.8).

VI. Data Protection by Design and by Default

385. Taking into account the state of the art, the cost of implementation and the nature, scope, context and purposes of processing, as well as the risks of varying likelihood and severity for rights and freedoms of natural persons posed by the processing, the controller implements, both at the time of the determination of the means for processing and at the time of the processing itself, appropriate technical and organisational measures, such as pseudonymisation, which are designed to implement data protection principles, such as data minimisation, in an effective manner and to integrate the necessary safeguards into the processing in order to meet the requirements of the GDPR and protect the rights of data subjects (Article 25.1). Pseudonymisation means the processing of personal data in such a manner that the personal data can no longer be attributed to a specific data subject without the use of additional information, provided that such additional information is kept separately and is subject to technical and organisational measures to ensure that the personal data are not attributed to an identified or identifiable natural person (Article 4(5)). The likelihood and severity of the risk to the rights and freedoms of the data subject should be determined by reference to the nature, scope, context, and purposes of the processing. Risk should be evaluated on the basis of an objective assessment, by which it is established whether data processing operations involve a risk or a high risk (*see* Recital 76 in the Preamble). The controller has to implement appropriate technical and organisational measures to ensure that, by default, only personal data which are necessary for each specific purpose of the processing are processed. That obligation applies to the amount of personal data collected, the extent of their processing, the period of their storage and their accessibility. In particular, such measures have to ensure that by default, personal data are not made accessible without the individual's intervention to an indefinite number of natural persons (Article 25.2).

VII. Communication of a Personal Data Breach to the Data Subject

386. Personal data breach means a breach of security leading to the accidental or unlawful destruction, loss, alteration, or unauthorised disclosure of, or access to, personal data transmitted, stored, or otherwise processed (Article 4(12)). When the personal data breach is likely to result in a high risk to the rights and freedoms of natural persons, the controller has to communicate the personal data breach to the data subject without undue delay (Article 34.1). This communication to the data subject describes in clear and plain language the nature of the personal data breach and contains at least the following information and measures: the name and contact details of the data protection officer or other contact point where more information can be obtained, the likely consequences of the personal data breach and the measures taken or proposed to be taken by the controller to address the personal data breach, including, where appropriate, measures to mitigate its possible adverse effects (Article 34.2). The communication to the data subject is not required if any of the following conditions are met: (a) the controller has implemented appropriate technical and organisational protection measures, and those measures were applied to the personal data affected by the personal data breach, in particular, those that render the personal data unintelligible to any person who is not authorised to access it, such as encryption; (b) the controller has taken subsequent measures which ensure that the high risk to the rights and freedoms of data subjects is no longer likely to materialise; (c) it would involve disproportionate effort. In such a case, there has instead to be a public communication or similar measure whereby the data subjects are informed in an equally effective manner (Article 34.3).

VIII. Data Protection Impact Assessment

387. Where a type of processing, in particular, using new technologies and taking into account the nature, scope, context and purposes of the processing, is likely to result in a high risk to the rights and freedoms of natural persons, the controller has, prior to the processing, to carry out an assessment of the impact of the envisaged processing operations on the protection of personal data. A single assessment may address a set of similar processing operations that present similar high risks (Article 35.1).

IX. Designation of a Data Protection Officer When Health Data or Genetic Data Are Processed on a Large Scale

388. The controller and the processor have to designate a data protection officer in any case where the core activities of the controller or the processor consist of processing on a large-scale health data or genetic data (Article 37.1c). Large-scale processing operations aim to process a considerable amount of personal data at regional, national, or supranational levels, which could affect a large number of data subjects and are likely to result in a high risk. The processing of personal data is not considered to be on a large scale if the processing concerns personal data from patients by an individual physician or other healthcare professional. In such cases, a data protection officer is not mandatory (analogues to Recital 91 in the Preamble).

Chapter 3. End-of-Life Care (Palliative Care and Euthanasia)

§1. Introduction

389. End-of-life issues are amongst the most controversial bioethical issues. While most individuals would agree that human dignity should be at the centre of end-of-life care, it is challenging to agree on what dignity means in concrete end-of-life situations.

390. Historically, a reflection process on end-of-life issues was initiated in the Luxembourg Parliament in 1996. In 1998, the CNE organised the first national ethics day around the question of euthanasia and assisted suicide.[375] A special Ethics Commission of the Luxembourg Parliament elaborated reports on end of life, palliative care, therapeutic obstinacy and euthanasia in 1999 and 2003, followed each time by an orientation debate in the Plenary of Parliament.[376] Amongst others, the Medical College adopted in 2002 a position opposed to the legalisation of euthanasia and assisted suicide.[377]

The reflection process within politics and society was partially controversial and showed a political and societal divide across political party lines. After a long-lasting process, palliative care and physician-assisted dying have not been regarded as irreconcilable by the legislator.[378] Parliament adopted on 18 December 2008, in a vote not subject to party discipline, both the Law on palliative care, advance directive and end-of-life support and the Law on euthanasia and assisted suicide. The adoption of the Law on euthanasia and assisted suicide led to a constitutional crisis, as the Grand Duke initially objected to signing the law.[379] After political negotiations, an amendment to the Constitution was adopted to omit discretionary 'sanctioning' of Laws by the Grand Duke. Although the debate on euthanasia was controversial, all political parties supported the amendment of the Constitution. Grand Duke Henri finally promulgated both Laws on 16 March 2009.

375. Harpes, J.-P. & Wagner, E., *Actes de la Première Journée Nationale d'Ethique du 15 mai 1998*, Les Cahiers de la C.N.E. (1998), https://cne.public.lu/dam-assets/fr/publications/autres_publications/actes.pdf.

376. Chambre des Députés, Commission spéciale d'éthique, *L'encadrement en fin de vie*, Rapport en vue du débat d'orientation sur la médecine palliative, l'acharnement thérapeutique et l'euthanasie, doc. parl. 4408 (1999) https://www.chd.lu/de/techdossier/410, et doc. parl. 4934 (2003), https://www.chd.lu/de/techdossier/1209.

377. Avis du Collège médical du 7 juin 2002 concernant l'euthanasie et les soins palliatifs.

378. In the view of the Council of State, the draft law on palliative care and the draft law on euthanasia and assisted suicide were proposals that cannot be reconciled. At a certain point within the legislative procedure, the Council of State refrained to provide a detailed opinion on the proposal on euthanasia and assisted suicide (Conseil d'Etat, Avis complémentaire, 11 déc. 2007, doc. parl. 4909/05 et 5584/10).

379. Heuschling, L., *Luxembourg: Grand Duke Henri's refusal, in 2008, to sign the bill legalizing euthanasia*, in: Hazell, R. & Morris, B., (eds), *The Role of Monarchy in Modern Democracy: European Monarchies Compared,* Hart Publishing (2020), https://orbilu.uni.lu/handle/10993/38953.

391. As a result, Luxembourg has today a comprehensive legal framework on end-of-life issues.[380] While the legislator has considered that palliative care and physician-assisted dying are complementary, the historical process explains why end-of-life questions are split over two different legal instruments. The Law on patient rights and obligations, adopted in 2014, plays a subsidiary role. A national plan aiming to further develop end-of-life care (2023–2026) was adopted in July 2023 and confirmed by the Government elected in October 2023.[381]

§2. Palliative Care

I. Introduction

392. The development of palliative care in Luxembourg started in the 1980s. The main association for the promotion of palliative care ('Omega90') was founded in 1990. The first hospital unit dedicated to palliative care opened in March 1994 in the South of Luxembourg (CHEM). Palliative care is offered today in a variety of settings: in general hospitals, in a dedicated hospice centre ('Haus Omega'), in residential facilities for the elderly or disabled, as well as at home.

393. From a legal point of view, the 1998 Law on hospital establishments formalised for the first time a patient's right to palliative care and to an end of life in dignity. The current Law on hospitals foresees that every general hospital must dispose of a palliative care unit (CHdN: six beds; HRS, CHL and CHEM: ten beds each). Palliative care is present in other units, with the support of mobile palliative care and support teams attached to the palliative care unit of hospitals.

394. The Law of 16 March 2009 on palliative care, advance directives, and end-of-life support,[382] hereinafter 'Law on palliative care', governs end of life except for euthanasia and physician-assisted suicide. It results from a governmental initiative in 2006, which replaced and took up core elements from the first governmental proposal deposited in 2004.[383] The Law was significantly influenced by the Law on patient rights in end-of-life situations adopted in France in 2005 (called 'Loi Leonetti').

380. Braum, S., *Euthanasie et assistance au suicide au Luxembourg: antécédents, contenu et effets de la nouvelle loi*, Ann. dr. lux., Vol. 19, pp. 219–236 (2010).

381. *Plan national fin de vie et soins palliatifs 2023–2026: Vers une meilleure prise en charge et accompagnement en fin de vie*, Luxembourg Government Press Release (2023), https://gouvernement.lu/fr/actualites/toutes_actualites/communiques/2023/09-septembre/01-plan-national-fin-vie.html.

382. Loi du 16 mars 2009 relative aux soins palliatifs, à la directive anticipée et à l'accompagnement en fin de vie et modifiant: (1) le Code de la sécurité sociale; (2) la loi modifiée du 16 avril 1979 fixant le statut général des fonctionnaires de l'Etat; (3) la loi modifiée du 24 décembre 1985 fixant le statut général des fonctionnaires communaux; (4) le Code du travail, Mem. A – 46 du 16.03.2009, http://data.legilux.public.lu/eli/etat/leg/loi/2009/03/16/n1/jo.

383. Projet de loi 5303 relatif aux soins palliatifs et à l'accompagnement en fin de vie, https://www.chd.lu/de/dossier/5303.

II. Definition, Access, and Promotion of Palliative Care

395. The Law on palliative care addresses the rights of patients in an end-of-life situation having recourse to palliative care. According to the first article, any person in an advanced or terminal phase of a serious and incurable disease, whatever the cause, has access to palliative care. Palliative care in tandem with curative treatment may be appropriate for patients with serious illnesses beyond such situations. Generally, Article 6bis, §1, of the Law concerning the exercise of the medical profession stresses that any physician shall provide his patients with the preventive, curative or palliative care required by their state of health, in accordance with scientific knowledge and professional ethics. Palliative care is defined by Article 1 as 'active, continuous, and coordinated care, practised by a multidisciplinary team with respect for the dignity of the person being cared for. It aims to cover all the physical, psychological, and spiritual needs of the person being cared for and to support the family and friends. It includes the treatment of pain and psychological suffering'.

396. It was the intention of the 2009 legislator to promote both access to and quality of palliative care. The parliamentary documents specify that palliative care is 'an individual right to which all those who can benefit from it must have equitable access, without prejudice to the strict respect of their will. It is therefore necessary to create and make available the necessary structures and resources and to integrate them into the basket of care provided for by social security'.[384] Palliative care is to be provided in a hospital, in a nursing home or long-term care institution, or at home. For patients cared for at home, in a nursing home or long-term care institution, the close cooperation of a hospital must be ensured according to the law.

397. The promotion of access to palliative care in end of life is pursued through specific social security entitlements. If a person becomes eligible for palliative care, the treating physician submits a request to the CMSS. If the right to palliative care is granted, the person is entitled to receive a range of specific benefits for a period of thirty-five days. At the request of the treating physicians, the palliative care entitlement can be renewed by CMSS for one or more additional thirty-five-day periods.[385] The benefits cover the costs of services and benefits in kind provided to the patient. To promote quality and coordination of care, the patient receives a specific care booklet ('carnet de soins') in which the various health professionals record the supplies, services and care provided. Quality of palliative care is further promoted by training of healthcare professionals and through norms that impose a minimum number of trained healthcare professionals in institutional care.

384. Exposé de motifs, doc. parl. 4909.
385. Règlement grand-ducal du 28 avril 2009 précisant les modalités d'attribution du droit aux soins palliatifs, Mem. A – 91 du 4.05.2009.

III. Life-Shortening Effect of Pain Relief

398. Even before the entry into force of the Law on palliative care, it was an accepted medical practice to alleviate the intensive pain of patients even if this had an unintended life-shortening effect. Article 3 of the Law on palliative care, after recalling that the physician has an obligation to effectively relieve the physical and psychological suffering of the patient facing end of life, requests the physician to inform the patient about a potentially life-shortening effect and to obtain his specific consent.

IV. Cessation of Treatment at the Patient's Actual Request

399. It is a general patient's right to accept or refuse any diagnostic or therapeutic intervention after receiving adequate information from the attending physician.[386] The physician has a right to treat solely insofar as the patient capable of doing so has given his or her consent. Beyond the care refused, the patient continues to have a right to access any other care or treatment that may meet his or her needs. This involves discussing what remains to be done in terms of palliative care. It further involves, in our view, an obligation to hear and discuss a possible request for euthanasia or assisted suicide despite the right of the treating physician not to practise euthanasia himself or herself because of conscious objections.

V. Presumed Patient Will, Advance Directive and Person of Trust

400. Chapter III of the Law on palliative care regulates how to proceed if a patient is not (or no longer) able to express his or her will. It further clarifies the status of advance directives. According to Article 4, 'If the person at the end of life (…) is not able to express his or her will regarding the end of life, including the conditions, limitation, and cessation of treatment, including pain treatment, (…), the physician shall seek to establish his or her presumed will. To establish this will, the physician shall call upon the person of trust designated (…). He may call upon any other person likely to know the will of the person at the end of life.'

401. Article 5 recognises the right of every person to express in advance his/her will ('volonté') with regard to end-of-life issues, including the conditions, limitation and cessation of treatment, pain management, as well as psychological and spiritual support. This written advance expression will is called 'advance directive' ('directive anticipée'). If the patient is physically incapable of writing and signing, two witnesses must certify that the advance directive is in accordance with the free will of the patient. The certificate of the two witnesses must be joined to the advanced directive.

386. *See*: Part II., Ch. 1., §12. Refusal or Withdrawal of Consent *supra*.

Article 5 further foresees the possibility to designate a person of trust within an advance directive, in which case the physician is obliged to hear the person of trust. The status of the person of trust is identical to the one under the Law on patient rights and obligations.[387]

402. The Law on palliative care specifies the effect of an advance directive. According to Article 6, §1, the physician must 'take into account' the advance directive that is documented in the patient file or of which he has obtained knowledge. It further gives several precise indications as to the circumstances in which the physician may depart from an advance directive. According to Article 6, §3, the physician must assess whether the provisions of an advance directive correspond to the situation envisaged by the patient. In this context, the physician may consider the evolution of medical knowledge since the advance directive was drawn up. If the advance directive is contrary to the convictions of the physicians treating the patient, he or she must, in consultation with the person of trust or the family, transfer the patient within twenty-four hours to a colleague willing to respect the advance directive. Finally, the reasons for departing from an advance directive must be documented in the medical file of the patient. The physician further must inform the person of trust or, if no person of trust is available, the relatives. Article 6 must be read in conjunction with Article 4, requesting the physician to establish the patient's presumed will. The Law establishes a flexible mechanism whose aim is to ensure, as far as possible, that the patient's will is respected. The parliamentary documents describe the mechanism as follows: 'The physician will proceed informally. He or she will speak to those people from whom he or she thinks he or she can expect to get relevant information. This may be the patient's family, a friend or life partner, or a member of the nursing staff to whom the patient has confided. If, in an advance directive, the patient has designated a person of trust, this person will be the physician's main contact. However, the physician will hear other persons if the person of trust says that he or she doesn't know the patient's presumed wishes or has only very old statements from the patient on the subject.'[388]

403. It has been written that the wording 'take into account' does not ensure a strong binding effect to advance directives.[389] The legislator indeed aimed to introduce a certain flexibility. Advance directives do, however, in our view, not merely record wishes. They document the patient's will (at a certain point in time). The intention of the legislator was to ascertain the patient's (presumed) will in the light of, according to the circumstances, the dialogue with the person of trust (if designated) or, if required, any other person likely to know the patient's will. In our view, the flexibility introduced by the wording 'take into account' does, however, by no means allow it to go against the patient's self-determination.

---

387. *See:* Part II., Ch. 1., §8. Person of Trust *supra.*
388. Projet de loi 5584, Commentaire d'article (Art. 4), doc. parl. 5584/00, p. 14.
389. Pierrat, M., *Soins et respect de la volonté de la personne en fin de vie – Rapport luxembourgeois aux journées suisses de l'Association H. Capitant*, Ann. dr. lux., Vol. 19, pp. 189–218 (2009).

404. The aim of the advance directive is to document the patient's will. It may be amended or revoked at any time. The last will of the patient is always to follow, even if the patient omitted to update the advance directive. Therefore, oral expressions may overrule an advance directive.

405. The initial law proposal limited the right to draw an advance directive to legally competent adults. During the parliamentary process, this limitation has been omitted at the demand of the High Council of Disabled Persons.[390] According to the formulation retained in the parliamentary process 'any person' may draw an advance directive under the 2009 law. Persons under a legal protection regime may thus express their will in writing. Any possible cognitive impairment at the time of drafting an advance directive may, in our view, be considered when the physician must decide whether to follow or depart from the content of an advance directive.

406. In opposition to end-of-life provisions, there is no mandatory registration of advance directives. It is therefore crucial that the patient, the person of trust or a next of kin bring the existence of an advance directive to the attention of the treating physician. An advance directive may be deposited in the patient's file. It may also be added to the DSP.

VI. Cessation of Treatment Without Prospect

407. According to Article 2: 'It is not a criminal offence and cannot give rise to a civil action for damages for a physician to refuse or refrain from carrying out, in the advanced or terminal phase of a serious and incurable disease, whatever the cause, examinations and treatment inappropriate to the condition of the person at the end of life and which, according to the medical knowledge of the time, would not bring the person at the end of life any relief or improvement in his or her condition or any hope of recovery.' While maintaining a right to palliative care, Article 2 aims to avoid that care without prospect is initiated or continued. It allows for the cessation of such treatment or diagnostic means by decision of the treating physician. The physician is, in such circumstances, protected against legal action thereof.

VII. End-of-Life Support Leave

408. Chapter III of the Law on Palliative Care introduces a specific end-of-life support leave. The benefit of this leave is limited to persons accompanying the end-of-life of a first-degree relative in ascending or descending line (mother/father, mother/father-in-law, daughter/son or daughter/son-in-law); or a second-degree relative in collateral line (sister/brother, sister/brother-in-law); or a spouse or (legally recognised) partner.

---

390. Avis du Conseil supérieur des personnes handicapées, doc. parl. 5584/7.

409. The duration of the end-of-life support leave cannot exceed five working days (or forty hours) per calendar year and relative accompanied. It may be split up into several periods and may be taken on a part-time basis. Several persons can share the leave granted but its total duration cannot exceed forty hours.

§3. Euthanasia and Assisted Suicide

I. Introduction

410. The modified Law of 16 March 2009 on euthanasia and assisted suicide,[391] hereinafter 'Law on euthanasia and assisted suicide', results from a parliamentarian initiative in 2002 ('proposition de loi Err-Huss') based on the Belgian Law on Euthanasia adopted the same year. It legalises both euthanasia and physician-assisted suicide under certain conditions. While there are many similarities with the Belgian Law, some differences exist and are mentioned below.

II. Definition of Euthanasia and of Assisted Suicide

411. The first article defines euthanasia and assisted suicide. The definition of euthanasia has its origin in the Belgian Law of 2002, with some minor adaptations. Euthanasia is defined as 'the act, performed by a physician, of intentionally ending a person's life at that person's express and voluntary request'. Like in the Netherlands, but unlike in Belgium,[392] it also covers physician-assisted suicide. Suicide is defined as 'the fact that a physician intentionally helps another person to commit suicide or provides another person with the means to do so, at that person's express and voluntary request'.

412. It results from these definitions that euthanasia and assisted suicide are acts to be performed by are acts reserved for the medical profession. If a non-physician performs euthanasia or assisted suicide, these acts do not benefit from the depenalisation. The acts covered are intentional acts performed at the express and voluntary request of the person (patient). There can be no euthanasia performed without a patient's request. The wording 'act, performed by a physician' may be read as including omissions.[393] In our view, pure omissions (e.g., not initiating a treatment on which the patient's life depends) and withdrawal or cessation of a procedure at the patient's request should not be considered 'euthanasia'. It can be assumed that the legislator did not intend a cumulative application of both laws of 16 March 2009. Such acts should be considered to fall exclusively within the scope of the Law

391. Loi du 16 mars 2009 sur l'euthanasie et l'assistance au suicide, Mem. A – 46 du 16.03.2009, doc. parl. 4909, http://data.legilux.public.lu/eli/etat/leg/loi/2009/03/16/n2/jo.

392. Nys, H., 'The Ambiguous Legal Status of Physician Assisted Suicide in Belgium', 7 *Journal für Medizin- und Gesundheitsrecht*, pp. 191–194 (2022).

393. Braum, S., *supra* n. 380, p. 222.

on palliative care. An advance expression of the patient requesting to omit a life-sustaining treatment must likewise be considered an 'advance directive' governed by the Law on palliative care.

413. The additional requirements and procedures that must be fulfilled for a physician to be allowed to perform euthanasia or physician-assisted suicide are analysed below.

III. Actual Request for Euthanasia or Assisted Suicide: Requirements and Procedure

414. Article 2 distinguishes between substantive requirements, enumerated in paragraph 1 and formal and procedural requirements, enumerated in paragraph 2. This distinction is of upmost importance insofar as the consequences and procedures foreseen in case a requirement is not respected are fundamentally different.

A. *Substantive Requirements*

415. A physician's compliance with a request for euthanasia or physician-assisted suicide is not criminally sanctioned and cannot give rise to a civil action for damages, if the following substantive requirements are met:

(1) the patient has attained the age of majority, is legally competent and conscious at the time of the request;
(2) the request is made voluntarily, thoughtfully considered and, where appropriate, repeatedly, and is not the result of external pressure;
(3) the patient is in a medically futile condition and reports constant and unbearable physical or psychological suffering with no prospect of improvement, resulting from an accidental or pathological condition;
(4) the patient's request for euthanasia or assisted suicide is documented in writing.

416. It results from condition 1) that euthanasia is currently not allowed under the age of 18. Euthanasia remains thus unlawful with regards to a minor with the full discernment or even for minors emancipated by a Court decision. Patients under the protective measure of tutelage are further excluded as they are not legally competent.

417. According to the introductory phrase, there is no criminal sanction or civil action for damages, if the substantive conditions enumerated are met. The criminal protection is further ensured through Article 397-1 of the Criminal Code, disposing that the section on homicide shall not apply 'if a physician responds to a request for euthanasia or assisted suicide in accordance with substantive conditions set out in the Law of 16 March 2009 on euthanasia and assisted suicide'. Here again, the formal and procedural requirements are not mentioned. This immunity against criminal or civil consequences is far-reaching. In the absence of a substantive condition, the criminal and civil liability protection of the physician is, however, no longer given. Consequently, if the *ex post* control concludes to the absence of a substantive condition, the National Control and Evaluation Commission, hereinafter 'Commission', must turn the case over to the public prosecutor's office.[394]

B. Formal and Procedural Requirements

418. The physician must, in all cases, before carrying out euthanasia or physician-assisted suicide, comply with the following seven formal and procedural requirements:

(1) inform the patient of his or her state of health and life expectancy, consult with the patient on his or her request for euthanasia or assisted suicide, and discuss with the patient the remaining therapeutic options and the possibilities of palliative care and its consequences. The physician must be convinced that the patient's request is voluntary and that, in the patient's view, there is no other acceptable solution in his or her situation. The discussions are recorded in the medical record, and the recording is considered a valid proof of the information exchanged;
(2) be certain of the persistence of physical or mental suffering and of the patient's recently expressed or reiterated will. To this end, the physician has several conversations with the patient spread out over a reasonable period of time, taking into account the evolution of the patient's condition;
(3) consult another physician about the serious and incurable nature of the condition, stating the reasons for the consultation. The physician consulted reviews the medical file, examines the patient, and makes certain that the patient's physical or mental suffering is constant, unbearable and without any prospect of improvement. The physician consulted reports on his or her findings. The physician consulted must be independent of the patient as well as of the attending physician and must be competent in the pathology concerned. The treating physician informs the patient of the results of this consultation;
(4) unless the patient objects, discuss the request with the healthcare team in regular contact with the patient or members of the team;
(5) unless the patient objects, discuss the request with the person of trust designated by the patient in his or her end-of-life arrangements or at the time of the request for euthanasia or assisted suicide;
(6) ensure that the patient has had the opportunity to discuss his or her request with the persons he or she wishes to meet;
(7) enquire at the Commission whether any end-of-life provisions on behalf of the patient are registered.

394. Article 8, Law on euthanasia and assisted suicide.

With regards to point 3), one notes that the criterion 'serious and incurable nature of the condition' ('caractère grave et incurable de l'affection') do not exactly correspond to the terms used in Articles 2, §1, 3) 'medically futile condition' ('situation médicale sans issue'). As stressed by doctrine, this should be redressed.[395]

419. Furthermore, Article 2 describes the formal conditions under which the patient's actual request must be documented in writing. The request of the patient must be drawn up, dated and signed by the patient. It is not required that he or she has written it by hand; it can be typed or written on a computer and printed out.

If the patient is not capable of writing and signing, a person designated by the patient writes the document. This person must have attained the age of majority. The person designated by the patient drafts the document in the presence of the physician whose name must be mentioned in the document. The fact that the patient is incapable of formulating his or her request in writing and the reasons why are testified.

The document is added to the patient file. The patient may revoke his request at any time, in which case the document is removed from the medical file and returned to the patient.

420. According to Article 3, the treating physician may be accompanied or advised by an expert of his choice and place the latter's opinion or certificate of intervention in the patient's file.

421. All the requests formulated by the patient, as well as any actions by the attending physician and their results, including the report(s) of the consulted physician(s), are regularly documented in the patient file.

422. In cases where the requesting patient is in a futile situation but not expected to die in the near future, Belgian law foresees a mandatory independent assessment by two physicians and a waiting period of at least one month. The Luxembourg Law on euthanasia and assisted suicide does not foresee such a specific procedure. In view of the findings of the ECtHR in the case of *Mortier v. Belgium*, it is uncertain whether sufficient formal safeguards are currently in place in Luxembourg.[396] Even if not mandatory, Luxembourg physicians are well advised to make use of the possibility of further consultations foreseen in Article 3 and to apply for a waiting period of at least one month.

423. Failure to comply with these formal and procedural requirements does not lift the criminal and civil liability protection of a physician. If the *ex post* control by the Commission reveals such a failure, the Commission turns the case over to the Medical College that decides on disciplinary action.[397]

395. Braum, S., *supra* n. 380, p. 227.
396. ECtHR 4 Oct. 2022, *Mortier v. Belgium*, No. 78017/17; Nys, H. & Schwebag, M., *The Mortier Case and What It Means for the Belgian and Luxembourg Legal Frameworks on Euthanasia*, RLDS, No. 15, pp. 22–27 (2023).
397. Article 8, Law on euthanasia and assisted suicide.

IV. Advance Request for Euthanasia (End-of-Life Provisions)

A. Scope and Drafting of End-of-Life Provisions

424. According to Article 4, every legally competent adult person may express in his or her end-of-life provisions ('dispositions de fin de vie') an advance request that a physician performs euthanasia if the physician finds that:

- the patient suffers from a serious and incurable disorder caused by illness or accident;
- the patient is no longer conscious;
- this condition is irreversible, given the current state of medical science.

425. These conditions imply that the physician verifies that the patient is in a state of irreversible unconsciousness. This requirement could be read strictly or as including persons in a state characterised by diminished minimal discernment without being strictly unconscious. It results, however, without doubt from the parliamentary documents that the legislator exclusively targeted patients within a state of unconsciousness in the sense of a state of irreversible coma. According to the parliamentary documents, the irreversible state of advanced dementia does therefore not allow to perform euthanasia.[398]

426. Contrary to advance directives, end-of-life provisions must be registered by the Commission to be valid. End-of-life provisions may be amended or revoked at any time. Every change needs to be registered. There is no time limit for the validity of end-of-life provisions. The Commission has, however, to ask every five years whether a person confirms his or her end-of-life provisions.

427. The person drawing up an end-of-life provision may designate a person of trust ('personne de confiance') who informs the attending physician about the patient's will. In case the patient has already designated a person of trust pursuant to the Law on rights and duties of the patient, this designation is also valid in an end-of-life situation and vice-versa.[399] End-of-life provisions may further contain arrangements for burial and the funeral ceremony.

428. End-of-life provisions may be drafted at any moment. They must be drafted in writing, dated, and signed by the drafter. In case the person who wishes to draft end-of-life provisions is permanently physically incapable of writing and signing, he or she designates an adult person to draft the provisions in the presence of two witnesses who have attained the age of majority. The end-of-life provisions must indicate that the person in question is incapable of writing and signing and why. The provisions must be dated and signed by the person chosen to draft them, by the witnesses, and by the person of trust, if applicable. A medical certificate must be

398. Explanatory note to amendment 10 adopted by the Committee on Health and Social Security, doc. parl. 4909/12, p. 4.
399. Article 12, §5, Law on Patient rights and obligations.

annexed proving that the person in question is permanently physically incapable of drafting and signing the end-of-life provision.

429. The physician taking care of a patient in an end-of-life condition who is no longer able to express his or her will has to enquire at the Commission whether any end-of-life provision is registered on behalf of his patient. This obligation is, however, in practice frequently not met, so patients and the person of trust must take the necessary precautions to make sure that the provisions are at the disposal of the treating physician.

B. Euthanasia Based on End-of-Life Provisions

430. According to Article 4, the physician who performs euthanasia in compliance with valid end-of-life provisions cannot be criminally sanctioned and there is no ground for civil action when he or she ensures that the following substantive requirements are met:

- the patient suffers from a serious and incurable disorder caused by illness or accident;
- the patient is unconscious;
- this condition is irreversible, given the current state of medical science.

As seen above, the scope of Article 4 corresponds to patients in a state of irreversible coma.

431. The physician must, in all cases and before proceeding with euthanasia, respect the following formal and procedural requirements:

(1) consult another physician about the irreversibility of the patient's medical situation, informing him/her of the reasons for the consultation. The consulted physician takes note of the patient's file and examines the patient. He or she draws up a report on his or her findings. If a person of trust is designated in the end-of-life provision, the physician in charge of the patient's care must inform the person of trust of the results of this consultation. The consulted physician must be impartial towards the patient and the physician treating him or her and must be competent in the pathology concerned;
(2) if there is a healthcare team in regular contact with the patient, the physician must discuss the content of the end-of-life provision with the healthcare team or members thereof;
(3) if the end-of-life provision designates a person of trust, the physician must discuss the patient's wishes with that person;
(4) if the end-of-life provision designates a person of trust, discuss the patient's wishes with the patient's relatives whom the trusted person designates.

432. The end-of-life provision, as well as all actions by the attending physician and their results, including the report of the consulted physician, is documented in the patient file.

V. Role and Functioning of the National Control and Evaluation Commission

A. *Composition of the Commission*

433. The Commission is composed of nine members, appointed based on their knowledge and experience in the issues belonging to the Commission's missions: three members are physicians; three are legal experts (one professor of law, one practising lawyer, one judge); one member is a non-medical healthcare professional; two are patient representatives. The members of the Commission elect the chairperson. There is an equal number of alternate members. The Grand Duke appoints the members of the Commission for a period of three years. The mandate is renewable three times. Membership in the Commission cannot be combined with a function as a Member of Parliament, of the Council of State or of the Government.[400]

B. *Mandatory Notification to the Commission*

434. Any physician who has performed euthanasia or physician-assisted suicide is required to fill in a registration form drawn up by the National Control and Evaluation Commission. It must be sent to the Commission within eight working days.[401] The mandatory registration form consists of two parts.

435. The first part of the mandatory registration form must be placed under seal by the physician. It includes the following information:

- the patient's full name and address;
- the full name, address, and health insurance registration number of the physician;
- the full name, address, and health insurance registration number of the physician(s) consulted about the request;
- the full name, address, and capacity of all persons consulted by the attending physician and the date of these consultations; and
- if there exists an end-of-life provision in which a person of trust is designated, the full name of the person of trust.

The first part of the registration document is confidential. The Commission can only consult it following a specific decision. Under no circumstances may the Commission use this document for its evaluation.

400. Article 6, §2, Law on euthanasia and assisted suicide.
401. Article 5, Law on euthanasia and assisted suicide.

436. The second part of the mandatory registration form is also confidential but not sealed. It includes the following information:

- whether end-of-life provisions have been drafted or whether an actual request was formulated;
- the patient's sex and date of birth;
- the nature of the serious and incurable condition caused by accident or illness from which the patient suffered;
- the nature of the constant and unbearable suffering;
- the reasons why this suffering was considered without prospect to be alleviated;
- the elements underlying the assurance that the request is voluntary, well-considered and repeated, and not the result of any external pressure;
- the procedure followed by the physician;
- the capacity of the physician(s) consulted, the recommendations, and the information from these consultations;
- the capacity of the persons and of further experts consulted by the physician and the date of these consultations;
- the manner in which euthanasia or physician-assisted suicide was performed and the means used.

C. Functioning and Control by the Commission

437. The Commission's decisions are taken by a simple majority of the members present and are only valid if seven members (principal or alternate members replacing a member) are present (Article 6, §2). The Commission may draw up its own internal rules of procedure (Article 6, §3).

438. The Commission analyses the completed registration form submitted to it by the attending physician. Based on the second part of the registration form, the Commission decides whether euthanasia or physician-assisted suicide was performed in accordance with the conditions and the procedure stipulated in the Law. In cases of doubt, the Commission may decide by simple majority to lift the anonymity and examine the first part of the registration form. The Commission may request the attending physician to provide any information that is relevant.

439. The Commission hands down a verdict within two months. If, in a decision taken with a specific two-third majority, the Commission is of the opinion that the substantive conditions for euthanasia or assisted suicide[402] (Article 2, §1) or euthanasia based on an end-of-life provision (Article 4, §3) have not been fulfilled, it turns the case over to the public prosecutor's office. In case the substantive conditions

---

402. *See:* para. 415 *supra.*

are respected but a formal and procedural requirement is not fulfilled, the case is turned over to the Medical College that decides on disciplinary action.

440. No physician who is practising euthanasia or assisted suicide has been prosecuted so far in Luxembourg.

441. In the case of *Mortier v. Belgium*, the ECtH considered that leaving it to the sole discretion of the member of the Commission concerned to remain silent when he finds that he was involved in the euthanasia under anonymous review cannot be considered sufficient to ensure the independence of the review process by the Commission. As the review processes applied in Luxembourg and Belgium are identical, there is a need to reconsider the current functioning of the Commission.[403]

D. Bi-annual Report

442. The Commission drafts a bi-annual report deposited in Parliament, which includes:

- a statistical report processing the information from the second part of the completed registration forms submitted by physicians;
- a report in which the implementation of the law is clarified and evaluated;
- if required, recommendations that could lead to new legislation or other measures concerning the execution of the Law on euthanasia and assisted suicide.

443. For the purpose of carrying out this task, the Commission may seek additional information from the various public services and institutions. The information gathered is confidential. None of these documents may reveal the identity of any persons named in the dossiers submitted to the Commission for the purposes of the review.

444. The Commission can decide to supply statistical and purely technical data, without any personal information, to research teams that submit a reasoned request for such data.

445. The Commission can hear experts. Any person who is involved, in whatever capacity, in implementing the Law on euthanasia and assisted suicide is required to maintain confidentiality regarding the information provided to him or her in the exercise of his or her function.[404]

403. ECtHR 4 Oct. 2022, *Mortier v. Belgium*, No. 78017/17; Nys, H. & Schwebag, M., *The Mortier Case and What It Means for the Belgian and Luxembourg Legal Frameworks on Euthanasia,* RLDS, No. 15, pp. 22–27 (2023).

404. Article 12, Law on euthanasia and assisted suicide.

446. Within six months of submitting the first report and the Commission's recommendations, if any, a debate is to be held in the Parliament. The six-month period is suspended during the time that Parliament is dissolved and/or during the time there is no government having the confidence of Parliament.[405]

VI. Objection of Conscience

447. No physician may be compelled to practise euthanasia or assisted suicide. No other person may be compelled to assist in practising.[406] The Law on euthanasia and assisted suicide thus recognises the conscious objection of physicians and healthcare providers. Contrary to the Belgian Law on euthanasia, it does not specify explicitly that requests for euthanasia or physician-assisted suicide are not legally binding. It is, however, generally admitted that a right to euthanasia or physician-assisted suicide does not exist; only a right to request euthanasia or physician-assisted suicide is recognised.

448. If the physician consulted refuses to practise euthanasia because of conscious objections, then he or she must inform the patient and the person of trust, if any, of this fact within twenty-four hours after the request for euthanasia and explain his or her reasons for such refusal.[407]

449. The question has risen whether hospitals, care centres for the elderly and other institutional actors may prohibit physicians from practising euthanasia or assisted suicide within their institution. Indeed, Article 15 disposes that no person may be compelled to assist in practising euthanasia. This could be read as including legal persons. With regard to this interrogation, the Department of Health has stated that the freedom of conscience is, by nature, an individual freedom, not an institutional one. It would not be in line with the intention of the legislator if an institution could invoke the objection of conscience to justify prohibiting a physician from performing euthanasia or physician-assisted suicide within its institution.[408] Furthermore, euthanasia and assisted suicide are legally defined as acts reserved for physicians. A hospital infringes thus the sphere of competence reserved to the medical profession by forbidding a physician to practise euthanasia or assisted suicide. This infringement would violate both the general principle of therapeutic freedom and Article 33(6) of the Law of 8 March 2018 on hospital establishments and hospital planning, which prohibits hospitals from interfering in the individual relationship between the physician and the patient.

405. Article 13, Law on euthanasia and assisted suicide.
406. Article 15, Law on euthanasia and assisted suicide.
407. *Ibid.*
408. Reply of the Minister of Health to the parliamentary question 151 of 8 Oct. 2009; reply of the Minister of Health to the parliamentary question 2029 of 24 Feb. 2016.

VII. Insurance Contracts

450. A person who dies as a result of euthanasia or assisted suicide in accordance with the provisions of the Law on euthanasia and assisted suicide is deemed to have died of natural causes in respect of the performance of contracts to which he or she was a party.[409]

409. Article 15bis, Law on euthanasia and assisted suicide.

Chapter 4. Patients Not Capable to Exercise Their Rights (Autonomously)

451. We will hereafter present the specific framework applicable to minor patients, adult patients under a legal protection regime, and psychiatric patients.

§1. Minor Patient[410]

I. Introduction

452. Of minor age is the person who has not attained fully the age of 18 years.[411] A minor is subject to parental authority until the age of majority or, in rare cases, emancipation before that age. According to general civil law, a non-emancipated minor person lacks the legal capacity to contract and is represented by the holder(s) of parental authority. At the same time, the parents are requested to involve their minor child according to his or her age and degree of maturity.[412]

Since the 2023 revision, the Constitution disposes that the child's best interests shall be a primary consideration; it recognises the right of children to express their views freely in all matters affecting them. It finally recognises the right to such protection, measures, and care necessary for their well-being and development.[413]

453. The legal status of minors with regard to questions concerning their health tends to consider both the role assigned to the holder(s) of parental authority laid down in civil law (II.) and the need to imply minor patients progressively in health-care matters (III.).

II. Rights and Obligations Assigned to the Holder(s) of Parental Authority

454. According to Article 13, §1, of the Law on patient rights and obligations, the rights of a minor and not emancipated patient are exercised by his or her parents or by any other legal representative.

The provisions of the Civil Code regulating parental authority have been modified in 2018.[414] Since the 2018 reform, Article 372 defines parental authority as 'all the rights and duties aimed at meeting the best interests of the child'. Parental authority includes rights and duties with the aim of ensuring the best interests of the minor in various areas, in particular regarding his or her safety, health and personal

410. Schwebag, M., *Le patient mineur et ses parents face aux soins de santé*, RLDS, Nos 9–10, pp. 11–23 (2022).
411. Article 488, Code civil.
412. Article 372, Code civil.
413. Article 15, §5, Constitution.
414. Loi du 27 juin 2018 instituant le juge aux affaires familiales, portant réforme du divorce et de l'autorité parentale, Mém. A –589 du 12 juillet 2018, https://legilux.public.lu/eli/etat/leg/loi/2018/06/27/a589/jo.

development. Issues relating to the health of the minor patient are indeed a fundamental component of parental rights and duties. The 2018 reform of parental authority has introduced the principle of joint parental authority. The two parents, regardless of whether they are married or not, generally exercise parental authority in common. In conjunction with the principles governing parental authority, both parents are generally jointly exercising the patient rights of their minor patient. If one parent is deceased, the remaining parent exercises parental authority. Exceptionally, a Court decision may assign parental authority to one parent or to a guardian.

455. It results from the principle of joint parental authority that both parents generally need to give consent. Article 375-1 of the Civil Code establishes, however, a certain flexibility by providing that: 'With regard to third parties in good faith, each parent is deemed to act with the agreement of the other when he or she alone performs a customary act of parental authority in relation to the person of the child.' Transposed to healthcare, Article 375-1 means that a physician may accept the consent of one parent for care that does not expose the minor patient to any particular danger (e.g., care for superficial wounds, benign infections, etc.) as well as for care that has already been routinely given before (e.g., the continuation of a well-supported ongoing treatment).[415] The Civil Code allows in such circumstances to presume that the parent present acts with the agreement of the parent not present. If a physician is, however, aware of the other parent's disagreement or hesitation, he or she may not accept the parent present to decide alone.

III. Gradual Involvement and Autonomy of the Minor Patient

456. Healthcare rights are personal rights. Within certain limits, young patients have the right to have their physical integrity respected and the right to dispose of it.

457. According to Article 13, §1, of the Law on patient rights and obligations, minor patients must, as far as possible, be involved in the exercise of their rights according to their age and maturity. The obligation to involve the minor patient is incumbent on both the parents and the physician. The involvement of the minor patient must bear in mind his or her age and level of maturity. Depending on the age of the minor, the language and information provided need to be adapted pursuant to the general principle that communication must take place in a clear and comprehensive language adapted to each individual patient.

458. According to Article 13, §2, of the Law on patient rights and obligations, a minor patient who has the discernment to reasonably assess his or her interests on his or her own may be admitted by the attending physician to exercise his or her healthcare rights autonomously. Granting complete autonomy to a minor patient is,

415. Article 375-1 of the Civil Code, identical in wording to Art. 372-2 of the French Civil Code.

however, not automatic. It may prove inappropriate from the point of view of family psychology. It is up to the physician to assess the situation *in concreto* and take a decision based on the circumstances: the patient's characteristics, mainly his age and capacity of discernment; the scope and complexity of the decision to be taken; and the socio-family environment.

459. In case the physician authorises a young patient to exercise his or her rights autonomously, this decision does not automatically exclude his or her parents. According to Article 13, §2, unless the minor patient actively objects to involve his legal representative(s) in the exercise of his rights, the physician is not bound by professional secrecy towards the legal representative(s). The physician may thus inform parents or guardians unless the minor actively objects to it. The physician, the minor patient and the parents may thus co-decide that the minor patient may exercise his patient rights while keeping his or her parents informed. If the physician accepts that a young patient exercises his or her rights without keeping the parents informed, the minor patient is allowed to directly exercise the right to reimbursement of the healthcare costs paid by the social security bodies.

IV. Conflictual Situations

460. In conflictual situations, the Family Court Judge ('Juge aux affaires familiales') may be seized by one of the parents or by the minor patient. Based on the arguments of both parents and the opinion of the minor, the Family Court Judge decides according to the best interest of the minor principle. The Family Court Judge may not intervene at the request of the physician. If a minor patient's health is seriously compromised, a physician may always refer the matter to the Youth Judge ('Juge de la Jeunesse').

V. Urgent Need for Care

461. In case of a serious and immediate danger to the life or the health of a minor patient, Article 13, §3, of the Law on patient rights and obligations authorises a physician to take all the medical measures that the situation requires, despite the opposition or the impossibility to contact the parents or legal representatives in good time. The medical intervention must be urgent to avoid a substantial risk. In terms of potential consequences, it is not necessary for the risk incurred to be vital. By delaying the act, a serious and immediate danger to the health of the minor patient must, however, exist. If these conditions are given, all the medical measures that the situation requires can be taken by the physician. In case the protection of the minor patient commands to override the opinion of the parents or custodian, the physician must report within three working days to the State Prosecutor.

§2. ADULT PATIENT UNDER PROTECTIVE MEASURES

I. Introduction

462. Any person who has attained the age of 18 years is considered an adult (Civil Code, Article 488) and the capacity for discernment is presumed until proven otherwise (Civil Code, Article 489).

463. The Guardianship Judge ('juge des tutelles') may decide on a protective measure when a person's mental faculties are impaired. The Civil Code currently provides for three types of protective measures: judicial safeguard[416] ('sauvegarde de justice'), curatorship[417] ('curatelle') and tutelage[418] ('tutelle'). These protective regimes may limit the legal capacity of the protected adult, the most protective being the tutelage regime. The decision of the Guardianship Judge may adapt the protective measure to the individual circumstances.

464. Requests for protection may come from the concerned person, a relative, a physician, a hospital, a nursing home, or a retirement home. The guardianship judge must dispose of a medical report from a neurologist, psychiatrist, neuropsychiatrist, geriatrician, or internist before a protective measure may be ordered.

465. There is a consensus that the current provisions of the Civil Code regulating these protective measures need reform. As a first step, a recent Law project aims to introduce a 'future protection mandate' ('mandat de protection future') inspired by French Law.[419]

II. Influence of Protective Regimes on the Exercise of Patient Rights

466. The legal status of adults under a protective measure is addressed by Article 14 of the Law on patient rights and obligations. Article 14 distinguishes between patients under a tutelage and those under a curatorship.

467. In principle, tutelage is established when a person needs to be permanently represented in the acts of civil life. Tutelage always implies legal representation. According to Article 14, the interests of the patient under a tutelage regime are, in principle, exercised by his or her person of trust. If a person of trust was appointed before the tutelage was opened, this person continues to exercise healthcare rights. In the absence of the designation of a trusted person, the tutor of the patient exercises by default the interests of the patient with regard to healthcare matters. The guardianship judge may, however, appoint a specific representative for healthcare

416. Code civil, Art. 461 à 461-1.
417. Code civil, Art. 508 à 515.
418. Code civil, Art. 492 à 507.
419. Projet de loi 8133 relatif au mandat de protection future, https://www.chd.lu/fr/dossier/8133.

matters when deciding to open a tutelage or in a subsequent judgment. The patient under tutelage must, as far as possible, be involved in the exercise of his or her rights according to his or her abilities.

468. According to civil law, the impairment of mental faculties required for the opening of a curatorship is less serious than for a tutelage. Curatorship is a system of assistance. The person under curatorship remains legally capable of acting while needing advice or supervision. Accordingly, unless authorised by the guardianship judge to exercise his or her health rights autonomously, a patient under curatorship exercises his rights with the assistance of his or her curator.

III. Urgent Need for Care

469. In case of serious and immediate danger to the life or health of a patient, Article 14, §3 authorises a physician to take all the medical measures that the situation requires, despite the opposition or the impossibility of contacting the legal representative. Medical decisions must be made urgently to avoid considerable risks. In terms of potential consequences, it is not necessary for the risk incurred to be vital. By delaying the act, a serious and immediate danger to the health of the patient must, however, exist. If these conditions are given, all the medical measures that the situation requires can be taken. The patient must, as far as possible, be involved in the exercise of his or her patient rights according to his or her abilities. In case the protection of a patient commands to override the opinion of the tutor or curator, the physician must report within three working days to the State Prosecutor.

§3. Patients De Facto Not Capable of Exercising Their Patient Rights

470. A patient may be de facto incapable of exercising his or her rights without being under a legal protection regime. In case a patient is temporarily or permanently incapable of expressing his/her wishes, the physician must establish his/her presumed will.[420] The written expression of will of the patient (advance directive or end-of-life provision), as well as the person of trust are key elements to determine the (presumed) patient will. The physician may further consult any other person likely to know the patient's will. There is no specific legal rule requesting to imply a specific next of kin, and the relatives do not have an automatic right to decide on behalf of the patient. The physician should always consider the likelihood that the opinion of a parent or a person with close ties corresponds to the patient's will. Any person designated as a person of trust must be implied in the decision-making process.

471. In a medical emergency, when a patient is not able to make decisions about his or her health and his or her will is not established, any urgent measures that the

420. Article 11, §1, Law on patient rights and obligations; Art. 4, Law on palliative care.

situation requires may immediately be taken in the patient's best interest.[421] This provision presumes consent when the patient's will is unknown and when there is not sufficient time available to determine the patient's will.

§4. Psychiatric Patients and Hospitalisation Without Consent

I. Introduction

472. In the early 1960s, the 'Sunier report' led to the first transformation of psychiatry. The psychiatric hospital ('Maison de Santé'), the later CHNP, was modernised and community psychiatry started to be developed.[422] The organisation of psychiatry has further undergone important changes since the 1990s. The 'Häfner report' set an important impulse in the early 1990s and was followed in 2005 by the 'Rössler plan'.[423]

473. Acute psychiatric hospital care is currently provided by the four general hospitals. The focus of the CHNP is on active psychiatric rehabilitation, as well as on support for people with mental disabilities. The CHNP further runs a residential care setting for the elderly. Initial acute hospitalisation is done in the closed psychiatric department of the hospital closest to the person's place of life or stay. In the event of a disturbance of public order, the person may, however, be placed under observation at the hospital on duty in the region in which he or she is present at that moment.

474. A person with a mental disorder has the same rights and obligations as any other patient. Persons with mental disorders are treated as far as possible in the environment in which they live. Hospitalisation in psychiatric care is done, as far as possible, with the patient's consent. By exception, if a person constitutes a danger to himself or to others, the Law allows hospitalisation against the will of the person concerned or without the consent of a person unable to give consent validly. Such hospitalisation in a psychiatric environment is regulated by the amended Law of 10 December 2009 on the hospitalisation without the consent of persons with mental disorders,[424] hereafter 'Law on the hospitalisation without consent'. The law distinguishes hospitalisation without consent at the request of a third party (II.) and hospitalisation without consent based on a placement order when a person is not criminally responsible according to Article 71 of the Criminal Code (III.).

---

421. Article 11, §3, Law on patient rights and obligations.
422. Substantially by the 'Ligue Luxembourgeoise d'Hygiène Mentale' founded in 1956 (www.llhm.lu), followed by a diverse local offer since (https://www.prevention-psy.lu/aide/information-sur-la-sante-mentale/).
423. Häfner, H., Rössler, W. & Salize, H.-J., *Gemeindepsychiatrie – Grundlagen und Leitlinien: Planungsstudie Luxemburg,* Verlag Integrative Psychiatrie (1993); Rössler, W. & Koch, U., *Psychiatrie Luxemburg – Planungsstudie 2005 – Bestandaufnahme und Empfehlungen,* Universität Zürich (2005).
424. Loi modifiée du 10 décembre 2009, (a) relative à l'hospitalisation sans leur consentement de personnes atteintes de troubles mentaux, (b) modifiant la loi modifiée du 31 mai 1999 sur la Police et

II. Hospitalisation at the Request of a Third Party

475. The Law on hospitalisation without consent foresees substantive and formal conditions for such a hospitalisation at the request of a third party. It distinguishes the initial period of observation followed, if necessary, by placement and treatment in a specialised institution. It further regulates certain modalities of non-consensual treatment and organises specific safeguards and controls to avoid any abuse or arbitrariness.

A. *Justifying Condition: Constitute a Danger to Oneself or to Others*

476. Hospitalisation without consent always presupposes a serious mental disorder, making the person dangerous to himself or to others. Hospitalisation must thus respond to a need for protection, which is the result of a serious mental disorder. The mere impairment of a person's mental faculties due to ageing is not, in itself, a sufficient reason for non-consensual hospitalisation. Similarly, failure to adapt to the moral, social, political, or other values of society cannot, in itself, be considered a justification for such hospitalisation.[425]

B. *Application for Admission*

477. Hospitalisation without consent requires a written request supported by a medical certificate. Article 7, §1, determines the persons and the authorities authorised to request such non-consensual hospitalisation. Admission can be requested by:

- the person in charge of a tutelage or curatorship, if such a protective measure has been taken;
- a family member;
- any other interested person: this may, if necessary, be a health professional in contact with the patient.

If the person concerned endangers public order or security, admission may also be requested by:

- the mayor of the municipality (or his delegate) on whose territory the person is located;
- the head of the police station (or, in his absence, any officer) of the Grand-Ducal Police;

---

l'Inspection générale de la Police et (c) modifiant l'article 73 de la loi communale modifiée du 13 décembre 1988, Mém. A – 263 du 31.12.2009, https://legilux.public.lu/eli/etat/leg/loi/2009/12/10/n1/consolide/20220807; Malmendier–Muehlschlegel, A. & Power, N.C., 'Mental Health Legislation in Luxembourg, a Small Country in Western Europe', 19(3) *BJPsych Int.*, pp. 70–72 (2022).

425. Article 3, Law on the hospitalisation without consent.

– the State Prosecutor of the judicial district in which the person concerned is located.

478. The written application for admission must explain the main factual circumstances on which it is based. If admission is not requested by one of the authorities entitled to do so, the person applying for admission must indicate the degree of kinship or the nature of the relationship with the person concerned.[426] The law requires to attach to the application for admission a medical certificate not more than three days old. This certificate must describe the symptoms of the mental disorder observed and must attest to the need for hospitalisation. The certifying physician, who may not be attached to the psychiatric department of the hospital of admission, must first examine the person concerned.[427]

479. Generally, the application has to be made prior to the admission. In the event of imminent danger witnessed by a doctor of the requested hospital, the patient may, however, be hospitalised without a prior formal application. The application must follow within twenty-four hours, failing which the person may leave the institution if he or she wishes so.[428]

C. Initial Observation Period[429]

480. Admission to a closed psychiatric ward begins with a period of observation, which, in principle, may not exceed thirty days. From the first days of the observation period, the decision to maintain the observation of the patient is a judicial decision: the supervisory judge of the district where the initial admission takes place is informed on the same day of each admission. He or she immediately examines the formal regularity of the admission procedure, including the existence of an application for admission and a medical certificate.

481. During the period of observation, the attending psychiatrist gathers the necessary information to assess whether further maintenance appears necessary. From the sixth day of the observation period, the attending psychiatrist must submit a reasoned report to the supervisory judge. Within a maximum period of three days from receipt of this report, the supervisory judge decides whether to maintain the person's observation or not. The judge can thus quickly put an end to a hospitalisation that was unjustified or is no longer justified after treatment of a brief episode of acute crisis. This decision to maintain the observation is not subject to appeal. If the observation is maintained, the person or any interested person may, however, call at any time to the District Court of the place of establishment.

426. Article 7, §1, Law on the hospitalisation without consent.
427. Article 9, Law on the hospitalisation without consent.
428. Article 8, Law on the hospitalisation without consent.
429. Articles 11–14, Law on the hospitalisation without consent.

482. Before the end of the observation period, the attending psychiatrist sends a reasoned report in which he expresses his opinion on the advisability of maintaining hospitalisation beyond the observation period.

D. Judicial Decision on Release or Placement[430]

483. The observation period ends following the decision of the supervisory judge ordering the discharge or the placement of the patient. The supervisory judge takes a formal decision on exit or placement at the latest at the end of the maximum observation period of thirty days. The supervisory judge hears the patient and informs him of the conclusions of the report of his psychiatrist. The patient may be assisted on this occasion by a person of his choice. His legal representative may also attend the hearing. The judge may hear the psychiatrist together or separately with the patient. If he considers it necessary, the supervisory judge may order any additional measures he deems useful for the collection of information.

484. Following the hearing, the judge issues an order either for placement or for release. The order is communicated to the concerned patient and to the attending physician. If the order has ordered a placement, it becomes effective on the date of the order. The order is not subject to appeal; the person placed or any interested person may, however, call the District Court of the place of establishment at any time.

485. After a placement decision, as the condition of the person placed requires long-term hospitalisation, the patient is transferred to a specialised psychiatric institution. In Luxembourg, specialised care is generally provided at the CHNP.

E. Treatment and Conditions of Stay[431]

486. During hospitalisation, the patient is entitled to medical treatment that is proper for his condition and is oriented towards reintegration into society. He shall be associated as far as possible.

1. Involuntary Treatment

487. A patient may be subjected to involuntary treatment in relation to his or her mental disorder only if his or her condition poses a risk to his or her health or others. Involuntary treatment must be proportionate to the patient's state of health. The law specifies that preference should always be given to the least invasive treatment. In particular, a patient may be subjected to isolation or restraint only for the purpose of preventing imminent harm to himself or others. The principle of minimum restriction is applied. Patients who are in isolation or restraint must receive regular

430. Articles 18–22, Law on the hospitalisation without consent.
431. Chapter 4, Law on the hospitalisation without consent.

follow-up. An isolation or restraint measure may only be taken under medical supervision. However, in an emergency, temporary restraints may be applied. Staff carrying out such temporary restraints must immediately inform the psychiatrist on duty.

488. The patient, his legal representative or, failing that, his person of trust, shall be consulted before the application of an involuntary treatment. The involuntary treatment, the duration, and its modalities must be recorded in the patient's medical record.

2. Permission to Leave

489. To promote the patient's recovery, rehabilitation or social reintegration, the attending psychiatrist may grant permission to leave the institution on a trial basis. He may also grant accompanied outings depending on the patient's condition. If the patient leaves the institution without authorisation, or if he does not comply with the conditions attached to his discharge, the State Prosecutor may take all necessary measures to bring him back into the institution.

3. Visits

490. Hospitalised patients have the right to receive visits. The internal regulations of the establishment determine the modalities of visits by external persons. If the patient or the person who intends to visit him considers that the right of visit is too limited, he may refer the matter to the Supervisory Commission. The Commission may extend a patient's right to visit if it considers these limits to be disproportional.

F. End of Hospitalisation Without Consent[432]

491. If the attending psychiatrist is of the opinion that his patient is cured or that there is an improvement in his state of health such that the placement is no longer necessary, he informs the patient and the judge. The patient can then immediately leave the facility. If the person leaves the establishment, the psychiatrist may impose conditions of residence and/or medical supervision.

492. The end of compulsory hospitalisation may also result from a decision of the supervisory judge or the District Court. The patient may indeed, at any time, apply to the supervisory judge or the District Court for his release.

---

432. Chapter 5, Law on the hospitalisation without consent.

493. Following the placement decision, a commission composed of a magistrate, a psychiatrist and a social hygiene assistant or social worker not attached to the institution carries out assessments of the need to maintain the placement. The first assessment is carried out by this commission one year after the date of the placement decision. If the placement is maintained, the Commission reviews the necessity every two years.

G. *Oversight*[433]

494. Non-consensual hospitalisation always constitutes an act of deprivation of liberty and persons treated in a closed environment are in a vulnerable situation. For this reason, the law organises specific guarantees and controls to avoid any abuse or arbitrariness.

1. Supervisory Judge

495. First, in each judicial district, a judge is responsible for supervising admissions to closed psychiatric institutions, making decisions on continued observation and decisions on release or placement, and subsequently supervising any placement. The right to apply to the supervisory judge, together with the obligation to inform patients, is an important safeguard against irregular detention.

2. District Court and Court of Appeal

496. In addition to the right to apply to the supervisory judge, a patient hospitalised without his consent (admitted or placed) or any interested person may at any time appeal to the District Court to request release. A new application is, however, not admissible until a final decision has been taken on a previous application. The decision of the District Court may be appealed to the Court of Appeal.

3. Supervisory Commission

497. In each judicial district, a five-member supervisory commission is responsible for ensuring compliance with the law and receiving complaints and grievances that patients may address. It conducts visits to the establishment.

433. Chapter 7, Law on the hospitalisation without consent.

4. External Control of Places of Deprivation of Liberty

498. The External Control of Places of Deprivation of Liberty ('CELPL'), attached to the Ombudsman, carries out monitoring visits and inspections of places of deprivation of liberty to prevent torture and other cruel, inhuman, or degrading treatment or punishment. In this capacity, it visits closed psychiatric services and makes recommendations.[434]

5. Information on Rights

499. The Law foresees a contact point to which patients can turn if they want to find out about their rights or if they want to be advised in legal or other cases that concern them in accordance with Article 47 of the amended Act of 10 December 2009 on the hospitalisation of persons with mental disorders without their consent.

III. Judicial Placement Order[435]

500. If a person commits a criminal offence while suffering from a mental disorder which has completely abolished his discernment or control of his actions, the investigating or sentencing court shall recognise his or her lack of criminal responsibility. In this case, if the court considers that the person continues to constitute a danger to himself or to others, it orders a judicial placement at the CHNP.

A. *Special Commission*

501. A special commission is responsible for the enforcement of judicial placement decisions. It is composed of a magistrate, a magistrate of the Public Prosecutor's Office, a medical specialist in psychiatry and a fourth member appointed by the Minister of Health and Social Security. Within two months of the admission, the attending psychiatrist shall draw up a report on the mental state of the patient and on the advisability of maintaining the placement and shall forward this report to the special commission. The latter decides within one month of receipt of the report. The special commission may visit the unit of placement or delegate one of its members.

502. The special commission reviews the condition of the judicial placement every year pursuant to a report of the attending psychiatrist.

---

434. Loi du 11 avril 2010, (1) portant approbation du protocole facultatif se rapportant à la Convention contre la torture et autres peines ou traitements cruels, inhumains ou dégradants, adopté par l'Assemblée Générale de l'Organisation des Nations Unies à New York, le 18 décembre 2002 et (2) portant désignation du médiateur en tant que mécanisme national de prévention et fixant ses attributions. Web site: https://www.ombudsman.lu/EN/CELPL-001.php.

435. Chapter 6, Law on the hospitalisation without consent.

503. If the attending physician is of the opinion that the judicial detainee has been cured or that his condition has improved in such a way that placement is no longer necessary, he must immediately inform the special commission, which shall decide within one month whether the placement should be maintained.

504. The special commission may order the permanent or probationary release of the person when his or her mental state has sufficiently improved and the conditions for social rehabilitation are met. It may also grant short, daily, or weekly permissions to leave, depending on the condition of the patient and on the advice of the attending psychiatrist.

B. District Court and Court of Appeal

505. The patient may at any time appeal to the district court requesting his release. The Court may also be called by any interested person who indicates in his application his degree of kinship with the patient or the nature of his relations with him. Discharge may be granted only if the Court has serious grounds for concluding that the patient no longer constitutes a danger to himself or to others. The decision may be appealed to the Court of Appeal sitting in chambers.

Chapter 5. Specific Activities and Issues

§1. Preventive Medicine

I. Introduction

506. While preventive medicine has always been part of medical activities, Luxembourg's health system traditionally focussed on curative rather than preventive medicine. First policies to develop preventive medicine started with a focus on perinatal care, childcare and school medicine, as well as on occupational health. Since the 2000s, preventive medicine programmes have been put up in collaboration with CNS. Organised prevention programmes further result from action plans elaborated with the main stakeholders of the healthcare system to address specific public health concerns, such as the HIV/aids action plan (1st plan in 2006) or the national cancer plan (1st plan in 2014). The initial referring doctor scheme (2010) aimed to further foster prevention through a specific prevention questionnaire ('fiche prévention'). It has, however, not effectively been taken up and was abandoned in 2015.[436] The Government elected in October 2023 plans to introduce health check-ups starting at the age of 30 years.[437]

We will give hereafter an overview of the disparate framework without listing all activities deployed.

II. Perinatal Care, Childcare and School Medicine

507. Pursuant to Chapter V – 'Birth Allowance' of the CSS, Luxembourg grants a relatively generous allowance to parents of a new borne.[438] The allowance is paid in three instalments of EUR 580, composed of a prenatal allowance, an actual birth allowance and a postnatal allowance. These three allowances are paid under several conditions, the main condition being to undergo compulsory medical examinations for the purpose of monitoring and following up the pregnancy, childbirth, and the child up to the age of 2 years. To receive the prenatal allowance, pregnant women must undergo at least five medical examinations and one dental examination. These examinations are both obstetric and general. They must be carried out by a physician specialised in gynaecology and obstetrics for obstetric examinations and by a physician specialised in internal medicine or a GP for the general examinations. A dentist must carry out a dental examination. To obtain the actual birth allowance, a

436. CNS, *Rapport annuel 2015*, pp. 39–41 (2016), https://cns.public.lu/dam-assets/publications/rapport-annuel/rapport-annuel-2015.pdf.

437. *Luxembourg Government, 2023–2028 Coalition Agreement*, p. 86, https://gouvernement.lu/fr/publications/accord-coalition/accord-de-coalition-2023-2028/accord-de-coalition-2023-2028.html.

438. CSS, Arts 276–305, https://www.secu.lu/prestations-familiales-et-indemnite-de-conge-parental/livre-iv/chapitre-iv-allocation-de-naissance/.

physician specialised in gynaecology and obstetrics must carry out one postnatal examination. Finally, to obtain the postnatal allowance, six medical examinations of the child must be carried out either by a paediatric specialist, an internal medicine specialist or a GP before the age of 2 years.

Implementing Grand-Ducal Regulations determines the procedures for the examinations, as well as the maternity booklet to be used to document these examinations.[439] Given the link with the payment of an allowance, Luxembourg scores high when it comes to monitoring and vaccinating[440] infants and young children below the age of 2. Numbers, however, drop significantly after the age of 2 years, when financial incentives stop.

Pursuant to the amended Law of 2 December 1987 regulating school medicine,[441] school medicine is deploying preventive medical measures and examinations carried out by school medical services to monitor the health and well-being of pupils (Article 1). All pupils, apprentices and students benefiting from basic, secondary, or higher education, differentiated education or occupational training are subject to mandatory school health measures and examinations (Article 2). A Grand-Ducal Regulation determines the content and frequency of school health measures and examinations.[442]

508. School medical services are coordinated and placed under the authority of the School Medical Division at the Directorate of Health. The School Medicine Division carries out health measures and examinations at the post-primary level. Local municipalities are responsible for organising school medicine for nurseries, primary schools, and special education. Most municipalities rely on the cooperation of health professionals from the 'Ligue médico-sociale'.[443]

III. Occupational Health

509. Occupational health has a mainly preventive role. Occupational health services protect employees by organising the provision of medical supervision of the staff employed and the prevention of occupational accidents and illnesses at work.

439. Règlement grand-ducal modifié du 8 décembre 1977 portant sur les modalités des examens médicaux et de l'examen dentaire de la femme enceinte et de l'examen postnatal de la mère, ainsi que sur le carnet de maternité, Mém. A –76 du 9.12.1977, https://legilux.public.lu/eli/etat/leg/rgd/1977/12/08/n2/jo; Règlement grand-ducal modifié du 8 décembre 1977 portant sur les modalités des examens médicaux des enfants en bas âge, sur la périodicité de ces examens et sur le modèle du carnet de santé et les inscriptions qui devront y être portées obligatoirement, Mém. A –76 du 9.12.1977, https://legilux.public.lu/eli/etat/leg/rgd/1977/12/08/n3/jo.

440. *Enquête de couverture vaccinale 2018 au Grand-Duché de Luxembourg*, Direction de la Santé (2019), https://sante.public.lu/fr/publications/e/enquete-couverture-vaccinale-lux-2018.html.

441. Loi modifiée du 2 décembre 1987 portant réglementation de la médecine scolaire, Mém. A – 96 du 9.12.1987, http://data.legilux.public.lu/eli/etat/leg/loi/1987/12/02/n1/jo.

442. Règlement grand-ducal du 24 octobre 2011 déterminant le contenu et la fréquence des mesures et examens de médecine scolaire et le fonctionnement de l'équipe médico-socio-scolaire, Mém. A – 219 du 28.10.2011, http://data.legilux.public.lu/eli/etat/leg/rgd/2011/10/24/n1/jo.

443. https://ligue.lu/en/home/translate-to-english-medecine-scolaire-4-13-ans.

The Labor Code currently governs occupational safety and occupational health services.[444] Employers who regularly employ more than 5,000 persons, or more than 3,000 persons with at least 100 in hazardous jobs, must set up an occupational health service within the company. All other employers may either set up an occupational health service or use the services of an external occupational health service. The Occupational Health Division of the Directorate of Health is responsible for the supervision and coordination of occupational health activities.

510. Occupational health services are in charge of identifying risks to health in the workplace and avoiding and combatting such risks. Occupational physicians exercise their function in complete professional independence from the employer. The function of occupational physician is incompatible with the private practice of the medical profession. Occupational physicians monitor workplace factors that may affect workers' health (e.g., noise, chemicals, harmful radiation) and make preventive recommendations. They further promote the adaptation of work to the individual worker, monitor the health of workers and carry out mandatory medical examinations.

IV. Preventive Medicine Measures in Collaboration with CNS

511. According to Article 17, §3 of the CSS, preventive medicine measures may be organised within the framework of partnership agreements concluded between the Ministers responsible for Health and Social Security, the National Health Fund and, where appropriate, specialised services.

As the first preventive medicine programme in collaboration with CNS, a programme for organised early detection of breast cancer by mammography was set up in 2003.[445] A tobacco cessation programme[446] was introduced in 2008 and an organised colorectal cancer screening programme followed in 2016.[447] Other preventive medicine programmes concern prenatal screening for congenital anomalies,[448] as well as certain vaccination programmes (vaccination with 'Rotarix' of infants;[449] vaccination of people at risk against pneumococcus).[450] A programme providing for free of charge access to contraceptives on medical prescription (reimbursement level at 100%) was introduced in 2023 and covers contraceptive pills, patches and rings, contraceptive injections and implants, as well as the 'morning-after pill' and tubal ligation or vasectomy.[451]

444. Code du Travail, Livre III., https://legilux.public.lu/eli/etat/leg/code/travail/20230915#title_18.
445. https://cns.public.lu/en/legislations/conv-etat-cns/cns-etat-mammographie.html.
446. https://cns.public.lu/en/legislations/conv-etat-cns/cns-etat-tabac.html.
447. https://cns.public.lu/en/legislations/conv-etat-cns/cns-etat-cancer-colorectal.html.
448. https://cns.public.lu/en/legislations/conv-etat-cns/cns-etat-anom-congen.html.
449. https://legilux.public.lu/eli/etat/leg/conv/2020/08/27/a723/jo.
450. https://cns.public.lu/en/legislations/conv-etat-cns/cns-etat-pneumocoque.html.
451. https://cns.public.lu/en/assure/vie-privee/sante-prevention/prevention/contraception.html.

V. Public Health Action Plans and Other Initiatives

512. In recent years, numerous specific national action plans have been established in collaboration with all concerned stakeholders (healthcare providers, patient associations, and governmental actors) under the coordination of the department of health. In their respective field, these plans generally set up a roadmap to improve all facets of care, starting with prevention and early screening/detection. As part of the national action plan against dementia, a comprehensive dementia prevention programme is deployed;[452] VIH/AIDS prevention is an important pillar of the national VIH/AIDS plan;[453] there is a national programme for the promotion of affective and sexual health[454] for rare diseases and[455] mental health,[456] etc.

§2. Prenatal Diagnosis, Genetic Testing and Genetic Counselling

513. The current legislative framework regarding prenatal diagnosis, genetic testing, or genetic counselling is disparate and completed by auto-regulation (operating rules of the NCG).

514. A preventive medicine programme to carry out and manage prenatal screening for congenital anomalies at national level has existed since 2007.[457] The prenatal diagnostic activity is exclusively carried out by the NCG of the LNS. In recent years, non-invasive prenatal testing (NIPT) has been made available for common foetal chromosomal abnormalities. Pre-implantation genetic testing is not formally regulated; it is currently not available in Luxembourg as it is not proposed by the national MAP laboratory at CHL.[458]

515. The LNS operates the NCG with the mission to carry out human, constitutional and somatic genetics, including the interpretation of these examinations and genetic counselling.[459] Diagnosis of human genetic diseases may not be offered by private laboratories.[460] The NCG is classified as a national diagnostic

452. Schroeder, V.E. et al., 'Programme Dementia Prevention (Pdp): A Nationwide Program for Personalized Prevention in Luxembourg', 97/2 *J. Alzheimers Dis.*, pp.791–804 (2024).
453. https://sante.public.lu/fr/publications/p/plan-action-national-sida-2018-2022.html.
454. https://sante.public.lu/fr/espace-professionnel/plans-nationaux/plan-national-sante-affective-sexuelle-2019.html.
455. https://sante.public.lu/fr/espace-professionnel/plans-nationaux/maladies-rares.html.
456. https://sante.public.lu/fr/publications/p/plan-national-sante-mentale.html.
457. Convention conclue entre l'État du Grand-Duché de Luxembourg et l'Union des caisses de maladie portant institution d'un programme de médecine préventive pour la réalisation et la prise en charge, au niveau national, du dépistage prénatal d'anomalies congénitales, Mém. A – 117 du 17.07.2007, https://cns.public.lu/en/legislations/conv-etat-cns/cns-etat-anom-congen.html.
458. *See:* §3. Medically Assisted Procreation *infra.*
459. Article 2, Loi modifiée du 7 août 2012 portant création de l'établissement public Laboratoire national de santé.
460. Article 1, Loi modifiée 6 juillet 1984 relative aux laboratoires d'analyses médicales.

centre pursuant to the Law on hospitals, with a monopoly to carry out human genetics, defined as tests relating to the heredity of malformations and anomalies, both physical and psychological, the molecular nature of these malformations and anomalies, or the fact of being a carrier of hereditary characteristics.[461] According to the Law on hospitals, it is mandatory for every hospital operating an oncology department to sign an agreement with CNG specifying the criteria and procedures for analysing samples; the Law on hospitals does, however, not further specify the contents thereof.[462]

516. According to the legal definitions, the mission of the CNG includes the interpretation of tests and genetic counselling. This could be read as attributing a monopoly of genetic counselling to LNS. However, such counselling is, by nature, part of the activities carried out by specialists in clinical genetics and the treating physician, particularly the treating oncologist.

517. Health insurance specifically covers genetic counselling by a specialist in clinical genetics through a lump tariff, including the establishment of the personal and family medical history, a family tree, personalised medical counselling, and a report to the treating physician. The fee varies depending on whether the test is included or excluded. If the test is included, prior written consent is required, and the lump tariff includes the announcement of the result with specific counselling. A lower tariff is available for a simple or majorated consultation with a specialist in clinical genetics.[463] In practice, such counselling by a specialist in clinical genetics is only available at the CNG and, partly, at the oncology department of CHL.

518. Prior written consent is required by the nomenclature of tariffs for the realisation of genetic testing to be reimbursed as part of genetic counselling by a specialist in clinical genetics. Furthermore, the CNG operating rules require a prior written consent form to be signed before carrying out genetic testing. This consent form offers patients a choice whether the test results may be used for counselling and testing of at-risk family members, whether secondary/additional findings concerning the patient shall be revealed to him or her, whether unused sample material may be used for teaching and research purposes, and whether the test results and associated data may be used in pseudonymised form for scientific research purposes.[464]

---

461. Article 1(2); Art. 6(3), Loi modifiée du 8 mars 2018 relative aux établissements hospitaliers et à la planification hospitalière.
462. Loi modifiée du 8 mars 2018 relative aux établissements hospitaliers et à la planification hospitalière, Annexe 2. – A, 'Oncologie'.
463. Nomenclature des actes et services des médecins pris en charge par l'assurance maladie, première partie, s. 1, sub 30), acte C75; s. 2, sub 12), acte C76; deuxième partie, chapitre 1, s. 10, actes 1A11 et 1A12, https://cns.public.lu/fr/legislations/ammd_dent/cns-ammd-med-tableau.html.
464. https://lns.lu/wp-content/uploads/2019/06/lns_consent_english-v1.1.pdf.

§3. Medically Assisted Procreation

I. Introduction[465]

519. MAP is carried out by physicians specialising in reproductive medicine in close collaboration with the patient's regular gynaecologist. Two hospital services are currently authorised: the 'Service Procréation Médicalement Assistée' within the maternity department of CHL, as well as the 'Centre de Traitement de l'Infertilité' within the HRS – Clinique Dr Bohler. Both services have recourse to the National Laboratory for MAP located at the maternity department of CHL.

520. Health insurance covers the costs of MAP by ovarian stimulation, artificial insemination, in vitro fertilisation, or intracytoplasmic sperm injection (ICSI). Coverage is generally subject to prior authorisation by the National Health Fund. Coverage of MAP ends on the woman's 43rd birthday and MAP is not covered after tubal ligation or vasectomy.[466]

II. Current Legislation and Soft Law

521. The current legal framework is disparate and completed by auto-regulation. De facto, the access rules of the national MAP lab contribute to a large extent to governing bioethical issues not governed by legislation. The absence of a comprehensive legal framework has not precluded the development of MAP services and has allowed flexible adaptations without giving rise to major difficulties. The lack of legislation and the reliance on soft law have, however, been questioned, in particular by the Council of State and the CNE.

522. Pursuant to the Law on hospitals, the national laboratory for MAP is considered a national hospital service. It has the mission to provide clinical and biological reproductive medicine services for in vitro conception, oocyte, germ tissue, embryo preservation, embryo transfer and artificial insemination.

The Law on human tissues and cells intended for human application applies to gametes or reproductive tissues to be used in the context of reproductive medicine.[467] It results thereof, that donation, procurement, processing, transformation, preservation, storage, and distribution activities are subject to licensing by the Minister of Health and Social Security. Afferent quality and safety requirements must be met.

523. Soft law governs essential parts of the framework notably via the charter of the national laboratory for MAP and the ministerial authorisation governing the

---

465. *Dossier 'La gestation pour autrui et la procréation médicalement assistée'*, RLDS, Nos 2 & 3 (2020).

466. Article 143bis of the statutes of CNS, https://cns.public.lu/en/legislations/textes-coordonnes/statuts-cns.html.

467. *See:* §6., II. Tissues and Cells Intended for Human Application *infra*.

establishment of the laboratory. The charter of the laboratory requires prior evaluation of causes of infertility and prior information and counselling. The candidates must sign a written agreement with the MAP laboratory. Access to MAP is given to single women and same-sex couples. Oocyte donation and embryo donation are not available. Pre-implantation genetic diagnosis is not offered. Embryo cryopreservation requires the consent of the woman or couple, and the embryos are stored for a period of one year, renewable at request, until the woman reaches the age of 45. Gestational surrogacy and *post mortem* insemination are currently excluded. In the absence of a dedicated legislative framework, supernumerary embryos and gametes are not available to other MAP candidates or for research purposes. If the parental project is abandoned, the embryos are destroyed.

Since 2018, hospital legislation has requested the national laboratory for MAP to dispose of a charter of good practice in MAP, approved by the national ethics committee and available to the public, as well as to audit compliance.[468] The current charter has, however, so far not yet been reviewed by the CNE and is currently not available to the public.[469] An ethical review of the charter would be an important first step forward and should, in our view, be accompanied by a public debate. Such a review and public debate could guide future legislative work in the area.

III. Regulatory Outlook

524. The CNE has called for a more comprehensive regulation and has stressed the need to establish an independent review process available to MAP candidates. It has expressed support for offering pre-implantation genetic testing within strictly limited medical conditions.[470] It has also supported the idea that supernumerary embryos and gametes are made available to other MAP candidates, and for research purposes.[471]

525. Several law proposals currently pending in the legislative process have a link to MAP and the legal consequences thereof.

Law proposal 5528, aiming to ratify the Oviedo Convention, as well as the three additional protocols adopted until the date of its introduction in Parliament, has been pending since 2006 without major advancement.[472] The opinion of the Council of

468. Law on hospitals, Annex 2 – D.
469. Information provided by CHL to the authors (March 2024).
470. National Ethics Commission (CNE), *PMA, GPA, accouchement anonyme: autant de défis éthiques pour la société*, Avis CNE No. 26 (2016).
471. National Ethics Commission (CNE), *La recherche sur les embryons surnuméraires au Luxembourg*, Avis CNE No. 24 (2013).
472. Projet de loi 5528 portant approbation – de la Convention pour la protection des Droits de l'Homme et de la dignité de l'être humain à l'égard des applications de la biologie et de la médecine: Convention sur les Droits de l'Homme et la biomédecine, ouverte à la signature, à Oviedo, le 4 avril 1997 – du Protocole additionnel à la Convention pour la protection des Droits de l'Homme et de la dignité de l'être humain à l'égard des applications de la biologie et de la médecine, portant interdiction du clonage d'êtres humains, ouvert à la signature, à Paris, le 12 janvier 1998 – du Protocole additionnel à la Convention sur les Droits de l'Homme et la biomédecine relatif à la transplantation d'organes et de tissus d'origine humaine, ouvert à la signature, à Strasbourg, le 24 janvier 2002 –

State recommended already in 2006 to elaborate a congruent regulation of key issues such as genetic testing and counselling, MAP, or biomedical research.

Law proposal No. 6568A reforming the law of filiation aims to provide a framework for couples having recourse to MAP, mainly through a section on MAP to be inserted in the Civil Code introducing a mandatory contract between the MAP centre and the candidates to MAP. It also intended to clarify issues related to filiation and inheritance.[473] The proposal further contains a national prohibition of gestational surrogacy while regulating legal status of such filiations abroad. In its complementary opinion, the Council of State has criticised the draft for being insufficiently clear and incomplete when it comes to the framework foreseen for MAP. In the Council of State's opinion, the Civil Code should regulate filiation questions and related issues, whereas issues relating to MAP procedures, such as definitions, the process to be followed, informed consent and retraction, as well as issues related to the allocation of embryos and gametes to a research programme, should be the subject of a specific law. The Council of State suggested finding inspiration in the Belgian Law of 2007 on MAP and the disposition of supernumerary embryos and gametes. We share this view.

The Government elected in October 2023 agreed to create a framework dedicated to MAP, which would exclude gestational surrogacy but recognise the filiation of children born after gestational surrogacy carried out abroad.[474] Finally, the child's right to know his or her origins is addressed by Law proposal No. 7674, organising access to knowledge of one's origins in the context of adoption or MAP with third-party donors.[475]

§4. Termination of Pregnancy (Abortion)

I. Introduction

526. Until 1978, abortion was prohibited on pain of criminal penalties for the pregnant woman and the physician or any other third party involved. Abortion was

---

du Protocole additionnel à la Convention sur les Droits de l'Homme et la biomédecine, relatif à la recherche biomédicale, ouvert à la signature, à Strasbourg, le 25 janvier 2005 et modifiant la loi du 25 novembre 1982 réglant le prélèvement de substances d'origine humaine, https://www.chd.lu/fr/dossier/5528.

473. Projet de loi 6568A portant réforme du droit de la filiation, modifiant – le Code civil, – le Nouveau Code de procédure civile, – le Code pénal, – la loi communale du 13 décembre 1988, – et la loi du 1er août 2007 relative aux tissus et cellules humains destinés à des applications humaines, https://www.chd.lu/fr/dossier/6568A.

474. *Luxembourg Government, 2023–2028 Coalition Agreement*, p. 98, https://gouvernement.lu/fr/publications/accord-coalition/accord-de-coalition-2023-2028/accord-de-coalition-2023-2028.html.

475. Projet de loi 7674 portant organisation de l'accès à ses origines dans le cadre d'une adoption ou d'une procréation médicalement assistée avec tiers donneurs, https://www.chd.lu/fr/dossier/7674.

first liberalised by the Law of 15 November 1978 on sexual information, the prevention of clandestine abortion and the regulation of termination of pregnancy,[476] thus following liberalising in France ('Loi Veil', 1975) and Germany (1976).[477] The legal framework for termination of pregnancy was further liberalised in 2011[478] and in 2014.[479] Under the outgoing government, a working group was set up to evaluate the current legal framework and its application.[480] An extension of the current time limit for abortion from twelve to fourteen weeks is discussed.[481]

527. The amended Law of 15 November 1978 on sexual information, the prevention of clandestine abortion and the regulation of termination of pregnancy will be referred to hereinafter as 'Law on the regulation of termination of pregnancy'. Besides regulating the voluntary termination of pregnancy, it contains a first chapter dedicated to measures promoting sexual education in schools and supporting centres that perform free-of-charge sexual information and family counselling. In addition to this mission, physicians carry out medical treatments relating to sexual hygiene in these centres.

II. Legal Conditions for Termination of Pregnancy

528. Article 1 of the Law on the regulation of termination of pregnancy enshrines the respect for human life from its very beginning: 'The Law guarantees respect for every human being from the beginning of life. This principle may not be infringed except in cases of necessity and in accordance with the conditions defined by this law.' Article 12 regulates the conditions under which, by exception to Article 1, the voluntary termination of a pregnancy with the consent of the pregnant woman is licit.

A. Termination Before the 12th Week of Pregnancy

529. Since the 2014 amendment to the law, a voluntary termination of pregnancy may generally be performed before the end of the twelfth week of pregnancy

476. Loi du 15 novembre 1978 relative à l'information sexuelle, à la prévention de l'avortement clandestin et à la réglementation de l'interruption volontaire de grossesse, Mém. A – 81 du 6 décembre 1978, http://data.legilux.public.lu/eli/etat/leg/loi/1978/11/15/n1/jo, doc. parl. 2146, https://wdocs-pub.chd.lu/docs/archive/25/19/3119449_pdf.

477. Nati R., *Réglementation de l'interruption volontaire de la grossesse*, in: *Le Conseil d'État face à l'évolution de la société luxembourgeoise*, pp. 395–402, Conseil d'Etat (2006).

478. Projet de loi 6103 portant modification des articles 351, 353 et 353-1 du Code pénal, https://www.chd.lu/fr/dossier/6103.

479. Projet de loi 6683 portant modification: (1) du Code pénal et (2) de la loi du 15 novembre 1978 relative à l'information sexuelle, à la prévention de l'avortement clandestin et à la réglementation de l'interruption volontaire de grossesse, https://www.chd.lu/fr/dossier/6683.

480. Answer of the Minister of Health, Parliamentary Question No. 7875, 5 May 2023, https://www.chd.lu/fr/question/25513.

481. Answer of the Minister of Health and the Minister of Justice, Parliamentary Question No. 6768, 7 Oct. 2022, https://www.chd.lu/fr/question/24254.

or before the end of the fourteenth week of amenorrhoea.[482] Additional procedural conditions are required; no medico-social indication is, however, necessary. The main criterion is the time limit.

B. *Therapeutic Termination of Pregnancy*

530. After the end of the twelfth week of pregnancy, or the fourteenth week of amenorrhoea, that voluntary termination of pregnancy is subject to a medical indication. A serious threat to the health or life of the pregnant woman or the foetus needs to be given and this medical indication needs to be certified in writing by two qualified physicians.[483] According to the parliamentary discussions, the notion of a serious threat to the health or life of the foetus includes cases where there is a strong probability that the unborn child will suffer from a particularly serious condition recognised as incurable at the time of diagnosis or with serious physical malformations or mental alterations.[484]

531. The law does not contain further details with respect to the competence or qualifications of the physician certifying the medical indication. Article 12, §1, second point, regulates the qualifications of the physician performing a termination of pregnancy. Even though this article does not specify so, it is considered that this provision also applies to late therapeutic termination of pregnancy.[485]

C. *Prior Consultation of a Physician Specialised in Gynaecology and Obstetrics*

532. The pregnant woman must consult a physician specialising in gynaecology and obstetrics at least three days before undergoing the procedure (reflection period).[486] The physician consulted must provide the patient with:

(a) a dated pregnancy certificate giving information on the exact location and age of the pregnancy, which will be given to the doctor who carries out the voluntary interruption of pregnancy;
(b) medical information on the various methods of voluntary termination of pregnancy available, as well as the medical risks and potential side effects of these methods;
(c) a list of hospitals approved to perform voluntary termination of pregnancy in accordance with the procedures, in case the consulted physician is unable, for whatever reason, to carry out such an intervention himself;

---

482. Article 12, §1, first sentence, Law on the regulation of termination of pregnancy.
483. Article 12, §4, Law on the regulation of termination of pregnancy.
484. CHD, *Rapport de la Commission juridique du 19.11.2014*, doc. parl. 6683/11, p. 11, https://www.chd.lu/fr/dossier/6683.
485. CHD, *Rapport de la Commission juridique du 19.11.2014*, doc. parl. 6683/11, p. 11, https://www.chd.lu/fr/dossier/6683.
486. Article 12, §1, point 1., Law on the regulation of termination of pregnancy.

(d) a standardised documentation, providing information about the rights of pregnant women, support for children and families, and the various options available to them in their situation, as well as their consequences. This documentation includes a list of the psychosocial assistance services.

D. Psychosocial Consultation

533. Before performing an abortion, the physician must inform the pregnant woman of her right, both before and after the voluntary termination of pregnancy, to consult a psychosocial assistance service.[487] These services provide information about alternatives to the decision to perform a termination of pregnancy, inform about the rights and assistance guaranteed by law to families and children and provide support and advice on how to find help to resolve any psychological and social issues in connection with the voluntary termination of pregnancy.

534. The consultation of a free-of-charge psychosocial assistance service is a patient right. Since the 2014 reform, it is, however, no longer mandatory for adult women to assist with such a consultation prior to an abortion. Consultation remains mandatory for non-emancipated minor women.

E. Termination of Pregnancy

535. Voluntary termination of pregnancy is reserved to physician specialising in gynaecology and obstetrics and must be performed in a hospital or another setting licensed by the Minister of Health and Social Security. A ministerial Order licensed the 'Planning Familial', which runs three centres performing free-of-charge sexual information and family counselling, as a setting where physicians may perform medically induced termination of pregnancy.[488] Any physician licensed to practise may further perform medically induced termination of pregnancy in private practice, but must, however, enter into an arrangement with a hospital that has a gynaecology and obstetrics department with twenty-four-hour emergency services.[489]

536. After a woman has decided to terminate her pregnancy, she may give written specific consent to the removal of embryonic or foetal tissues or cells for human applications. If the woman having undergone the termination of pregnancy is a minor or is the subject of a legal protection measure, the purpose of removal is limited to investigating the causes of the termination of pregnancy.[490]

---

487. Article 12, §2, Law on the regulation of termination of pregnancy.
488. https://legilux.public.lu/eli/etat/adm/amin/2023/02/02/b463/jo.
489. Article 12, §1, 2, Law on the regulation of termination of pregnancy.
490. Article 11, §2, Law on human tissues and cells intended for human applications.

F. Non-emancipated Minor Women

537. Specific conditions are applicable to non-emancipated minor women requesting a termination of pregnancy.[491] Consulting a psychosocial assistance service is mandatory for pregnant, non-emancipated minor women.

538. Written consent of one of the parents or of the holder of parental authority is generally required. Requesting the consent of only one parent is a derogation of the principle of joint parental authority.[492] Furthermore, if a minor patient wishes to keep the voluntary termination of pregnancy secret from her parents or from the holder of parental authority, the procedure may be performed on the condition that she is accompanied by a trusted adult of her choice.

539. After meeting with the psychosocial assistance services, the pregnant minor must consult the physician who delivers prior information.[493] The decision to undergo a voluntary termination of pregnancy must be confirmed in writing after having received the information from the physician. One of the parents, the holder of parental authority or the trusted adult accompanying the minor must co-sign the written confirmation of the minor woman's decision.

III. Objection of Conscience

540. No physician may be compelled to practise voluntary interruption of pregnancy. No health professional may be compelled to assist in practising voluntary interruption of pregnancy.[494]

IV. Illegal Termination of Pregnancy

541. Anyone who terminates or attempts to terminate the pregnancy or the presumed pregnancy of a consenting woman without respecting the conditions prescribed in Article 12 is punishable with imprisonment of two to five years and a fine of EUR 251 to EUR 25,000. A woman who terminates her pregnancy without respecting the conditions prescribed in Article 12 is punishable by a fine of EUR 250 to EUR 2,000.[495]

542. Performing an abortion without the consent of the woman remains punished by the Criminal Code. According to Article 348, anyone who, by means of food, drink, medication, violence, manoeuvers, or any other means, deliberately

491. Article 12, §3, Law on human tissues and cells intended for human applications.
492. *See:* para. 455 *supra*.
493. *See:* point 3. *Supra*.
494. Article 13, Law on the regulation of termination of pregnancy.
495. Article 15, Law on the regulation of termination of pregnancy.

causes or attempts to cause an abortion in a pregnant woman or a woman presumed to be pregnant who has not consented to the abortion will be punished by five to ten years of imprisonment. An attempt to cause an abortion punishable under Article 348 requires the following elements: the woman's actual or presumed state of pregnancy, the use of means likely to induce an abortion, the absence of voluntary withdrawal, a criminal intent, and the absence of the victim's consent.[496]

543. According to Article 349, where the abortion has been caused by violence exercised voluntarily but without the intention of inducing abortion, the guilty party will be punished by imprisonment of between three months and two years and a fine of between EUR 251 and EUR 3,000. If the violence is premeditated or committed with knowledge of the woman's condition, the prison sentence will be between six months and three years, and the fine will be between EUR 500 and EUR 5,000.

544. Finally, according to Article 351 of the Criminal Code, when the means used to induce an abortion cause death, the person who administers them or indicates them for this purpose will be sentenced to five to ten years of imprisonment if the woman has consented to the abortion and to ten to fifteen years of imprisonment if she has not consented.

§5. Vaccination

545. Vaccination is a medical activity generally reserved for physicians. A nurse may also perform a vaccination upon medical prescription and under the condition that a physician can intervene within a timeframe appropriate to the situation.[497]

546. Within the context of the COVID-19 pandemic, a specific framework was introduced to facilitate mass vaccination in dedicated vaccination centres.[498] The Law on combatting the COVID-19 pandemic further introduced the idea that pharmacists may vaccinate persons against COVID-19 within a pharmacy open to the public. The persons to vaccinate must be over 16 years and must have no known allergy against an excipient of the vaccine and no known reaction against a previous COVID-19 vaccination. The pharmacist must further have been specifically authorised to vaccinate against COVID-19 by the Minister of Health and Social

496. For an illustration of an such an attempt: Trib. Lux., 23 Jan. 2020, No. 202/2020 – Beating of a pregnant woman in public by a violent partner shouting 'I'll make you lose the child'.
497. Loi modifiée du 26 mars 1992 sur l'exercice et la revalorisation de certaines professions de santé, Annexe 1 relative à la profession d'infirmier, point 5.2.
498. Règlement grand-ducal modifié du 22 octobre 2009 relatif aux centres de traitement et aux centres de vaccination dans le cadre de la gestion d'une pandémie, Mém. A – 207 du 23.10.2009 https://legilux.public.lu/eli/etat/leg/rgd/2009/10/22/n1/consolide/20210518.

Security after undergoing a brief specific training course. No prescription by a physician is required to vaccinate. While most measures to combat COVID-19 have meanwhile been abolished, this measure has been maintained after the end of the pandemic.[499]

547. Since the abolition of compulsory vaccination against smallpox in 1977, there has been no compulsory vaccination. An amended Grand-Ducal Regulation of 18 October 2001 determines a list of officially recommended vaccinations.[500] Proof of vaccination against diphtheria, poliomyelitis, tetanus, hepatitis B, whooping cough and COVID-19 is further a precondition for admission to the school for health professions.

548. A Law of 4 July 2000 has introduced a specific liability for vaccinations that are compulsory or officially recommended. If a (compulsory) or recommended vaccination causes the death or results in permanent physical incapacity of the person vaccinated, the State is legally liable for the damage insofar as it is not compensable under the social security regime. Up to the amount of the compensation granted, the State is subrogated to the rights of the patient against those that might be responsible for the damage according to ordinary law. The Law does not detail the compensation scheme and the procedure to follow. It results from the parliamentary discussions that death or permanent physical incapacity are, besides being a severity criterion for accessing compensation, also the only damages to be compensated.[501] Physical incapacities must be irreversible, which excludes temporary incapacities that can be cured. This specific no fault liability of the State is without prejudice to any legal action that may be taken in accordance with ordinary civil law against the vaccinator, against the manufacturer of the vaccine or others. Pursuant to the mass vaccination against COVID-19, several requests were introduced, and the M3S has defined an ad hoc procedure for such requests.[502]

§6. Removal, Donation and Use of Human Bodily Material

549. Separate pieces of legislation govern, respectively, transplantation of organs (I.), donation of tissue and cells (II.) and blood donation (III.).

499. Article 10bis, Loi modifiée du 17 juillet 2020 relative à certaines mesures de suivi de l'évolution du virus SARS-CoV-2 et de lutte contre la maladie Covid-19, https://legilux.public.lu/eli/etat/leg/loi/2020/07/17/a624/consolide/20230701.

500. Règlement grand-ducal modifié du 18 octobre 2001 déterminant la liste des vaccinations recommandées, http://data.legilux.public.lu/eli/etat/leg/rgd/2001/10/18/n3.

501. Projet de loi 4440 relatif à la responsabilité de l'Etat en matière de vaccinations, https://www.chd.lu/fr/dossier/4440.

502. Official website: https://sante.public.lu/fr/espace-citoyen/dossiers-thematiques/v/vaccination/dommages-graves-vaccination.html.

I. Human Organs

A. *Introduction*[503]

550. Founded in 1983, Luxembourg Transplant is a not-for-profit organisation approved as the national coordination centre for organ donation and transplantation. Luxembourg Transplant is affiliated with the Eurotransplant Foundation.

551. Kidney transplantation activities took place in Luxembourg until 2010. Since then, all patients have been referred to a transplant centre in Europe, mainly in the neighbouring countries. Pre-transplant consultation with Luxembourg patients and inscription on the pre-transplant waiting list is done by Luxembourg Transplant. According to the Luxembourg Transplant activity report, 103 patients were on the national waiting list at the end of 2022. Three transplant coordinators in charge of organ donation organise the removal activity. In recent years, this activity has frequently been below the Eurotransplant average. In 2022, thirty-eight organs were removed from eight donors (13.6 donors/mil.), which is within the Eurotransplant average.

B. *Scope of the Law on Organs Intended for Transplantation*

552. The scope of the Law of 25 November 1982 covered initial sampling of all substances of human origin. The law was fundamentally amended in 2015, changing its title and scope. The amended Law of 25 November 1982 on organs intended for transplantation will hereinafter be referred to as 'Law on organs intended for transplantation'.

553. According to Article 1, the Law on organs intended for transplantation currently governs 'the removal of organs from living persons for therapeutic purposes for the benefit of a person other than the donor and any removal of organs from deceased persons for therapeutic or scientific purposes'.

It results thereof that autologous removal, for the benefit of the concerned donor, is excluded from the scope of the law and must be considered a standard medical act not subject to a specific regulatory framework.

The scope of the law with regard to removal of organs donated for research purposes is limited to deceased persons, as organs may not be removed on living donors for exclusively scientific purposes. Removal of organs for other purposes, such as industrial preparation, is not covered by the scope of the law.

554. Even though covered by two different pieces of legislation, donation of organs and of human cells and tissues have strong links and parallelisms. There are also legal links, as pursuant to Article 10 of the Law on human tissues and cells intended for human applications, Articles 6 to 13 of the Law on organs intended for

503. *Rapport d'activités 2022*, Luxembourg Transplant (2023), http://s293241499.onlinehome.fr/Luxtrans/.

transplantation are applicable to the removal of tissue and cells from deceased donors. Furthermore, as the Law on organs intended for transplantation does not contain any definitions, the definitions given in Article 2 of the Law on human tissues and cells intended for human applications must also be considered to apply in the context of organ donation. Point e) thereof defines the term 'organ' as 'a differentiated and vital part of the human body, made up of different tissues, which largely autonomously maintains its structure, vascularisation, and capacity to perform physiological functions'.

C. Donation and Removal from Living Persons

555. An organ may only be removed from an adult living donor disposing of mental capacity.[504] Thus, no removal of an organ may take place from a potential donor that is of minor age or not capable of expressing his or her will. The donor must further have no medical or psychological contraindications to the removal of the organ and there must be no risk that is disproportionate to the benefit of the potential recipient.[505] Before donation, appropriate medical examinations must be carried out to assess and reduce the risks to the health and life of the donor. Appropriate medical follow-up must further be offered to the donor after donation.[506]

556. The donor must give his or her specific prior informed consent in writing. He or she may withdraw consent at any time. Informing prior to consent is reserved for physicians. Information must include the possible consequences of the organ removal, in particular, the potential psychological consequences of the procedure, as well as the benefits of the procedure for the recipient. In addition, the donor must be informed of his or her right to receive independent information on the risks of the removal from a physician with appropriate experience who is not involved in the removal.[507]

557. The donation must, first, be in the direct therapeutic interest of a recipient known at the time of donation.[508] Second, the transplantation of the organ into the intended recipient must be likely to preserve that person's life, or it must be likely to cure or prevent the aggravation of a serious disease from which the recipient is suffering. Third, there must be no suitable organ from a deceased person. Fourth, there must further be no suitable therapeutic method or alternative therapeutic method of comparable effectiveness available.[509]

504. Article 2, §1, c), Law on organs intended for transplantation.
505. Article 2, §1, d), Law on organs intended for transplantation.
506. Article 4, Law on organs intended for transplantation.
507. Article 3, Law on organs intended for transplantation.
508. Article 2, §1, c), Law on organs intended for transplantation.
509. Article 2, §1, b), Law on organs intended for transplantation.

558. The donor must be the spouse, direct relative, brother or sister, uncle or aunt, first cousin of the recipient or related by a declaration of partnership within the meaning of the Law of 9 July 2004 on the legal effects of certain partnerships.[510]

By exception, donation is possible if the donor and the recipient have maintained a very close emotional relationship for at least one year or if there is a community of interest between them based on considerations other than financial or economic.[511] In that latter case, after approval of the removal for transplant by the expert committee, the consent must specifically be given before the president of the District Court or a magistrate delegated by the president.[512]

559. Article 2, §3, regulates the transplantation of organs removed for a purpose other than the donation in view of transplantation. In such circumstances, the organ may be transplanted if the consequences and possible risks are explained. The person must give his or her informed consent. In the case of a person who does not have the capacity to consent, the 'appropriate authorisation' must be obtained.

The text does not further specify what removal for a 'purpose other than donation in view of transplantation' means in practice. It is, however, difficult to imagine another purpose then an initial removal in the medical interest of the person from which the organ is removed, so that this disposition would regulate 'surgical leftovers'.

With regard to the need to obtain 'appropriate authorisation' it is reasonable to presume that this refers to consent being given by a representative according to the general rules laid down by the Civil Code and the Law on patient rights and obligations. The physician should further seek the association of the minor or protected patient according to the Law on patient rights and obligations.[513]

560. Any removal of a living person is further subject to approval by a committee of three experts appointed by the Minister of Health and Social Security, comprising at least a physician and a member with legal expertise. This committee ensures that the legal conditions for removal are met and that the donor's consent is given without any pressure.[514]

561. Any loss of income incurred by the donor, as well as the cost associated with the procedure, must be covered by the health insurance of the recipient.[515]

510. Article 2, §1, e), Law on organs intended for transplantation.
511. Article 2, §2, Law on organs intended for transplantation.
512. Article 5, §2, Law on organs intended for transplantation.
513. *See:* Part II., Ch. 4., §1. Minor Patients and §2. Adult Patients under Protective Measures.
514. Article 5, §1, Law on organs intended for transplantation.
515. Article 17, Law on organs intended for transplantation.

562. The Law does not specify that medical post-transplantation follow-up must be offered to the recipient. This may be deplored.[516] We believe, however, that post-transplantation follow-up must nevertheless be offered. Failure to do so would, in our view, violate the general obligation put upon physicians to ensure continuity of care.

D. Organ Removal from Deceased Persons

563. Removal of organs from a deceased adult is allowed unless it is established that a written objection to such removal has been expressed. This general opt-out system applies to both the removal of organs for therapeutic and scientific purposes.[517]

For minors or adults under a protection regime, the authorisation of the legal representative is, however, requested, unless the deceased person, disposing of the necessary discernment, expressed in writing his or her personal refusal to such a removal. If the parental authority of a minor donor is exercised jointly, the disagreement of the parents constitutes a refusal.[518]

564. Since an amendment introduced in 2021, the DSP has functioned as a non-mandatory register of the expression of will concerning organ donation. When a person opens his or her DSP for the first time, the electronic platform requests to indicate whether he or she is opposed to organ removal after his or her death.[519] This initial choice may be changed at any time.

Before removing an organ, physicians must verify the will of the patient via the DSP.[520] A patient may also express his or her opposition to organ removal in writing and entrust this to his or her person of trust.[521] In the absence of a DSP or in the event of its closure, the person of trust must therefore be consulted.[522] The efforts and investigations made to establish the absence of a refusal must be documented in writing.[523]

565. The deceased person must be a Luxembourg resident. Luxembourg residency is, however, presumed in case the official residence is unknown and if there is no fact or circumstance that makes the existence of a residence abroad certain or likely.[524]

516. Stoffel, D., *La réforme de la réglementation du don d'organes au Luxembourg,* Droit, Santé et Société, N. 1/Vol. 20 (2017).
517. Article 6, Law on organs intended for transplantation.
518. Article 7, Law on organs intended for transplantation.
519. Article 9, Law on organs intended for transplantation.
520. Article 10, Law on organs intended for transplantation.
521. Article 9, Law on organs intended for transplantation.
522. Article 10, Law on organs intended for transplantation.
523. Article 12, Law on organs intended for transplantation.
524. Article 8, Law on organs intended for transplantation.

566. Two physicians not involved in the subsequent transplant or research operations must diagnose the death of the person before the removal.[525] Each of the two physicians must carry out a clinical assessment in accordance with current scientific knowledge, applying a detailed procedure that includes a waiting period before the second test, pursuant to the procedure laid down by the Grand-Ducal Regulation of 3 December 2009 determining the procedures to be followed to establish death in view of organ removal.[526]

567. It is prohibited to reveal the identity of the donor to the recipient and that of the recipient to the donor's relative.[527]

568. During the removal procedure, the human body must be treated with respect and every reasonable measure must be taken to restore the appearance of the body after removal.[528]

569. The cost associated with the removal is covered by the State budget.[529]

E. Gratuity of Donation and Prohibition of Financial Gain

570. Without prejudice to the reimbursement of loss of income and any costs incurred, donation of organs must be free of charge. Any acceptance of payment and any assistance in obtaining an organ in return for payment or assistance to transfer an organ for payment is a criminal offence punishable by eight days to three years of imprisonment and/or a fine of EUR 251 to EUR 20,000.[530]

F. Further Provisions

571. Organ removal, characterisation and transplantation may only be carried out in hospitals that have the necessary infrastructure and are licensed to this effect by the Minister of Health and Social Security. The activity is limited to hospitals and the hospital must dispose of a resuscitation or intensive care unit, a medical imaging department with a facility for arteriography or with an axial computed tomography, a neurology department with an electroencephalograph or suitable equipment for researching evoked potentials, a biochemical and bacteriological

525. Article 11, Law on organs intended for transplantation.
526. Règlement grand-ducal du 3 décembre 2009 déterminant les procédés à suivre pour constater la mort en vue d'un prélèvement, Mem. A – 240 du 16.12.2009, https://legilux.public.lu/eli/etat/leg/rgd/2009/12/03/n3/jo; *Constat d'un décès par mort cérébrale en vue d'un prélèvement d'organes,* Conseil Scientifique du Domaine de la Santé (2021), https://conseil-scientifique.public.lu/fr/publications/neurologie/constat-d-un-deces-par-mort-cerebrale-en-vue-d-un-prelevement-d-organes.html.
527. Article 13, Law on organs intended for transplantation.
528. Article 13bis, Law on organs intended for transplantation.
529. Article 17, Law on organs intended for transplantation.
530. Article 16, Art. 18, Law on organs intended for transplantation.

analysis laboratory, as well as an operating theatre with the necessary equipment for organ removal. All the equipment and required services for taking samples must be available to ensure operations are carried out in accordance with the state of the art.[531]

572. A national coordination service for transplantation, designated by the Minister of Health and Social Security, ensures that patients have fair access to transplantation services and that organs are allocated according to transparent and duly justified rules, taking account of medical criteria. The coordination mission has been exercised since the 1980s by Luxembourg Transplant. It organises the collection and registration of the information needed to ensure the traceability of organs and registers patients waiting for a transplant on an official waiting list.[532] Grand-Ducal regulations further specify the terms and conditions of the ministerial approval and the functioning of the national coordination service.[533] The Directorate of Health is further in charge of operating a system for reporting, investigating and follow-up of serious adverse events. Hospital services carrying out organ removal, characterisation, and transplantation, as well as Luxembourg Transplant report towards the Directorate of Health.[534]

II. Tissues and Cells Intended for Human Applications

A. *Scope of the Law on Human Tissues and Cells Intended for Human Applications*

573. Removal of human tissues and cells intended for human applications is governed by the Law of 1. August 2007 on human tissues and cells intended for human applications,[535] hereinafter 'Law on tissues and cells for human application'.

574. According to Article 1, §2, the Law on tissues and cells for human application governs the procurement, testing, processing, preservation, storage and distribution of human tissues and cells intended for human applications and of manufactured products derived from human tissues and cells intended for human applications. The term 'application' means the use of tissues or cells on or in a human recipient and extracorporeal applications.[536] Manufactured products derived

531. Article 14, Law on organs intended for transplantation.
532. Article 15, Law on organs intended for transplantation.
533. Règlement grand-ducal modifié du 24 janvier 1984 relatif au service national de coordination pour le prélèvement d'organes, https://legilux.public.lu/eli/etat/leg/rgd/1984/01/24/n4/jo; Règlement grand-ducal du 18 juillet 2018 relatif à l'organisation et aux méthodes de travail du service national de coordination des dons d'organes, https://legilux.public.lu/eli/etat/leg/rgd/2018/07/18/a694/jo.
534. Article 15ter, Law on organs intended for transplantation.
535. Loi du 1er août 2007 relative aux tissus et cellules humains destinés à des applications humaines, https://legilux.public.lu/eli/etat/leg/loi/2007/08/01/n12/jo.
536. *See:* definition given in Art. 2, point 1).

from human tissues and cells are excluded, if covered by a specific legislation. Tissues and cells may further be removed for the production or testing of *in vitro* diagnostic medical devices or for quality control of medical biology analyses.[537]

575. The Law on human tissues and cells for human application does not apply to organs[538] as well as to blood and blood components[539] as these are covered by specific legislation. Tissues and cells used for autologous implantation as part of a single surgical operation are further excluded. Even though not specifically mentioned, research using human tissues and cells must be considered covered only when applied to a human. The Law applies thus to trials with an application of tissue and cell to the human body, but not to *in vitro* research with tissues and cells and not to animal models.

B. Removal for Donation from Living Persons

576. Tissues and cells may only be removed for donation with the express written consent of the donor. This consent may be revoked at any time. Revocation of consent does, however, not prevent the use of tissues and cells previously removed, except in the case of gametes removed for the purposes of MAP.[540]

577. No tissue or cell donation may be carried out on a living minor or on a living adult who is subject to one of the protective measures pursuant to the Civil Code. By exception, the removal of haematopoietic cells from bone marrow may be performed on a minor. There must, however, be no other therapeutic solution and no compatible donor of legal age. The recipient must further be a brother or a sister of the donor. Furthermore, each of the holders of parental authority, duly informed of the risks incurred by the minor, must give their informed consent in writing. If the minor is capable of expressing his or her wishes, he must be duly informed, and his or her refusal must be respected. Finally, a committee of three experts, including at least two physicians, must give their approval.[541]

578. The physician responsible for the removal must, prior to the donation, provide the donor or the person representing the donor with the necessary information in a clear and appropriate manner, using easily understandable terms. This prior information must include: (1) the need for prior consent; (2) the nature of the donation; (3) consequences and risks of the donation; (4) results of any analytical tests carried out; (5) storage and protection of data concerning the donor; (6) respect of medical confidentiality; (7) therapeutic objectives and their potential benefits; (8) safeguards intended to protect the donor. The person responsible for the removal

537. Article 11, §1, Law on human tissues and cells for human application.
538. *See:* I. Human Organs *supra*.
539. *See:* III. Blood and Blood components *supra*.
540. Article 8, §1, Law on human tissues and cells for human application.
541. Article 8, §2, Law on human tissues and cells for human application.

must also be informed of the right to receive clear and easily understandable confirmation of the results of the analytical tests and independent information on the risks of the retrieval by a health professional with appropriate experience who is not involved in the retrieval or in the subsequent stages of re-use.[542]

579. Tissues and cells may only be used for the purpose for which they were retrieved, as indicated during prior information, unless the donor, having been duly informed of another use, has not objected to it. In the case of reproductive tissues and cells, use for another purpose always requires the express written consent of the donor.[543]

C. Surgical Leftovers

580. According to Article 9, an opt-out regime applies to tissues and cells removed during a medical procedure carried out in the interest of the person undergoing it. Surgical leftovers may be used for human applications without explicit consent. The patient must be duly informed of the possible further use of the substances removed. Any objection expressed by the patient must be respected and recorded in a file, which must be consulted before any use is made of the substances removed. This opt-out regime for surgical leftovers does not apply to reproductive tissues and cells.[544]

D. Removal from Deceased Persons

581. Pursuant to Article 10 of the Law on human tissues and cells intended for human applications, Articles 6 to 13 of the Law on organs intended for transplantation are applicable to the removal of tissue and cells from deceased persons.

E. Allowed Purposes

582. Tissues or cells may only be removed for donation for human applications, the production or testing of in vitro diagnostic medical devices, or quality control of medical biology analyses without prejudice to specific provisions relating to the donation of gametes used in MAP.[545]

583. Embryonic or foetal tissues or cells may only be removed, preserved, and used following termination of pregnancy for human applications, if the woman who has undergone a termination of pregnancy gives her written consent after having

542. Article 13, Law on human tissues and cells for human application.
543. Article 8, §3, Law on human tissues and cells for human application.
544. Article 9, Law on human tissues and cells for human application.
545. Article 11, §1, Law on human tissues and cells for human application.

received appropriate information on the purposes of such removal. This information must be given after the woman has decided to terminate her pregnancy. If the woman having undergone the termination of pregnancy is a minor or is the subject of a legal protection measure, removal is only allowed for the purpose of investigating the causes of the termination of pregnancy. In this case, the minor woman must be informed in advance of her right to object to a sample being taken.[546]

F. Gratuity of Donation and Prohibition of Financial Gain

584. Without prejudice to the reimbursement of loss of income and any costs incurred, donation must be free of charge. Except when such operations are made between authorised hospital services, any acceptance of payment and any assistance in obtaining an organ in return for payment, or assistance to transfer an organ for payment, is a criminal offence and punishable by eight days to six months of imprisonment and/or a fine of EUR 2,000 to EUR 25,000.[547]

G. Further Provisions

585. With the aim to ensure quality and safety, there are further organisational and technical requirements, as well as control and inspection measures.

III. Blood and Blood Components

586. The Law of 15 March 1979 regulating blood transfusion governs blood transfusion[548] with the aim to ensure that the donation of blood is carried out without any profit motive and that the collection, storage and transfusion of blood are carried out under conditions that guarantee the safety of both recipient and donor.[549] It submits donation of blood, withdrawal of blood from third persons, and the supply of blood to an authorisation under the conditions and procedures it defines. The legal framework is further specified by Grand-Ducal regulations adopted for its implementation.[550]

587. Blood donation may not give rise to any payment.[551] Human blood or plasma may only be collected by or under the direction of a physician.[552] The collection of human blood or plasma in view of its delivery in the form of whole blood

546. Article 11, §2, Law on human tissues and cells for human application.
547. Article 12, Art. 32, Law on human tissues and cells for human application.
548. Loi du 15 mars 1979 portant réglementation de la transfusion sanguine, Mém. A – 30 du 17.04.1979, https://legilux.public.lu/eli/etat/leg/loi/1979/03/15/n4/jo.
549. Article 1, Law regulating blood transfusion.
550. Article 2, Art. 12, Law regulating blood transfusion.
551. Article 3, Law regulating blood transfusion.
552. Article 6, Law regulating blood transfusion.

or its components is submitted to a specific authorisation and must be a not-for-profit activity.[553] The import and export of human blood or its derivatives is further reserved for the holder of this authorisation, unless the products are industrially prepared and appear on a list established by Grand-Ducal regulation.[554] The Blood Transfusion Centre, run by the Luxembourg Red Cross, is currently the only organisation authorised to collect blood from donors in Luxembourg.

588. Immediate delivery of blood or its components to the recipient may be carried out by a hospital establishment under the authority of a physician responsible for the blood and blood derivatives.[555]

589. Failure to observe the provisions of the law and its implementing regulations is a criminal offence punishable by eight days to six months of imprisonment and/or a fine of EUR 251 to EUR 12,500.[556]

§7. Digital Health (eHealth)

I. Introduction

590. eHealth was first put on the political agenda in 2006 with the adoption of the first eHealth plan,[557] followed in 2010 by a service platform study.[558] The 2010 reform of the healthcare system[559] established the basic legal framework for the setting up of a dedicated eHealth Agency and charged it to build and manage a national electronic platform for health data, with the DSP as a key service.

II. National eHealth Agency and Services Platform

591. Article 60ter of the CSS establishes the National eHealth Agency ('Agence eSanté') under the supervision of the Minister of Health and Social Security. The function of the Agency is entrusted to an economic interest grouping, comprising the State, the CNS and the CCSS, as well as the bodies representing care providers and patient interests. The eHealth Agency has been operational since 2012.[560] It is funded by two-thirds of its budget by CNS and one third by the State.

553. Article 4, Law regulating blood transfusion.
554. Article 5, Law regulating blood transfusion.
555. Article 5, last phrase, Law regulating blood transfusion.
556. Article 15, Law regulating blood transfusion.
557. Groupe de travail eSanté, *Plan d'action eSanté,* Luxembourg Government (2006), https://sante.public.lu/fr/espace-professionnel/plans-nationaux/programme-esante.html.
558. *Luxembourg Ministry of Health eHealth Service Platform Study*, PwC Luxembourg (2010), https://sante.public.lu/dam-assets/fr/politique-sante/plans-action/programme-esante/agence-esante/pwc-report-ehealth-service.pdf.
559. Loi du 17 décembre 2010 portant réforme du système de soins de santé et modifiant: (1) le Code de la sécurité sociale; (2) la loi modifiée du 28 août 1998 sur les établissements hospitaliers, Mém. A – 242 du 27.12.2010, https://legilux.public.lu/eli/etat/leg/loi/2010/12/17/n12/jo.
560. Official website: www.esante.lu.

592. Pursuant to Article 60ter, §1, the eHealth Agency has the following missions:

(1) the creation, deployment, operation, and management of a national electronic platform for exchanging and sharing health data, as well as of health IT applications and systems, comprising:
  - the DSP referred to in Article 60quater;
  - other nationwide IT projects facilitating the exchange, sharing or better use of health data;
  - electronic communication systems with the platform and its applications, security mechanisms and other related basic services;
  - data exchange with similar platforms in other EU Member States.

(2) the promotion of interoperability and security in the implementation of health information systems by means of:
  - the production and promotion of standards contributing to the interoperability and security of health information systems;
  - implementing the convergence of health information systems through interoperability standards;
  - monitoring norms and standards for health information systems;
  - collaborating with international organisations responsible for standardisation in the field of health information systems.

(3) drawing up and updating a master plan for health information systems, setting out a national strategy in line with the country's health priorities and the exchange and sharing needs of the healthcare sector. This master plan shall organise the deployment of projects and activities directly or indirectly managed by the Agency, as well as other strategic information systems projects contributing to the sharing and exchange of health data managed by the actors of the healthcare sector;

(4) advising the authorities on strategic choices concerning health information systems;

(5) informing patients and service providers about operational procedures and security measures relating to the DSP and the national electronic platform.

593. Article 60ter further specifies security and data-protecting issues, as well as the running of a national patient reference directory and a national healthcare provider reference directory.

III. Electronic Healthcare Record ('Dossier de Soins Partagé')

594. The DSP, is regulated by Article 60quater of the CSS. The process of creation, closure and access rights of the patient and of the different categories of healthcare professionals are further specified by the Grand-Ducal Regulation of 9 December 2019 which specifies the terms and conditions for setting up the DSP.[561]

595. Pursuant to Article 60quater, a DSP is created by the eHealth Agency for all persons affiliated with Luxembourg Social Security under an opt-out regime. The DSP's aim is to support the exchange of patient data amongst healthcare providers through a nationwide EHR platform. It bridges but does not replace the patient files kept by health professionals or institutional healthcare providers. Patients not affiliated with a Luxembourg social security regime may request a DSP when benefiting from healthcare in Luxembourg.

596. Access to the DSP is limited to healthcare providers participating in healthcare delivery to the patient. Based on the category of the health profession, different default access rights are assigned to professionals. Thus, physicians have a larger access than, for instance, pharmacists. If a patient has chosen a reference doctor, this physician always has full access to the DSP. He is further charged to update the DSP with the patient summary of his patient.

597. The DSP is automatically created through an opt-out regime. Patients have a time limit after being informed of the creation of their DSP to opt-out. If no opt-out is exercised, the DSP is created and opened. Patients may, however, decide at any time to close their DSP or request the reopening of a closed DSP. Patients further have an electronic direct online access to their DSP and may designate a proxy to access it. Patients further have the possibility to restrict access at a document level, as different confidentiality levels can be assigned (standard, restricted or private). Patients may also assign individual professionals, or groups of them, to a blacklist, blocking thus all access to the EHR of the concerned patient. They may also add professionals to a whitelist, having full access to their DSP. Finally, the DSP functions as an electronic registry of patients with regard to donation of organs after death.[562] A patient may further inform his DSP about an advance directive or his person of trust.[563]

§8. Biomedical Research

I. Introduction

598. The main general legal provision governing biomedical research remains currently Article 27 of the 2018 Law on hospitals, completed by different texts governing specific domains of biomedical research, mainly to ensure *ad minima* transposition of relevant EU law.

561. Règlement grand-ducal du 6 décembre 2019 précisant les modalités et conditions de mise en place du dossier de soins partagé, Mém. A-909 du 28.12.2019, https://legilux.public.lu/eli/etat/leg/rgd/2019/12/06/a909/jo.
562. *See:* para. 564 *supra.*
563. *See:* para. 604 *infra.*

599. While certain issues are thus addressed, there is no comprehensive framework specifically addressing biomedical research. A Law project on biomedical research was submitted to Parliament in 2006; there has, however, been no follow-up and the existing proposal is outdated.[564] A Law project aiming to ratify the Oviedo Convention and its additional protocols, including the additional protocol on biomedical research, is further pending in Parliament.[565] Finally, a Law project aiming to create a Luxembourg Agency for Medicines and Health Products was submitted to Parliament in 2020.[566] Once adopted, the new Agency would be in charge of carrying out missions with regard to the authorisation and supervision of biomedical research and the legal framework will be amended accordingly.

II. Authorisation and Evaluation Pursuant to Article 27 of the Law on Hospitals

A. Field of Application

600. According to Article 27, §1, of the Law on hospitals, 'No trial, study or clinical experiment may be carried out on human beings with a view to developing biological or medical knowledge without prior authorisation from the Minister of Health, the opinions of the Health Directorate and the National Research Ethics Committee sought beforehand.'

601. This article gives rise to several hesitations, with regard to the field of application. First, no formal provision derogates from the general scope of the Law on hospitals, so Article 27 would normally only apply to hospital establishments; it is, nevertheless, in practice, applied to biomedical research carried out outside of the hospital sector.[567] Second, with regards to the type of research covered, the words 'trial, study or clinical experiment' are broad in scope and cover all forms of research activities. The Law does, however, not specify what exactly 'carried out on human beings' means. Conducting a clinical trial clearly falls within the scope

564. Projet de loi 5552 relatif à la recherche biomédicale, https://www.chd.lu/fr/techdossier/172.

565. Projet de loi 5528 portant approbation – de la Convention pour la protection des Droits de l'Homme et de la dignité de l'être humain à l'égard des applications de la biologie et de la médecine: Convention sur les Droits de l'Homme et la biomédecine, ouverte à la signature, à Oviedo, le 4 avril 1997 – du Protocole additionnel à la Convention pour la protection des Droits de l'Homme et de la dignité de l'être humain à l'égard des applications de la biologie et de la médecine, portant interdiction du clonage d'êtres humains, ouvert à la signature, à Paris, le 12 janvier 1998 – du Protocole additionnel à la Convention sur les Droits de l'Homme et la biomédecine relatif à la transplantation d'organes et de tissus d'origine humaine, ouvert à la signature, à Strasbourg, le 24 janvier 2002 – du Protocole additionnel à la Convention sur les Droits de l'Homme et la biomédecine, relatif à la recherche biomédicale, ouvert à la signature, à Strasbourg, le 25 janvier 2005 et modifiant la loi du 25 novembre 1982 réglant le prélèvement de substances d'origine humaine, https://www.chd.lu/fr/dossier/5528.

566. Projet de loi 7523 portant création de l'établissement public 'Agence luxembourgeoise des médicaments et produits de santé (ALMPS)', https://www.chd.lu/fr/dossier/7523.

567. The current Article originates from the 1998 Law on hospitals. The Council of State proposed the wording stressing the need to include non-hospital research. (Avis complémentaire du Conseil d'Etat, doc. parl. 3937/07).

of the Law. Is it, however, sufficient that a human being is the subject of a research question or, in a stricter reading, does there need to be a physical or psychological intervention or any other direct interference? In a strict interpretation, non-interventional retrospective research without any impact on the medical treatment or any contact with the person concerned is not covered. What about biomedical research carried out on existing biological material or on corpses? It must be questioned whether such research is carried out 'on human beings'. In the absence of a legislative clarification of the legal status of embryos, it is further uncertain whether *in vitro* research on embryos can be considered research 'on a human being'. Third, interpreting *a contrario* the words 'with a view to developing biological or medical knowledge' leads to consider that experiments not aiming to contribute to biological or medical knowledge are not covered.

602. In practice, Article 27 is very applied broadly. With regard to the activities covered, CNER has, for instance, issued a recommendation on secondary (re-)use of existing research data or biological material gathered for a first research project, although this may be clearly considered out of its legal mission.[568]

B. General Authorisation Process

603. Article 27 states that a prior authorisation from the minister in charge of health issues is required, and the opinions of the Health Directorate and the CNER are sought beforehand.

604. All biomedical research is thus submitted to an opinion of the CNER. This Committee is nominated by the Minister of Health and Social Security. It must be composed of a majority of people with expertise in medicine, pharmacy, biology or chemistry. It further must comprise persons with expertise in the ethical, social, or legal fields. The proportion of Committee members of each sex may not be less than 40%.[569] CNER issues its opinions with complete independence.[570] A Grand-Ducal Regulation further specifies the organisation and operation of CNER, as well as the amount of the fees to be charged.[571] Neither Article 27 nor the mentioned regulation specifies according to which criteria the Committee must assess applications. While this is precisely described for medical products for human use,[572] it is left to the Committee's appreciation and internal guidelines for all other matters. Even

568. https://cner.gouvernement.lu/fr/procedures/utilisation-secondaire-echantillons.html.
569. Article 27, §2, Law on hospitals.
570. Article 27, §3, Law on hospitals.
571. Règlement grand-ducal du 26 juin 2019 relatif – à l'organisation et au fonctionnement du Comité national d'éthique de recherche; – à la fixation des taxes à percevoir pour un projet de recherche; et modifiant le règlement grand-ducal modifié du 30 mai 2005 relatif à l'application de bonnes pratiques cliniques dans la conduite d'essais cliniques de médicaments à usage humain, Mém. A – 453 du 2.07.2019, https://legilux.public.lu/eli/etat/leg/rgd/2019/06/26/a453/jo.
572. *See:* III., Clinical Trials on Medicinal Products for Human Use *infra*.

though formally speaking, Luxembourg has not ratified it, CNER indicates on its website that it applies the Oviedo Convention and its additional protocol on biomedical research.[573]

605. Depending on the nature of the research submitted, the Health Directorate further assesses the respective application regarding the requirements for medical products, medical devices or any other pertinent legislation and submits its opinion to the Minister.

606. The final authorisation is issued by the Minister of Health and Social Security, without the ministerial decision being bound by the opinion of the Health Directorate or of the CNER. If the opinion of CNER is not favourable to the project or subjects it to conditions or restrictions deemed unacceptable by the research promoter, the latter may override it after referring the matter to the Minister, whose decision is binding on the research promoter and the investigator.[574] For clinical trials on medicinal products for human use, both the Minister of Health and Social Security and the CNER must both give their approval, respectively, a positive opinion, pursuant to the EU regulation.[575]

607. Neither the opinion of CNER nor the Minister's decision releases the research sponsor or the investigator from their liability.[576] An insurance must be concluded by the sponsor or investigator, covering the liability of all those involved.[577]

III. Clinical Trials on Medicinal Products for Human Use

A. Grand-Ducal Regulation of 30 May 2005

608. A Grand-Ducal Regulation of 30 May 2005 on the application of good clinical practice in the conduct of clinical trials on medicinal products for human use, as modified, faithfully implements the modified directive 2001/20/CE on the same matter.[578] Currently, newly introduced clinical trials fall within the scope of clinical trials regulation, which entirely repeals the directive and its national implementation after the transitional period (*See:* B. Clinical Trials Regulation *infra*).

573. https://cner.gouvernement.lu/fr/statuts-legislation.html.
574. Article 27, §3, Law on hospitals.
575. *See:* III. Clinical Trials on Medicinal Products for Human Use *infra*.
576. Article 27, §3, Law on hospitals.
577. Article 27, §4, Law on hospitals.
578. Directive 2001/20/EC of the European Parliament and of the Council of 4 Apr. 2001 on the approximation of the laws, regulations and administrative provisions of the Member States relating to the implementation of good clinical practice in the conduct of clinical trials on medicinal products for human use.

609. By derogation to Article 27, for clinical trials on medicinal products for human use governed by the clinical trials directive as transposed by the Grand-Ducal Regulation, the trial must receive a favourable opinion by CNER and the Minister of Health and Social Security must give his explicit or implicit approval.[579] Implicit approval by the Minister concerns clinical trials involving medicinal products which have been granted a marketing authorisation and which are not gene therapy or somatic cell therapy, including xenogeneic cell therapy, or contain genetically modified organisms. Such clinical trials benefit from an implicit authorisation after the expiry of a period which, in principle, is sixty days.[580] CNER must issue an opinion within a period which, in principle, is sixty days.[581] The opinion must specifically address the points enumerated in points a) to k) of Article 6, §3. Article 3 specifically concerns the protection of clinical trial subjects. Article 4 governs clinical trials on minors and Article 5 clinical trials on incapacitated adults not able to give informed consent.

B. Clinical Trials Regulation (Regulation 536/2014/UE)

610. Regulation 536/2014/UE on clinical trials on medicinal products for human use ('CTR') entered into force on 31 January 2022. The regulation foresees a three-year transition period for trials submitted under the clinical trials directive (Directive 2001/20/EC) ending on 30 January 2025. Since 31 January 2023, any new clinical trial must be submitted for approval via the Clinical Trials Information System (CTIS) operated by the European Medicines Agency (EMA) as a single portal for all Member States and is governed by the CTR. Any trial approved under the clinical trials directive and its national implementation legislation, which continues to run after 30 January 2025, will need to comply with the CTR, and the sponsor must record information for CTIS.

1. Field of Application

611. The CTR applies to all clinical trials conducted (Article 1). Although not explicitly specified, the Regulation is also applicable to a mono- or multicentre trial conducted only in one Member State. The Regulation does not apply to non-interventional studies.

'Clinical trial' means a clinical study which fulfils any of the following conditions: (a) the assignment of the subject to a particular therapeutic strategy is decided in advance and does not fall within normal clinical practice of the Member State concerned; (b) the decision to prescribe the investigational medicinal products is taken together with the decision to include the subject in the clinical study; or (c) diagnostic or monitoring procedures in addition to normal clinical practice are applied to the subjects (Article 2, §2, 2 CTR). On its turn, a 'clinical study' is

579. Article 8, §1, Grand-Ducal Regulation of 30 May 2005.
580. Article 8, §3, Grand-Ducal Regulation of 30 May 2005.
581. Article 6, §5, Grand-Ducal Regulation of 30 May 2005.

defined as any investigation in relation to humans intended: (a) to discover or verify the clinical, pharmacological or other pharmacodynamic effects of one or more medicinal products; (b) to identify any adverse reactions to one or more medicinal products; or (c) to study the absorption, distribution, metabolism and excretion of one or more medicinal products; with the objective of ascertaining the safety and/or efficacy of those medicinal products (Article 2, §2, 1 CTR).

Low-intervention clinical trials are subjected to a less regulated regime. A low-intervention clinical trial is a clinical trial which fulfils all of the following conditions: (a) the investigational medicinal products, excluding placebos, are authorised; (b) according to the protocol of the clinical trial; (i) the investigational medicinal products are used in accordance with the terms of the marketing authorisation; or (ii) the use of the investigational medicinal products is evidence-based and supported by published scientific evidence on the safety and efficacy of those investigational medicinal products in any of the Member States concerned; and (c) the additional diagnostic or monitoring procedures do not pose more than minimal additional risk or burden to the safety of the subjects compared to normal clinical practice in any Member State concerned (Article 2, §2, 3 CTR).

'A non-interventional study' means a clinical study other than a clinical trial (Article 2, §2, 4 CTR).

'Investigational medicinal product' means a medicinal product which is being tested or used as a reference, including as a placebo, in a clinical trial (Article 2, §2, 5 CTR).

'Normal clinical practice' means the treatment regime typically followed to treat, prevent, or diagnose a disease or a disorder (Article 2, §2, 6 CTR).

'Subject' means an individual who participates in a clinical trial, either as a recipient of an investigational medicinal product or as a control (Article 2, §2, 17 CTR).

2. Protection of Subjects of a Clinical Trial

a. Prior Authorisation, Validation and Consolidation

612. A clinical trial is subject to scientific and ethical review and must be authorised in accordance with the Regulation (Article 4 CTR). To obtain an authorisation, the sponsor must submit an application dossier to the intended Member States concerned through the CTIS portal referred to in Article 80 CTR. The sponsor must propose one of the Member States concerned as reporting Member State. The reporting Member State must notify the sponsor and the other Member States concerned that it is the reporting Member State through the CTIS within six days from the submission of the application dossier (Article 5, §1 CTR).

The reporting Member State is responsible for Part I of the assessment report (Article 6 CTR), whereas each Member State concerned is responsible for Part II of the assessment report (Article 7 CTR).

Each Member State concerned must notify the sponsor through the CTIS as to whether the clinical trial is authorised, whether it is authorised subject to conditions, or whether authorisation is refused (Article 8, §1 CTR).

b. General Provisions Concerning the Protection of Subjects of Clinical Trials

General Principle

613. A clinical trial may be conducted only if: (a) the rights, safety, dignity, and well-being of subjects are protected and prevail over all other interests; and (b) it is designed to generate reliable and robust data (Article 3 CTR).

Proportionality (Balance Between Benefits and Risks)

614. A clinical trial may be conducted only where the anticipated benefits to the subjects or to public health justify the foreseeable risks and inconveniences and compliance with this condition is constantly monitored (Article 28, §1, a) CTR).

Right to Information of the Subject

615. A clinical trial may be conducted only where the subjects have been informed in accordance with Article 29(2)–(6) (Article 28, §1, b) CTR). Inspectors are empowered to contact the trial subjects directly, in particular in case of reasonable suspicion that they were not informed adequately of their participation in the clinical trial (Article 10.6 Commission Implementing Regulation 2017/56).

Informed Consent of the Subject

616. A clinical trial may be conducted only where the subjects have given informed consent in accordance with Article 29(1), (7) and (8) (Article 28, §1, c) CTR.

According to Article 2, §2, 21 CTR informed consent 'means a subject's free and voluntary expression of his or her willingness to participate in a particular clinical trial, after having been informed of all aspects of the clinical trial that are relevant to the subject's decision to participate or, in case of minors and of incapacitated subjects, an authorisation or agreement from their legally designated representative to include them in the clinical trial'.

In order to certify that informed consent is given freely, the investigator should take into account all relevant circumstances which might influence the decision of a potential subject to participate in a clinical trial, in particular, whether the potential subject belongs to an economically or socially disadvantaged group or is in a situation of institutional or hierarchical dependency that could inappropriately influence her or his decision to participate (Recital 31 in the Preamble).

Informed consent shall be written, dated, and signed by the person performing the interview referred to in point (c) of §2 and by the subject. Where the subject is unable to write, consent may be given and recorded through appropriate alternative means in the presence of at least one impartial witness. In that case, the witness shall sign and date the informed consent document. The subject shall be provided with a copy of the document (or the record) by which informed consent has been given. The informed consent shall be documented. Adequate time shall be given for the subject to consider his or her decision to participate in the clinical trial (Article 29, §2 CTR).

Without prejudice to the GDPR, the sponsor may ask the subject to give his or her informed consent to the use of his or her data outside the protocol of the clinical trial exclusively for scientific purposes. That consent may be withdrawn at any time by the subject or his or her legally designated representative. The scientific research making use of the data outside the protocol of the clinical trial shall be conducted in accordance with the applicable Law on Data Protection (Article 28, §2 CTR).

Any subject may, without any resulting detriment and without having to provide any justification, withdraw from the clinical trial at any time by revoking his or her informed consent. Without prejudice to the GDPR, the withdrawal of the informed consent shall not affect the activities already carried out and the use of data obtained based on informed consent before its withdrawal (Article 28, §3 CTR).

Informed Consent in Cluster Trials

617. Article 30, §3, of the Regulation provides that informed consent may be provided in a simplified way for so-called cluster trials. The Regulation does not define what cluster trials are. Recital 33 in the Preamble contains the following clarification: 'It is appropriate to allow that informed consent be obtained by simplified means for certain clinical trials where the methodology of the trial requires that groups of subjects rather than individual subjects are allocated to receive different investigational medicinal products. In those clinical trials the investigational medicinal products are used in accordance with the marketing authorisations, and the individual subject receives a standard treatment regardless of whether he or she accepts or refuses to participate in the clinical trial, or withdraws from it, so that the only consequence of non-participation is that data relating to him or her are not used for the clinical trial. Such clinical trials, which serve to compare established treatments, should always be conducted within a single Member State.'

According to Article 30, §3, a) of the Regulation informed consent may only be obtained by the simplified means if 'the simplified means for obtaining informed consent do not contradict national law in the Member State concerned'. In the absence of national legislation covering this issue, simplified means may be applied.

Respect for the Integrity, the Privacy, and the Protection of Personal Data

618. A clinical trial may be conducted only where the rights of the subjects to physical and mental integrity, privacy and the protection of the data concerning them in accordance with the GDPR are safeguarded (Article 28, §1, d) CTR).

Minimal Pain, Discomfort, Fear, and Risks

619. A clinical trial may be conducted only where the clinical trial has been designed to involve as little pain, discomfort, fear and any other foreseeable risk as possible for the subjects and both the risk threshold and the degree of distress are specifically defined in the protocol and constantly monitored (Article 28, §1, e) CTR).

Medical Care

620. A clinical trial may be conducted only where the medical care provided to the subjects is the responsibility of an appropriately qualified medical doctor or, where appropriate, a qualified dental practitioner (Article 28, §1, f) CTR).

Further Information

621. A clinical trial may be conducted only where the subject has been provided with the contact details of an entity where further information can be received in case of need (Article 28, §1, g) CTR).

No Undue Influence

622. A clinical trial may be conducted only where no undue influence, including that of a financial nature, is exerted on subjects to participate in the clinical trial (Article 28, §1, h) CTR).

Ethical Review

623. A clinical trial shall be subject to ethical review. The ethical review shall be performed by an ethics committee in accordance with the law of the Member State concerned. As seen above, the competent national ethics committee for all clinical trials in Luxembourg is CNER (Article 27, Law on hospitals). The review by the ethics committee may encompass aspects addressed in Part I of the assessment report for the authorisation of a clinical trial as referred to in Article 6 and in Part II of that assessment report as referred to in Article 7 as appropriate for each Member State concerned. Member States shall ensure that the timelines and procedures for the review by the ethics committees are compatible with the timelines and procedures set out in this Regulation for the assessment of the application for authorisation of a clinical trial (Article 4 CTR).

Protection of the Subjects During the Clinical Trial

624. The sponsor of a clinical trial and the investigator shall ensure that the clinical trial is conducted in accordance with the protocol and with the principles of good clinical practice (Article 47 CTR).

To verify that the rights, safety, and well-being of subjects are protected, that the reported data are reliable and robust and that the conduct of the clinical trial is in compliance with the requirements of this Regulation, the sponsor shall adequately monitor the conduct of a clinical trial (Article 48 CTR).

The investigator shall be a medical doctor. The CTR foresees that national legislation may allow members of a health profession to have the necessary scientific knowledge and experience in patient care to act as investigators in clinical trials. No specific national legislation currently exits. Other individuals involved in conducting a clinical trial shall be suitably qualified by education, training, and experience to perform their tasks (Article 49 CTR).

The facilities where the clinical trial is to be conducted shall be suitable for conducting the clinical trial in compliance with the requirements of this Regulation (Article 50 CTR).

The sponsor shall notify the Member States concerned about a serious breach of the Regulation or of the version of the protocol applicable at the time of the breach through the EU portal without undue delay but not later than seven days of becoming aware of that breach. For the purposes of this Article, a 'serious breach' means a breach likely to affect to a significant degree the safety and rights of a subject or the reliability and robustness of the data generated in the clinical trial (Article 52 CTR).

Without prejudice to the Member States' competence for the definition of their health policy and for the organisation and delivery of health services and medical care, the costs for investigational medicinal products, auxiliary medicinal products, medical devices used for their administration and procedures specifically required by the protocol shall not be borne by the subject (Article 92 CTR).

Damage Compensation

625. Member States shall ensure that systems for compensation for any damage suffered by a subject resulting from participation in a clinical trial conducted on their territory are in place in the form of insurance, a guarantee, or a similar arrangement that is equivalent as regards its purpose and which is appropriate to the nature and the extent of the risk. The sponsor and the investigator shall make use of this system in the form appropriate for the Member State concerned where the clinical trial is conducted (Article 76, §§1–2 CTR). Luxembourg requests that an insurance contract, which sufficiently covers the liability issues, be submitted during the evaluation process. There is no further specific national requirement in place.

Information about the Outcome of the Clinical Trial

626. Irrespective of the outcome of a clinical trial, within one year from the end of a clinical trial in all Member States concerned, the sponsor shall submit to the EU database a summary of the results of the clinical trial. The content of that summary is set out in Annex IV. It shall be accompanied by a summary written in a manner that is understandable to laypersons. The content of that summary is set out in Annex V. However, where, for scientific reasons detailed in the protocol, it is not possible to submit a summary of the results within one year, the summary of results shall be submitted as soon as it is available. In this case, the protocol shall specify when the results are going to be submitted, together with a justification (Article 37, §4 CTR).

Inspection Procedures

627. Inspectors verify compliance with the requirements of the Regulation, including protection of the rights and well-being of the clinical trial subjects (Article 6 of Commission Implementing Regulation 2017/556).[582] Pursuant to national legislation, the Pharmacist-Inspectors of the Directorate of Health, Pharmacy and Medicines Division are in charge of conducing such inspections.

582. Commission Implementing Regulation (EU) 2017/556 of 24 Mar. 2017 on the detailed arrangements for the good clinical practice inspection pursuant to Regulation (EU) No. 536/2014.

3. Clinical Trials on Incapacitated Subjects

628. In the case of incapacitated subjects who have not given, or have not refused to give, informed consent before the onset of their incapacity, a clinical trial may be conducted only where, in addition to the conditions set out in Article 28, all of the conditions provided for in Article 31 are met (Article 31, §1 CTR). 'Incapacitated subject' means a subject who is, for reasons other than the age of legal competence to give informed consent, incapable of giving informed consent according to the law of the Member State concerned (Article 2, §2, 19 CTR). When an incapacitated person has before being incapacitated given informed consent or has refused to give such consent, Article 31 does not apply because the consent or the refusal remains valid after the person concerned became incapacitated.[583]

The informed consent of the legally designated representative of the incapacitated person has to be obtained (Article 31, §1, a) CTR). In accordance with national legislation, the legal representative is either a curator or a tutor and depends on the protection regime in place (*See:* Part II., Chapter 4., §2. Adult Patients under Protective Measures). The subject shall as far as possible take part in the informed consent procedure (Article 31, §3 CTR).

Apart from the informed consent of the representative of the incapacitated person, Article 31, §1 of the Regulation provides for the following conditions.

The incapacitated subjects have received the information referred to in Article 29(2) in a way that is adequate in view of their capacity to understand it (Article 31, §1, b). The explicit wish of an incapacitated subject who is capable of forming an opinion and assessing the information referred to in Article 29(2) to refuse participation in, or to withdraw from, the clinical trial at any time is respected by the investigator (Article 31, §1, c). No incentives or financial inducements are given to the subjects or their legally designated representatives, except for compensation for expenses and loss of earnings directly related to the participation in the clinical trial (Article 31, §1, d). The clinical trial is essential with respect to incapacitated subjects and data of comparable validity cannot be obtained in clinical trials on persons able to give informed consent or by other research methods (Article 31, §1, e). The clinical trial relates directly to a medical condition from which the subject suffers (Article 31, §1, f). There are scientific grounds for expecting that participation in the clinical trial will produce: (i) a direct benefit to the incapacitated subject outweighing the risks and burdens involved; or (ii) some benefit for the population represented by the incapacitated subject concerned when the clinical trial relates directly to the life-threatening or debilitating medical condition from which the subject suffers and such trial will pose only minimal risk to, and will impose minimal burden on, the incapacitated subject concerned in comparison with the standard treatment of the incapacitated subject's condition (Article 31, §1, g CTR).

Point (g) (ii) of §1 shall be without prejudice to more stringent national rules prohibiting the conduct of those clinical trials on incapacitated subjects where there are no scientific grounds to expect that participation in the clinical trial will produce a

583. J. McHale, 'Reforming the EU Clinical Trials Directive: Streamlining Processes or a Radical "New" Agenda?', 20 *Eur. J. Health L.* (363), 375 (2013).

direct benefit to the subject outweighing the risks and burdens involved (Article 31, §2 CTR). The CTL does not provide for more stringent rules than the Regulation.

Where the subjects are incapacitated subjects, specific consideration shall be given to the assessment of the application for authorisation of a clinical trial on the basis of expertise in the relevant disease and the patient population concerned or after taking advice on clinical, ethical and psychosocial questions in the field of the relevant disease and the patient population concerned (Article 10, §2 CTR).

4. Clinical Trials on Minors

629. A clinical trial on minors may be conducted only where, in addition to the conditions set out in Article 28, all the conditions provided for in Article 32 are met (Article 32, §1 CTR). The first condition is that the informed consent of their legally designated representative has been obtained (Article 32, §1, a) CTR). According to national legislation, informed consent of the two parents is generally necessary. By exception, a Court decision may have assigned parental authority to one parent or to a guardian (*See:* Part II., Chapter 4., §1. Minor Patients). The minor shall take part in the informed consent procedure in a way adapted to his or her age and mental maturity (Article 32, §2). If, during a clinical trial, the minor reaches the age of legal competence to give informed consent (18 years), his or her express informed consent shall be obtained before that subject can continue to participate in the clinical trial (Article 32, §3 CTR).

The other conditions provided for in Article 32, §1, of the Regulation are: the minors have received the information referred to in Article 29(2) in a way adapted to their age and mental maturity and from investigators or members of the investigating team who are trained or experienced in working with children (Article 32, §1, b CTR). The explicit wish of a minor who is capable of forming an opinion and assessing the information referred to in Article 29(2) to refuse participation in, or to withdraw from, the clinical trial at any time is respected by the investigator (Article 32, §1, c CTR). No incentives or financial inducements are given to the subject or his or her legally designated representative except for compensation for expenses and loss of earnings directly related to the participation in the clinical trial (Article 32, §1, d CTR). The clinical trial is intended to investigate treatments for a medical condition that only occurs in minors, or the clinical trial is essential with respect to minors to validate data obtained in clinical trials on persons able to give informed consent or by other research methods (Article 32, §1, e CTR). The clinical trial either relates directly to a medical condition from which the minor concerned suffers or is of such a nature that it can only be carried out on minors (Article 32, §1, f CTR). There are scientific grounds for expecting that participation in the clinical trial will produce: (i) a direct benefit for the minor concerned outweighing the risks and burdens involved; or (ii) some benefit for the population represented by the minor concerned and such a clinical trial will pose only minimal risk to, and will impose minimal burden on, the minor concerned in comparison with the standard treatment of the minor's condition (Article 32, §1, g CTR).

Where the subjects are minors, specific consideration shall be given to the assessment of the application for authorisation of a clinical trial on the basis of paediatric expertise or after taking advice on clinical, ethical and psychosocial problems in the field of paediatrics (Article 10, §1 CTR).

5. Clinical Trials on Pregnant or Breastfeeding Women

630. A clinical trial on pregnant or breastfeeding women may be conducted only where, in addition to the conditions set out in Article 28, the following conditions are met: the clinical trial has the potential to produce a direct benefit for the pregnant or breastfeeding woman concerned, or her embryo, foetus or child after birth, outweighing the risks and burdens involved (Article 33, a CTR). Or if such clinical trial has no direct benefit for the pregnant or breastfeeding woman concerned, or her embryo, foetus or child after birth, it can be conducted only if: (i) a clinical trial of comparable effectiveness cannot be carried out on women who are not pregnant or breastfeeding; (ii) the clinical trial contributes to the attainment of results capable of benefitting pregnant or breastfeeding women or other women in relation to reproduction or other embryos, foetuses or children; and (iii) the clinical trial poses a minimal risk to, and imposes a minimal burden on, the pregnant or breastfeeding woman concerned, her embryo, foetus or child after birth (Article 33, b CTR). Where research is undertaken on breastfeeding women, particular care is taken to avoid any adverse impact on the health of the child (Article 33, c CTR). No incentives or financial inducements are given to the subject except for compensation for expenses and loss of earnings directly related to participation in the clinical trial (Article 33, d CTR).

Where the subjects are pregnant or breastfeeding women, specific consideration shall be given to the assessment of the application for authorisation of a clinical trial on the basis of expertise in the relevant condition and the population represented by the subject concerned (Article 10, §3 CTR).

6. Clinical Trials on Other Vulnerable Subjects

631. Member States may maintain additional measures regarding persons performing mandatory military service, persons deprived of liberty, persons who, due to a judicial decision, cannot take part in clinical trials, or persons in residential care institutions (Article 34 CTR).

Recital 35 in the Preamble gives the following clarification: 'Persons performing mandatory military service, persons deprived of liberty, persons who, due to a judicial decision, cannot take part in clinical trials, and persons, who due to their age, disability or state of health are reliant on care and for that reason accommodated in residential care institutions, that is accommodations providing uninterrupted assistance for persons who necessitate such assistance, are in a situation of subordination or factual dependency and therefore may require specific protective measures. Member States should be allowed to maintain such additional measures.'

If, according to the protocol, a clinical trial provides for the participation of specific groups or subgroups of subjects, where appropriate, specific consideration shall be given to the assessment of the application for authorisation of that clinical trial on the basis of expertise in the population represented by the subjects concerned (Article 10, §4 CTR).

7. Clinical Trials in Emergency Situations

632. By way of derogation from points (b) and (c) of Article 28, §1, from points (a) and (b) of Article 31, §1, and from points (a) and (b) of Article 32, §1, informed consent to participate in a clinical trial may be obtained, and information on the clinical trial may be given, after the decision to include the subject in the clinical trial, provided that this decision is taken at the time of the first intervention on the subject, in accordance with the protocol for that clinical trial and that all of the following conditions are fulfilled: (a) due to the urgency of the situation, caused by a sudden life-threatening or other sudden serious medical condition, the subject is unable to provide prior informed consent and to receive prior information on the clinical trial; (b) there are scientific grounds to expect that participation of the subject in the clinical trial will have the potential to produce a direct clinically relevant benefit for the subject resulting in a measurable health-related improvement alleviating the suffering and/or improving the health of the subject, or in the diagnosis of its condition; (c) it is not possible within the therapeutic window to supply all prior information to and obtain prior informed consent from his or her legally designated representative; (d) the investigator certifies that he or she is not aware of any objections to participate in the clinical trial previously expressed by the subject; (e) the clinical trial relates directly to the subject's medical condition because of which it is not possible within the therapeutic window to obtain prior informed consent from the subject or from his or her legally designated representative and to supply prior information, and the clinical trial is of such a nature that it may be conducted exclusively in emergency situations; (f) the clinical trial poses a minimal risk to, and imposes a minimal burden on, the subject in comparison with the standard treatment of the subject's condition (Article 35, §1 CTR).

Following an intervention pursuant to §1, informed consent in accordance with Article 29 shall be sought to continue the participation of the subject in the clinical trial, and information on the clinical trial shall be given in accordance with the following requirements: (a) regarding incapacitated subjects and minors, the informed consent shall be sought by the investigator from his or her legally designated representative without undue delay and the information referred to in Article 29, §2, shall be given as soon as possible to the subject and to his or her legally designated representative; (b) regarding other subjects, the informed consent shall be sought by the investigator without undue delay from the subject or his or her legally designated representative, whichever is sooner and the information referred to in Article 29, §2, shall be given as soon as possible to the subject or his or her legally designated representative, whichever is sooner. For the purposes of point (b), where informed consent has been obtained from the legally designated representative, informed consent to continue the participation in the clinical trial shall be obtained from the subject as soon as he or she is capable of giving informed consent (Article 35, §2 CTR).

If the subject or, where applicable, his or her legally designated representative does not give consent, he or she shall be informed of the right to object to the use of data obtained from the clinical trial (Article 35, §3 CTR).

In any application for authorisation of a clinical trial in emergency situations, specific consideration shall be given to the circumstances of the conduct of the clinical trial (Article 10, §5 CTR).

IV. Medical Devices

633. Medical devices may be part of an investigation falling under the scope of Article 27 of the Law on hospitals.[584] The grand-ducal regulations applicable to the different types of medical devices contain further provisions. According to Article 10 of the amended Grand-Ducal Regulation of 5 February 1993 on active implantable medical devices, for devices intended for clinical investigations, the manufacturer or his representative in the EU must notify a declaration to the Minister for Health at least sixty days before the start of the investigations. This declaration must be according to Annex VI of the regulation. The clinical investigations in question may, however, begin before the expiry of the period of sixty days, if CNER has issued a favourable opinion on the programme of investigations in question, including the clinical investigation protocol. A comparable notification process and further requirements are foreseen by Article 13 of the amended Grand-Ducal Regulation of 11 August 1996 on medical devices and Annexes VIII, section 2.2, and X thereof.

V. Human Bodily Material

A. Organs

634. The modified Law of 25 November 1982 on organs intended for transplantation applies to removal for scientific purposes. Organs may not be removed from living donors for exclusively scientific purposes.[585] Removal of organs from a deceased adult is, in general, under an opt-out regime.[586]

B. Tissues and Cells

635. The Law of 1 August 2007 on human tissues and cells intended for human applications applies to trials with an application of tissue and cell to the human body, but not to *in vitro* research with tissues and cells and not to animal models. There is no specific framework for the latter. An opt-out regime generally applies to 'left-over' tissues and cells removed during a medical procedure carried out in the

584. *See:* para. 600 *supra.*
585. *See:* para. 553 *supra.*
586. *See:* para. 563 *supra.*

interest of the person undergoing it. Pursuant to Article 10 of the Law of 1 August 2007 on human tissues and cells, Articles 6 to 13 of the Law on organs are applicable to the removal of tissue and cells from deceased persons.[587]

636. A woman who has undergone a termination of pregnancy may give her written consent to the removal, preservation, and use of embryonic or foetal tissues or cells after having received appropriate information on the purposes of such removal. This information must be given after the woman has already decided to terminate her pregnancy. Removal from minors is not licit for research purposes.[588]

C. *Supernumerary Embryos, Gametes and Stem Cells*

637. Both the Law proposal on biomedical research and the proposal aiming to ratify the Oviedo Convention[589] (2006) proposed to ban research on supernumerary embryos and gametes. The CNE has been in favour of allowing research on supernumerary embryos and the Council of State formally opposed the wording of the proposed ban. A draft framework for research on supernumerary embryos was advised favourably by the CNE in 2013.[590] None of these initiatives have been adopted so far. Donation of supremacy embryos is currently not accepted by the unique Luxembourg MAP laboratory and remains thus de facto banned.

§9. Declaration of Death and Causes of Death, Autopsies and Mortal Remains

I. Declaration of Death and Causes of Death

638. According to the Civil Code,[591] deaths must be declared to the civil registrar of the commune where a death takes place. The declaration is made by a close

---

587. *See:* §6, II., Tissues and Cells Intended for Human Applications *supra*.
588. Article 11, §2, Law on human tissues and cells intended for human application.
589. Projet de loi 5552 relatif à la recherche biomédicale, https://www.chd.lu/fr/techdossier/172; Projet de loi 5528 portant approbation – de la Convention pour la protection des Droits de l'Homme et de la dignité de l'être humain à l'égard des applications de la biologie et de la médecine: Convention sur les Droits de l'Homme et la biomédecine, ouverte à la signature, à Oviedo, le 4 avril 1997 – du Protocole additionnel à la Convention pour la protection des Droits de l'Homme et de la dignité de l'être humain à l'égard des applications de la biologie et de la médecine, portant interdiction du clonage d'êtres humains, ouvert à la signature, à Paris, le 12 janvier 1998 – du Protocole additionnel à la Convention sur les Droits de l'Homme et la biomédecine relatif à la transplantation d'organes et de tissus d'origine humaine, ouvert à la signature, à Strasbourg, le 24 janvier 2002 – du Protocole additionnel à la Convention sur les Droits de l'Homme et la biomédecine, relatif à la recherche biomédicale, ouvert à la signature, à Strasbourg, le 25 janvier 2005 et modifiant la loi du 25 novembre 1982 réglant le prélèvement de substances d'origine humaine, https://www.chd.lu/fr/dossier/5528.
590. *La recherche sur les embryons surnuméraires au Luxembourg*, Avis No. 24, Commission consultative nationale d'éthique (2013), https://cne.public.lu/dam-assets/fr/publications/avis/Avis_24.pdf; Schwebag, M. & Stoffel, D., *L'embryon humain en droit luxembourgeois*, RLDS, No. 3 (2020).
591. Articles 77–87, Code civil.

relative, a neighbour, or the person in whose home a person died. In case of a death in a hospital or any other healthcare institution, the declaration must be made within twenty-four hours by the management of the institution. The declarant must submit a certificate of death drawn up by the attending physician or any other physician charged thereof. The reporting of death causes to a medical inspector of the Directorate of Health is further mandatory.[592]

639. A Grand-Ducal Regulation establishes the compulsory procedure to follow and the mandatory official form to be used by physicians in view of declaration of death and of causes of death.[593] The mandatory form to be used consists of three sheets. The first sheet is used during declaration of the death to the civil registrar. The civil registrar, after receiving the declaration, detaches this sheet intended for him. He or she sends the remaining part of the declaration, without opening it, to the Directorate of Health. These remaining two sheets are used to report the causes of death and draw statistics thereof.

640. The mandatory form requests to certify whether there are signs or indications of violent death or other circumstances giving rise to suspicion. In such circumstances, police must be informed without delay and an enquiry is opened.

II. Autopsies

641. An autopsy may be ordered as part of an investigation or may be requested by a physician.

642. When there are signs or indications of a violent death or other circumstances giving rise to suspicion, an enquiry is opened. The examining magistrate is leading the inquiry with the police. He generally orders a forensic autopsy. The department of forensic medicine at LNS is generally charged with carrying out such autopsies.[594] The next of kin may not be denied the right to see the body of the deceased, even if a forensic autopsy is ordered. However, the examining magistrate who ordered the autopsy decides when the body of the deceased may be shown to them.[595]

643. If no forensic autopsy was ordered, an autopsy may further be requested by a physician or at the next of kin. Such autopsies full under the scope of the Law of 17 November 1958 concerning autopsies, moulding and the use of human cadavers

592. Article 6, Loi du 31 décembre 1952, portant abrogation de la loi du 18 mai 1902, concernant l'institution des médecins-inspecteurs et l'exercice de leurs attributions et nouvelle organisation du service des médecins-inspecteurs, Mém. A- 2 du 14.01.1953, https://legilux.public.lu/eli/etat/leg/loi/1952/12/31/n1/jo.
593. Règlement grand-ducal modifié du 20 juin 1963 rendant obligatoire la déclaration des causes de décès, Mém. A – 43 du 27 juillet 1963, https://legilux.public.lu/eli/etat/leg/rgd/1963/06/20/n1/jo.
594. https://lns.lu/en/departement/departement-of-forensic-medicine/.
595. Article 44, Code de procédure pénale.

for scientific or therapeutic purposes.[596] In general, such autopsies can only take place twenty-four hours after the death and after the declaration of death to the civil registrar. They may only be done with prior authorisation of the deceased or, in the absence of a refusal by the deceased, with authorisation of his parents or spouse, in the order in which they are called to the succession. A written authorisation from a medical inspector of the Directorate of Health is required. In hospitals, such autopsies may, even without the authorisation of the medical inspector and in the absence of any consent from the parents or spouse, be carried out without delay if there is a scientific or therapeutic interest in doing so, unless the deceased, the parents or the spouse have manifested their opposition. The death must first be certified by two physicians, who are required to draw up a report certifying the date and time of death, the reasons for and circumstances of the autopsy and the completion of all prescribed formalities. A copy of the report must be sent to a medical inspector of the Directorate of Health.

III. Burial, Cremation and Mortal Remains

644. The mandatory form used by physicians to certify a death request to state whether there are signs or indications of a violent death or other circumstances giving rise to suspicion. In such circumstances, am enquiry is opened. Burial or incineration may then only take place with the agreement of the State Prosecutor. A judicial autopsy is generally ordered.

645. A Law of 1 August 1972 regulates the burial and cremation of mortal remains.[597] Human bodies may only be buried in cemeteries. Cremation may only take place based on a document expressing the deceased's wish to be cremated or, failing this, at the request of the family. Cremation needs an authorisation by the civil registrar of the place of death, which must be refused in circumstances giving rise to suspicion.

646. A Grand-Ducal Decree of 14 February 1913 regulates the transport of corpses.[598] Transport is subject to a permit. This permit is issued by the civil registrar of the commune in whose territory the death occurred, generally when the death is declared. It is issued by a medical inspector of the Directorate of Health when the transport is carried out by rail, requires the crossing of a border, or when its purpose is to bury an exhumed corpse in another cemetery.

---

596. The provisions of this law which relate to the removal of organs and other human bodily materials are repealed. Loi modifiée du 17 novembre 1958 concernant l'autopsie, le moulage, ainsi que l'utilisation de cadavres humains dans un intérêt scientifique ou thérapeutique, Mém. A – 61 du 4.12.1985, https://legilux.public.lu/eli/etat/leg/loi/1958/11/17/n1/jo.

597. Loi du 1er août 1972 portant réglementation de l'inhumation et de l'incinération des dépouilles mortelles.

598. Arrêté grand-ducal du 14 février 1913 réglant le transport des cadavres.

Part III. The Physician in Relation to the Healthcare System

Chapter 1. Collegial Relationships

§1. Professional Duties Towards Colleagues

647. Articles 80–83 of the Code of Medical Ethics concern the duty of 'Good fellowship among physicians'. Physicians must demonstrate loyal professional collaboration when working with colleagues or with other health professionals in the diagnosis and treatment of the patient.[599] Physicians shall maintain good fraternal relations and support each other in adversity, demonstrating solidarity and mutual assistance in the accomplishment of their medical mission. It is prohibited to calumny or defame a colleague, to speak bad of him or to echo remarks likely to harm him.[600] A disagreement between physicians shall not give rise to public polemics. In case of a dispute, physicians are required to seek conciliation or mediation, if needed, through the Medical College.[601] Relations between physicians must be marked by courtesy and loyalty. Physicians must refrain from any action likely to harm a colleague.[602]

648. According to Article 83, except for the patient's express free request, physicians may not divert patients from their usual physician. Article 83 considers the following circumstances as a breach of this duty: as an on-call or replacement physician, the act of continuing to treat a patient for whom the physician on-call or on replacement is not the usual physician; as a specialist, continuing to treat a patient after giving a specialist opinion and no longer referring the patient to his usual treating physician; as a hospital physician, continuing to treat a patient on an outpatient basis even though the treatment after hospitalisation could be continued by the patient's usual physician.

599. Article 80, Code of Medical Ethics.
600. Article 81, Code of Medical Ethics.
601. Article 82, Code of Medical Ethics.
602. Article 83, Code of Medical Ethics.

§2. Associations of Physicians

649. Private group practices traditionally regrouped only physicians active in the same field, as deontological rules were opposed to multidisciplinary regroupings. This has, however, evolved over the last decade. Since 2013, the Code of Medical Ethics no longer limit associations of physicians to an association of GPs or of physicians of the same medical specialty.

650. According to Article 110 of the Code of Medical Ethics, physicians may create associations. Such associations should be regulated by a contractual agreement submitted for prior approval to the Medical College. According to Article 111, the following types of associations may be concluded:

- association with sharing of costs without pooling of medical fees;
- association with sharing of costs and pooling of medical fees between physicians in the same speciality;
- association with sharing of costs and pooling of medical fees for physicians in related specialities, subject to authorisation by the competent authorities (CNS);
- a temporary association with shared costs but no pooling of medical fees between established physicians and physicians in training who hold a temporary authorisation to practise in the same discipline.

651. Article 113 prohibits any association, direct or via an intermediary, with third parties who are not physicians or companies, in particular any agreement between third parties or companies in which a counterpart depends on a physicians percentage of turnover; any agreement in the form of commercialisation of medical activity involving remuneration (salaries) of the physician or payment of expenses other than that authorised in an association; any incorporation of a company or third party which executes in the association the rights and obligations of an associated physician; any agreement which requires the physician to pay a lump sum which is not justified by the operating requirements of the association or by the transfer of tangible or intangible assets and which subjects the doctor to the payment of an entry fee to an association or of an indemnity in full discharge in the event of leaving the association; any non-competition agreement; any termination agreement with an abnormally short period of advance notice (less than one month).

652. According to Article 114, the association contract must comprise:

(1) safeguards ensuring the free choice of the physician;
(2) safeguards ensuring professional independence of each associate;
(3) safeguards ensuring protection of professional secrecy;
(4) professional and civil liability insurance for physicians and staff;
(5) allocation of fees and expenses according to the form of association: (a) association with pooling of fees and sharing of costs (rental of premises and installations, operating costs); (b) association with shared costs but no pooling of fees;

(6) working hours, organisation of leave, scientific activities, continuing training and continuing professional development;
(7) regulations in the event of illness, pregnancy, disability, death or other causes of absence;
(8) procedures for the admission and departure of a physician from the association;
(9) procedures for the operation of the association in the event of disciplinary sanctions affecting an associate member's right to practise;
(10) obligation to notify associate members of any disciplinary, criminal or administrative sanction;
(11) procedures for settling disputes;
(12) procedures for the early dissolution of the association: transfer of files, continuity of care;
(13) a non-competition clause obliging a member who leaves the association not to set up in a place whose immediate proximity could constitute a factor of direct competition, except with the written agreement of the associate(s) or the authorisation of the Medical College;
(14) a declaration in honour of the absence of a counter-letter.

653. Pursuant to Article 8 of the Agreement between CNS and AMMD, concluded pursuant to Articles 61 et seq. of CSS, the practice as an association is only binding on the health insurance if the associated physicians all practise the same medical discipline.[603] It results thereof that associations of different specialities may not proceed to a pooling of fees through a shared common CNS identification code.

654. According to Article 20 of the Law on the medical profession, any agreement between members of the medical and dental professions or between them and a hospital providing for the sharing of medical fees or for discounts on prescribed medicines shall be null and void, without prejudice to the provisions concerning the remuneration of physicians laid down by the organic laws relating to certain hospital establishments.

655. The Medical College has elaborated standard contract terms for medical associations, which consider these points. In practice, the restrictions mentioned, which aim to avoid commercialisation of medicine, are partly disregarded, and the first private healthcare centre financed by private investors opened.[604]

603. Convention entre la Caisse nationale de santé et l'Association des médecins et médecins-dentistes, conclue en exécution de l'article 61 et suivants du Code des assurances sociales, https://cns.public.lu/en/legislations/ammd_dent/cns-ammd-med-convention.html.
604. *See:* Ch. 3., §2. Private Healthcare Centres and Hospital Antennas *infra.*

Chapter 2. Relationship with Other Professions

§1. PHARMACISTS

656. The practice of pharmacy is regulated by the amended Law of 31 July 1991 determining the conditions for authorisation to practise the profession of pharmacist,[605] hereinafter 'Law on the profession of pharmacist'. The exercise of pharmacy is subject to a specific authorisation delivered by the Minister of Health and Social Security.[606] The authorisation procedure is comparable to the procedure described for the authorisation to practise medicine. Temporary service provision by nationals of an EU member country legally established in an EU member country other than Luxembourg is subject to a notification.[607]

657. The Medical College functions as a common professional order for physicians, dentists, pharmacists, and psychotherapists. It maintains the ordinal register for the profession of pharmacist.[608] The Medical College is mandated to establish a Code of Professional Ethics for pharmacists.[609] The current Code of Deontology for Pharmacists has been approved by the Ministerial Order of 11 July 2011.[610] The functioning of the Medical College and the exercise of disciplinary action against pharmacists obey the modified Law of 8 June 1999 relative to the Medical College as described supra for physicians.[611]

658. Pharmacists exercise an autonomous health profession. Pharmacists have a legal monopoly on the practice of pharmaceutical activities. Article 45, §2, of the amended Law on the recognition of professional qualifications defines the following pharmaceutical activities reserved to pharmacists duly authorised: (a) preparation of the pharmaceutical form of medicinal products; (b) manufacturing and control of medicinal products; (c) control of medicinal products in a laboratory for the control of medicinal products; (d) storage, preservation and distribution of medicinal products at the wholesale stage; (e) supply, preparation, testing, storage, distribution and dispensing of safe and effective medicinal products of the required quality in pharmacies open to the public; (f) preparation, control, storage and dispensing of safe and effective medicinal products of the required quality in hospitals; (g) providing information and advice on medicinal products, including their correct use; (h) reporting to the competent authorities on the number of adverse reactions to pharmaceutical products; (i) personalised assistance for self-medicating patients; (j) contributing to local or national public health campaigns.

605. Loi du 31 juillet 1991 déterminant les conditions d'autorisation d'exercer la profession de pharmacien, Mém. A – 60 du 29 août 1991, https://legilux.public.lu/eli/etat/leg/loi/1991/07/31/n3/jo.
606. Article 1, Law on the profession of pharmacist.
607. Article 12bis and 12ter, Law on the profession of pharmacist.
608. Article 5, Law on the profession of pharmacist.
609. Article 9, Law on the profession of pharmacist.
610. Arrêté ministériel du 11 juillet 2011 approuvant le code de déontologie des pharmaciens édicté par le Collège médical, Mem. A – 160 du 01.08.2011, http://data.legilux.public.lu/eli/etat/leg/amin/2011/07/11/n1/jo.
611. *See:* Part I., Ch. 4., §1. Medical College and Rules of Professional Conduct *supra*.

659. The exercise, even free of charge, of such a pharmaceutical activity by a person not authorised to practise constitutes an illegal practice of pharmacy. By derogation, the following activities are authorised: the dispensing of medicinal products for veterinary use by veterinary surgeons in accordance with the legislation in force; the possession of medicinal products for personal use; the provision of information and advice on medicinal products and the supply of samples of medicinal products to physicians, dentists, veterinary surgeons and pharmacists; the practice of the pharmaceutical activities by pharmacy students who are nationals of an EU Member State undergoing training under the responsibility of a pharmacist authorised to practice the profession in Luxembourg.[612] Illegal exercise of pharmacy is a criminal offence.[613]

660. The authorisation to practise, as well as the notification of the temporary service provider, entitles to use the official protected title 'pharmacien', as well as the titles 'Apdikter' and 'Apotheker'.[614] Undue use of one of these professional titles constitutes usurpation and is an offence.[615]

661. Like for the medical profession, specific legislation attributes further domains of activity to pharmacists. During the COVID-19 pandemic, the possibility for pharmacists to vaccinate against COVID-19 within a pharmacy open to the public was introduced. While most measures to combat COVID-19 have meanwhile been abolished, this measure has been maintained after the end of the pandemic.[616] The persons to vaccinate must be over 16 years and have no known allergy against an excipient of the vaccine and no known reaction against a previous COVID-19 vaccination. The pharmacist must further have been specifically authorised to vaccinate against COVID-19 by the Minister of Health and Social Security after undergoing a short specific training course. No prescription by a physician is required to vaccinate.

662. The simultaneous practice of pharmacy and the medical profession (medicine, veterinary medicine, or dentistry) is forbidden, even in the case of persons holding diplomas authorising them to practise each of these professions.[617]

663. By derogation to the monopoly for the practice of pharmaceutical activities, veterinarians are authorised to hold a stock of veterinary medicines and use them for the treatment of the animals under their care. Furthermore, physicians, dentists and veterinarians are authorised to keep an emergency kit of medicines.[618] The

612. Article 13, Law on the profession of pharmacist.
613. Article 14, Law on the profession of pharmacist.
614. Article 8, §1, Law on the profession of pharmacist.
615. Article 15, Law on the profession of pharmacist.
616. Article 10bis, Loi modifiée du 17 juillet 2020 relative à certaines mesures de suivi de l'évolution du virus SARS-CoV-2 et de lutte contre la maladie Covid-19, https://legilux.public.lu/eli/etat/leg/loi/2020/07/17/a624/consolide/20230701.
617. Article 12, Law on the profession of pharmacist; Art. 38, Law concerning the exercise of the medical profession.
618. Article 4, §6 and §7, Law of 25 Nov. 1975 on the supply of medicines to the public.

list of medicinal products that may be carried as part of the emergency kit, the storage conditions, and the management of the medicinal products included are supposed to be specified by a Grand-Ducal Regulation; no such regulation has, however, been adopted so far. Besides these emergency medicines, physicians may not hold a stock of medicinal products.

§2. Psychotherapists

664. The practice of psychotherapy is regulated by the amended Law of 14 July 2015, creating the profession of psychotherapist,[619] hereinafter 'Law on the profession of psychotherapist'. The exercise of psychotherapy is subject to a specific authorisation delivered by the Minister of Health and Social Security.[620] The Law fixes the general minimal criteria for psychotherapy training that is required to be authorised.[621] Physicians already authorised as specialists in psychiatry, neuropsychiatry or child psychiatry may be authorised as psychotherapists after completion of an abridged (450h) complementary training in psychotherapy.[622] The authorisation procedure is comparable to the one described for the authorisation to practise medicine. The exercise of psychotherapy by a person not authorised to practise constitutes an illegal practice of psychotherapy and is an offence.[623] The authorisation to practise allows using the official protected title 'psychothérapeute'[624] Undue use of the professional title constitutes usurpation of the protected title and is an offence.[625]

665. The Law on the profession of psychotherapist created a 'Scientific council of psychotherapy' collaborating in determining establishing recognised psychological means, setting up training in psychotherapy, participating in the recognition of foreign diplomas and giving advice on other questions related to psychotherapy, including professional ethics.[626] The Medical College functions as a common professional order for physicians, dentists, pharmacists, and psychotherapists. The Medical College maintains the ordinal register for the profession of psychotherapist.[627] In their professional practice, psychotherapists are subject to the ethical and disciplinary action of the Medical College.[628] The Medical College is mandated to establish a Code of professional ethics for psychotherapists. The current Code of

619. Loi modifiée du 14 juillet 2015 portant création de la profession de psychothérapeute, Mém. A – 136 du 21 juillet 2015, https://legilux.public.lu/eli/etat/leg/loi/2015/07/14/n1/jo.
620. Article 2, Law on the profession of psychotherapist.
621. Article 2, Law on the profession of psychotherapist.
622. Article 2ter, Law on the profession of psychotherapist.
623. Article 14, Law on the profession of psychotherapist.
624. Article 3, §1, Law on the profession of psychotherapist.
625. Article 12, Law on the profession of psychotherapist.
626. Article 6, Law on the profession of psychotherapist.
627. Article 7, §3–§9, Law on the profession of psychotherapist.
628. Article 7, §1, Law on the profession of psychotherapist.

Professional Ethics for the profession of psychotherapist was adopted on 31 October 2018.[629] The functioning of the Medical College and the exercise of disciplinary action against psychotherapists obey the modified Law of 8 June 1999 relative to the Medical College as described for physicians.[630]

666. Psychotherapists have a legal monopoly on the practice of psychotherapy. According to Article 1, a psychotherapist 'makes exclusive use of recognised psychological means in order to treat mental disorders in adults, adolescents and children'. Psychotherapy is further defined as 'psychological treatment for a mental disorder, behavioural disturbance or any other problem causing psychological suffering or distress, with the aim of promoting beneficial changes in the patient's cognitive, emotional, or behavioural functioning, interpersonal system, personality, or state of health. This treatment goes beyond the provision of psychological help to deal with common difficulties, or a counselling or support activity'. Further to the entry into force of the law, psychologists not recognised as psychotherapists continue to exercise as an unregulated profession. It results from the last phrase of the definition that psychological counselling and support activities do not infringe on the monopoly of psychotherapists. Such psychologists may, however, not strive to treat a mental disorder.

667. Psychotherapists practise their profession independently.[631] Psychotherapists are thus autonomous from physicians and free to determine the psychotherapeutic procedures together with their patients without having to follow a medical prescription with regard to the psychotherapeutic means they apply. At the same time, not all psychotherapeutic procedures are eligible for reimbursement by social security. In order to be reimbursed, psychotherapy must currently be prescribed by a physician who certifies that there is no medical contraindication to psychotherapy. This prescription is not requested for reimbursement of the introductory psychotherapy session; however, a medical prescription must be issued within ninety days of the introductory session for which reimbursement is claimed.

§3. Law on the Practice and Revalorisation of Certain Health Professions

I. Introduction

668. Besides dentistry, considered part of medicine, only pharmacists (§1) and psychotherapists (§2) are governed by a specific Law. The amended Law of 26 March

629. The 2015 Law establishing the profession of psychotherapist does not foresee a ministerial validation or an official publication procedure. The Code is however made available online by the Medical College: http://www.collegemedical.lu/Doc/Code_de_deontologie_des_psychotherapeutes_2018.pdf.
630. *See:* Part I., Ch. 4., §1. Medical College and Rules of Professional Conduct *supra*.
631. Article 5, Law on the profession of psychotherapist.

1992 on the practice and revalorisation of certain health professions, in combination with Grand-Ducal Regulations adopted for its implementation, regulated until recently all other 'paramedical' professions recognised as healthcare professions. On 4 June 2021, the Constitutional Court declared unconstitutional Articles 1 and 7 of this Law because, in matters reserved to the Law, such as regulating a healthcare profession, the essential part of the normative framework must result directly from the Law, including the purposes, conditions, and modalities according to which the less essential elements may be regulated by the lower norm. Only minor issues may be relegated to regulations. The Court held that the Law may not unconditionally delegate the determination of the status, attributions, and rules of practice of a healthcare profession to Grand-Ducal Regulations. To avoid the legal vacuum created, the Constitutional Court postponed the effects of the declaration of unconstitutionality until 30 June 2023 to allow the legislator to remedy the situation.[632] On 29 June 2023, Parliament adopted an amendment to the Law of 26 March 1992 to formally comply with the decision of the Constitutional Court by transferring the substantial elements of the former regulations into annexes of the amended Law.[633] This necessary reform left, however, unchanged the substantial content of the framework. It is generally accepted that a reform of the partly outdated framework is desirable. The Government elected in October 2023 agreed to redefine the roles and responsibilities of the different health professions.[634]

II. Healthcare Professions Covered

669. According to Article 1, §1, the Law applies to the following healthcare professions: (1) nurse ('infirmier'); (2) anaesthetics and intensive care nurse ('infirmier en anesthésie et réanimation'); (3) paediatric nurse ('infirmier en pédiatrie'); (4) psychiatric nurse ('infirmier psychiatrique'); (5) head nurse ('infirmier gradué'); (6) midwife ('sage-femme'); (7) healthcare assistant ('aide-soignant'); (8) medical technical assistant ('assistant technique médical'); (9) laboratory assistant ('laborantin'); (10) social and hygiene worker ('assistant d'hygiène sociale'); (11) social worker ('assistant social'); (12) curative pedagogue ('pédagogue curatif'); (13) dietician ('diététicien'); (14) occupational therapist ('ergothérapeute'); (15) psychomotor therapist ('rééducateur en psychomotricité'); (16) masseur ('masseur'); (17) physiotherapist ('masseur-kinésithérapeute'); (18) osteopath ('ostéopathe'); (19) speech therapist ('orthophoniste)'; (20) orthoptist ('orthoptiste'); (21) chiropodist ('podologue').

632. C. Const., 4 juin 2021, Arrêt No. 0166, https://legilux.public.lu/eli/etat/leg/acc/2021/06/04/a440/jo.
633. Loi du 29 juin 2023 portant modification de la loi modifiée du 26 mars 1992 sur l'exercice et la revalorisation de certaines professions de santé, Mém. A – 334 du 29.06.2023., https://legilux.public.lu/eli/etat/leg/loi/2023/06/29/a334/jo, doc. parl. 8108, https://www.chd.lu/fr/dossier/8108.
634. *Luxembourg Government, 2023–2028 Coalition Agreement*, p. 91, https://gouvernement.lu/fr/publications/accord-coalition/accord-de-coalition-2023-2028/accord-de-coalition-2023-2028.html.

III. Overview of the Legal Framework

670. The exercise of any of the professions mentioned in Article 1 is subject to a specific authorisation delivered by the Minister of Health and Social Security. The procedure is comparable to the one described for the authorisation to practise medicine.[635] Temporary service provision by nationals of an EU member country legally established in an EU member country other than Luxembourg is subject to a notification.[636]

671. A person authorised to practise one of these professions is allowed to use the official protected title corresponding to that profession.[637] The exercise of any of these professions by a person not authorised to practise constitutes illegal practice and the undue use of the title constitutes usurpation of the protected title with criminal sanctions.[638]

672. Since the 2023 amendment, for each of these professions, a specific Annex contains the definition, attributions, and specific rules applicable to the practice of the concerned profession. The annexes describe, with a varying degree of precision, the level of autonomy with regard to physicians. They distinguish autonomous attributions and attributions that may only be carried out following a medical prescription or under the supervision of a physician. The profession with the most far-reaching autonomy is midwives. Midwives may, amongst other attributions, autonomously monitor uncomplicated pregnancies, practise physiological childbirth, prescribe drugs, analyses and medical devices for the monitoring of uncomplicated pregnancies, the practice of normal childbirth and the care of healthy newborns.

673. The Law establishes the Higher Council for Certain Health Professions as a common professional order for all the paramedical professions covered.[639] The Higher Council maintains the ordinal register for the professions[640] and is mandated to establish a Code of professional ethics.[641] In their professional practice, the members of any of the professions covered are subject to ethical and disciplinary action by the Higher Council. Chapter 2 establishes the disciplinary jurisdictions and the procedure to be applied.

635. Article 2, Law on the practice and revalorisation of certain health professions.
636. Article 4, Law on the practice and revalorisation of certain health professions.
637. Article 5, Law on the practice and revalorisation of certain health professions.
638. Article 16, Law on the practice and revalorisation of certain health professions.
639. Article 19, Law on the practice and revalorisation of certain health professions.
640. Article 8, Law on the practice and revalorisation of certain health professions.
641. Article 19, Law on the practice and revalorisation of certain health professions.

Chapter 3. Relationship with Healthcare Institutions

§1. Hospitals

I. General Overview

674. The amended Law of 8 March 2018 on hospital establishments and hospital planning ('Law on hospitals') sets the general legal framework applicable to hospital establishments. Article 1 applies to 'hospitals, establishments for people at the end of their lives, spa establishments and diagnostic centres' and these categories are further defined by the Law. Article 1 further defines the mission of hospital establishments: 'to provide inpatient or outpatient healthcare in a multidisciplinary context, under the required and appropriate medical, medico-technical, professional and logistical conditions and frameworks, for or to patients who are admitted because their state of health requires this type of care, in order to treat or alleviate the disease, restore or improve the state of health or stabilise injuries as quickly as possible'.

675. The general organisation of hospitals, foreseen by the Law on hospitals, comprises different levels of governance:

(a) Governing board (or equivalent): the governing board fixes the general policy and the strategic choices and defines the activities of the establishment. It exercises control over the activities of the establishment. Physicians are represented in the governing board through at least on delegate with a deliberative vote and one with an advisory vote designated by the medical council.[642] The governing board must similarly comprise delegates representing the employees of the hospital. It further comprises the government hospital commissioner, who has a consultative vote. The Government elected in October 2023 intends to review the current legal framework to further ensure a representation of patients in the governing board of hospitals.[643]
(b) Board of directors: the governing board appoints the board of directors. Management is in the hands of a general director, who must be a physician, assisted by a medical director, a care director, and an administrative and financial director.
(c) Three Departments: a medical department, a care department and an administrative and technical department.

The medical director heads the medical department. He or she is assisted by medical coordinators ('médecins coordinateurs') nominated by the governing board, the position of medical coordinator being incompatible with the position of general director, head of the medical department or chairman of the medical council. The

642. Law on hospitals, Art. 23, §4.
643. *Luxembourg Government, 2023–2028 Coalition Agreement*, p. 102, https://gouvernement.lu/fr/publications/accord-coalition/accord-de-coalition-2023-2028/accord-de-coalition-2023-2028.html.

medical coordinators assist the medical director in the coordination and development of the medical activity of a medical department or a cluster of departments.[644] Given the strong attachment to therapeutic freedom and liberal practice of medicine, the medical activity remains at the same time less hierarchically organised than in other countries and the coordinating physician has no strong direct hierarchical authority.[645]

The director of care heads the department of care. Below the director of care, different levels of hierarchy exist within the care department, usually mirroring the medical organisation. Contrary to the medical department, there is a strongly hierarchical organisation, not to mention the specific attributions of the different categories of non-medical healthcare professionals.

An administrative and financial director heads the administrative department generally comprising administrative, financial and support functions such as IT.

676. Each hospital has a medical council ('Conseil médical)' representing the doctors, pharmacists and heads of laboratories practising in the hospital. The members are elected by their pairs. Members are not financially compensated for the burden of their mandate. The medical council is the main body allowing participation in the organisation of the hospital and must be called upon to give its opinion on key matters: the general internal regulation; budget and building maters; medical or medico-technical departments and important medical acquisitions; appointment of physicians, heads of laboratories and pharmacists; hospital ethics committee. It further oversees the discipline of the professions it represents, ensures compliance with the legal and regulatory provisions and rules of professional conduct, as well as good relations between doctors, pharmacists, and laboratories without prejudice to the powers of the Medical College, the general director and medical director.[646]

(*See also:* General Introduction, Chapter 2., §1., I. Hospital Establishments and Hospital Care; and*:* Part I., Chapter 4., §4, II. Ethics Committees in Hospitals).

II. Practice of Hospital Medicine

677. According to the Law on hospitals, any physician attached to one or more hospital units must comply with the general regulations of the hospital and the department(s) to which he or she is attached, to internal procedures and to the directives that concern his or her practice. He or she must participate in the reporting and monitoring system of quality and safety and respect afferent recommendations. He or she must further participate in maintaining the continuity of care and must participate in on-call duty and the service plan to ensure medical permanence. Hospital physicians shall further keep the patient records up to date.[647] At the same time, given the strong attachment to therapeutic freedom and liberal practice of medicine, hospital physicians exercise their profession without any medical subordination

644. Law on hospitals, Art. 31, §6.
645. *See:* para. 681 *infra.*
646. Article 32, Law on hospitals.
647. Article 33, §1–§5, Law on hospitals.

concerning an individual patient. Individual decisions taken by the physician in the interest of the patient are a matter of therapeutic freedom and the hospital may not intervene in the individual relationship with his patient.[648]

678. Most of Luxembourg's hospitals operate as 'open regime' ('régime ouvert') hospitals, with physicians that are admitted by the hospitals to work as self-employed liberal professionals. Such self-employed liberal hospital physicians need to be registered with the hospital based on a collaboration contract. This contract must contain a common minimum content, as laid down by a standard model contract, determined by mutual agreement between the representative association of physicians (AMMD) and hospitals (FHL). In case no such agreement is reached within twelve months, the Minister of Health and Social Security may determine the content. The essential content of this standard collaboration contract must include: (1) its purpose and the medical activities that the doctor carries out in the hospital establishment; (2) compliance with the quality and safety objectives; (3) the duration of the contract and its extension rules; (4) the conditions of access to care units as well as the conditions of rational and scientific use of medico-technical equipment and infrastructures; (5) the procedures for managing doctors' absences; (6) the obligation for doctors to take out civil liability insurance; (7) out-of-court settlement of disputes between hospitals and doctors; (8) the practical application of the rights and obligations of the physician and the consequences for the collaboration contract in the event of non-compliance by one of the contracting parties, in compliance with the procedures.[649] The currently applicable standard contract model negotiated between AMMD and FHL dates from 2004.[650] If the hospital operates as a 'closed regime' hospital, the employment contract or internal directives govern these matters.

679. The distinction between open and closed regime hospitals has important legal implications concerning civil liability. If the hospital operates as an 'open regime' hospital, there is a division of tasks and responsibilities: the hospital assumes responsibility for hospital care, while the physician assumes responsibility for medical care. If the hospital operates as a 'closed regime' hospital, the hospital's liability includes medical care delivered by its employed physicians.

680. According to Article 20 of the Law on the medical profession, any agreement between members of the medical and dental professions or between them and a hospital providing for the sharing of fees or for discounts on prescribed medicines shall be null and void, without prejudice to the provisions concerning the remuneration of physicians laid down by the organic laws relating to certain hospital establishments.

---

648. Article 33, §6, Law on hospitals.
649. Article 33, §7, Law on hospitals.
650. https://fhlux.lu/web/wp-content/uploads/2013/03/Contrat_Agement_type_hopitaux_medecins.pdf.

681. The medical coordinators assists in coordination and planning of the medical activity of one or more department(s). He or she ensures: (1) the smooth running of the department(s) and the quality of services provided; (2) the standardisation of patient care; (3) the efficient use of available resources. This mission is carried out in collaboration with the head of the department of care and the pharmacist in charge. In carrying out his duties, the medical coordinator monitors the activities of all those involved in the concerned department(s).[651]

A Grand-Ducal Regulation of 27 February 2015 further specifies the status, duties, and powers of the medical coordinators, as well as the procedures for their appointment.[652] According to this regulation, the medical coordinator is in charge of coordinating the medical care. He or she draws up the on-call roster and duty schedule for the physicians in the department(s) for which he is responsible. He or she coordinates and ensures the implementation of explicit patient management processes in his department or group of departments, with a view to continuously improving clinical outcomes and contributes to optimising patient flows in his/her department or group of departments, determines the conditions of access to and use of technical platforms and equipment and coordinates the outpatient activities of the department(s). He or she ensures the quality of documentation, traceability, and transparency of the medical activity of the department(s) he/she coordinates.

The medical coordinator monitors the medical activities of the department or group of departments whose activities he or she coordinates. However, except in emergencies, he or she may not intervene or take a decision relating to the medical treatment of a patient under the care of a physician in his or her department or group of departments. Access to the patient file is subject to the concerned patient's express consent and solely allowed for the purposes of accomplishing his or her duties.

§2. Private Healthcare Centres and Hospital Antennas

682. Luxembourg has traditionally a relatively hospital-centric healthcare system, characterised by the absence of intermediate healthcare institutions offering out-of-hospital ambulatory healthcare.

Article 19 of the amended Law of 29 April 1983 concerning the exercise of the medical profession prohibited physicians from disposing of equipment listed in a Grand-Ducal Regulation, currently the Grand-Ducal Regulation of 17 June 1993. The regulation bans a list of twenty-one equipment and appliances, including MRI, any equipment required for general anaesthesia and any medical biology equipment, allowing to perform more than five analytical parameters on the same biological sample. This regulation de facto limited the scope of ambulatory care that can be offered by physicians in private healthcare centres by indirectly attributing a monopoly of a large range of necessary equipment to hospital establishments. This

651. Article 31, §6–§8, Law on hospitals.

652. Règlement grand-ducal du 27 février 2015 relatif au statut, aux modalités de désignation et aux attributions du médecin-coordinateur, Mém. A – 46 du 12.03.2015, https://legilux.public.lu/eli/etat/leg/rgd/2015/02/27/n4/jo.

limitation was seen as less appropriate, and there were initiatives to compose multidisciplinary teams that would have access to adequate equipment, including so-called heavy equipment such as MRI, to be able to offer a broader range of healthcare in private ambulatory healthcare centres. In a case where the Minister of Health and Social Security had refused to allow the acquisition of an MRI for the purposes of a private healthcare centre, the legal mechanism consisting of establishing a list of prohibited equipment within a Grand-Ducal Regulation was declared incompatible with the Constitution. The Constitutional Court ruling is, in substance, based on the formal ground that the Law of 29 April 1983 does not sufficiently circumscribe the purposes, conditions and procedures according to which a Grand-Ducal Regulation may ban a type of equipment.[653] It results thereof that the aforementioned Grand-Ducal Regulation, even though never formally abrogated, is no longer enforceable.

683. In view of the Constitutional Court ruling, the opening of a privately owned ambulatory care centre comprising an MRI was announced in late 2021. This centre, called 'Centre Médical Potaschbierg', opened its doors after the judgment of the Constitutional Court, although the Minister of Health had declared that it considered this activity to be in breach of the Law on hospitals, an aspect not legally decided by the case submitted to the Constitutional Court. An agreement was finally reached, with the Minister declaring to allow the continued operation of the MRI as a 'pilot project' between CHL hospital and the physicians at the origin of the creation of the centre.[654] This evolution can be paralleled by the thwarted tentative to establish a birthing house to be run by a group of midwives, even though the latter closed its door.[655]

684. In May 2022, a Law project was submitted to Parliament to amend the Law on hospitals such as to reserve to hospitals any medical equipment and appliances worth more than EUR 250,000 (excl. VAT) as well as any use of equipment reserved to the hospital sector by Annex 3 of the Law on hospitals. This list of 'medical equipment and appliances requiring national planning, highly qualified personnel or requiring special conditions of use' includes twenty-one equipment and appliances, including MRI, as well as any equipment required for general anaesthesia, endovascular and urological lasers, surgical robots, or mammography equipment. The

653. C. Const., 5 juillet 2019, Arrêt No. 148/19, Mem. A – 491 du 12.07.2019, https://legilux.public.lu/eli/etat/leg/acc/2019/07/05/a491/jo; Laurincella, P., *L'arrêt du 5 juillet 2019 de la Cour Constitutionnelle: vers le libre accès d'acquérir du matériel pour les professionnels de la santé en milieu extrahospitalier ?* RLDS, No. 3 (2020); Wolter, T., *La protection sociale face à la médecine libérale: l'arrêt de la Cour constitutionnelle du 5 juillet 2019*, Cahier juridique No. 1, IGSS (2021).

654. Feist, P., *Die vielen neuen IRM*, d'Lëtzebuerger Land (2021), https://www.land.lu/page/article/674/338674/DEU/index.html; Pallier, P., *Pas d'IRM à Grevenmacher sans régularisation, insiste Lenert*, Paperjam (2022); *IRM Potaschberg: signature de la convention entre l'État et le CHL*, Luxembourg Government (2022), https://paperjam.lu/article/pas-irm-a-grevenmacher-sans-re; https://sante.public.lu/fr/actualites/2022/12/convention-irm-chl.html.

655. *See:* para. 42 *supra*.

amendment to the Law on hospitals further allows general hospitals to run 'antennas' providing exclusively ambulatory care outside of the main or secondary hospital site, either directly operated as a service branch or operated by a general hospital in collaboration with a group of physicians. These additional 'antennas' are considered part of the main hospital service and are dedicated to ambulatory healthcare. Every general hospital may dispose of a maximum of two such antennas for each of the following hospital services: dialysis, non-surgical day hospitalisation, medical imaging and oncology.

In its opinion on the draft law, the Council of State stressed that reserving such equipment and appliances for the purposes of medical treatment to hospital establishments and hospital antennas constitutes a restriction on the exercise of the liberal profession of physicians. While recognising the legitimacy of the objectives of cost control, quality control and ensuring skilled providers, the Council of State questioned the appropriateness and proportionality of the proposed measures. In the Council of State's opinion, it was not demonstrated in a factual manner that each of the equipment and appliances listed objectively requires national planning, highly qualified personnel or represents an investment cost requiring national planning. In its complementary opinion, the Council of State further stressed that, according to the case, the restrictions put in place may be challengeable before the administrative jurisdictions in an individual case. The Luxembourg Competition Authority made similar serious reservations concerning respect for the principle of freedom of trade and industry, freedom of establishment and the principle of proportionality. Notwithstanding these legal reservations, Parliament adopted the proposal and the amendment entered into force on 3 August 2023.[656]

685. A further private healthcare centre financed by private investors and comprising equipment traditionally reserved for hospitals opened its doors in the south of Luxembourg[657] before the entry into force of the amendment of the Law on hospitals, reserving such activities to hospital antennas. Not having been able to sign a collaboration with a general hospital, it closed the concerned activities in March 2024 after the Minister of Health and Social Security had stressed it considered this activity to be in breach of the Law on hospitals as amended. Legal procedures were announced.[658]

686. A Law proposal was further submitted to Parliament in May 2022, which aimed to allow healthcare professionals to regroup in a civil law company that could

656. Loi du 29 juillet 2023 portant modification: (1) de la loi modifiée du 8 mars 2018 relative aux établissements hospitaliers et à la planification hospitalière; (2) de la loi modifiée du 29 avril 1983 relative à l'exercice de la profession de médecin, de médecin-dentiste et de médecin-vétérinaire; (3) du Code de la sécurité sociale, https://legilux.public.lu/eli/etat/leg/loi/2023/07/29/a478/jo.

657. Feist, P., *Arztpraxen als Geschäftsidee*, d'Lëtzebuerger Land (2023), *See*: https://www.hygie-group.lu/en/.

658. Montaigu, G., *Hygie Group, dépité, contre-attaque*, Le Quotidien (2024), https://lequotidien.lu/a-la-une/hygie-group-depite-contre-attaque/.

be authorised to exercise a healthcare profession. This controversially discussed proposal was withdrawn in February 2024.[659]

687. In parallel to these recent legal developments, there is an ongoing political and societal debate concerning the legal framework necessary to ensure the interests of the social security system and public health needs when ambulatory healthcare centres are created by private initiatives. Some see the traditional universal, solidarity-based Luxembourg healthcare system threatened by privatisation and commercialisation of healthcare. Others stress the patients' interest in unlocking innovation, granting quicker access to care, and delivering a more flexible service. Hospitals fear losing not only parts of their current ambulatory activity but also the collaboration of qualified physicians within a context of increasing scarcity of medical resources. They point to a risk of 'cherry picking' by delivering the most lucrative part of healthcare out-of-hospital while not having to participate in hospital duty services. There are also worries that such centres would not have to respect the same norms and that their employees would not benefit from the group contract that applies to employees in the hospital sector. Given the lack of afferent regulation, there is a risk that such centres do not put in place comparable quality and safety management procedures when not being part of a hospital service.

688. The Government elected in October 2023 agreed to amend the Law on hospitals with the objective of reducing the restrictions concerning medical equipment allowed in privately run healthcare centres. It further agreed to create a legal framework allowing healthcare professionals to regroup in a civil law company, stressing that such companies should solely be composed of physicians and other health professionals and that professionals established outside the hospital would have to participate in duty services.[660]

§3. Long-Term Care Institutions

689. Providers of long-term care are governed by the Law governing relations between the State and organisations working in the social, family, and therapeutic fields and its executing Grand-Ducal Regulations. The Law on the quality of services for the elderly further applies to accommodation facilities for the elderly, home help and care services and day centres for the elderly.[661]

690. Long-term care residential facilities are considered a home-replacing environment. The medical responsibility generally rests with a liberal GP, who visits his

659. Projet de loi 8013 portant modification: (1) de loi modifiée du 29 avril 1983 concernant l'exercice des professions de médecin, médecin-dentiste et de médecin-vétérinaire; (2) de la loi modifiée du 26 mars 1992 sur l'exercice et la revalorisation de certaines professions de santé; (3) de la loi modifiée du 14 juillet 2015 portant création de la profession de psychothérapeute, https://www.chd.lu/fr/dossier/8013.

660. *Luxembourg Government, 2023–2028 Coalition Agreement*, p. 89, https://gouvernement.lu/fr/publications/accord-coalition/accord-de-coalition-2023-2028/accord-de-coalition-2023-2028.html.

661. *See:* General Introduction, Ch. 2., §1., IV. Long-Term Care.

patients regularly. Unlike the Law on hospitals, the legislative framework currently does not foresee a legal requirement for physicians to register with long-term care facilities based on a collaboration contract. It has, however, in practice, become a requirement of almost all long-term care institutions that physicians regularly visiting sign a contract and institutions keep a list of registered GPs. Patient choice is de facto limited to these physicians. In 2021, AMMD and COPAS[662] agreed upon a model contract that is the basis of such contracts.[663]

662. 'Fédération COPAS' is regrouping providers of long-term care. (www.copas.lu).
663. https://www.ammd.lu/media/611fa2d4b3090_57302_ammd_corps_medical_03_2021_bro_web.pdf.

Chapter 4. Relations with Social Security

691. Physicians practising in Luxembourg are obliged to contract with social security (§1.). Besides other legal sources, conventional provisions apply in their dealings with patients (§2.), and medical fees are further defined by the nomenclature (§3.). Finally, specific litigation may arise in relation to the respect of social security legislation (§4.).

§1. Mandatory Contracting with Social Security

692. Luxembourg ensures access to healthcare by means of a compulsory, generalised and automatic contracting of physicians with social security. The term 'contracting' ('conventionnement') is insofar misleading, as relations with social security are automatic and compulsory ('conventionnement obligatoire, généralisé et automatique'). No physician may practise his profession outside of the social security system; the insurance is at the same time obliged to admit all authorised physicians.

693. Before taking up their duties, physicians need to notify CNS of their authorisation to practise and their professional address. Thereof, physicians are assigned an individual physician code by CNS. This code is used in relation to social security and, more generally, the healthcare system (on prescriptions, reports, etc.).

§2. Convention for Physicians and Dentists

694. Pursuant to the CSS, the relationship between the insurance and healthcare providers is governed by conventions negotiated between the CNS and the representative groups of the providers. Once signed, such conventions are submitted for control of legality to the Minister of Health and Social Security. Duly approved and published, these conventions are generally applicable to all providers.[664] It results thereof, as recalled by the Code of Medical Ethics[665] that all practising physicians and dentists must comply with the provisions of the convention agreed upon between CNS and AMMD. Article 64, §2, CSS fixes a non-limitative list of mandatory issues to be covered in the convention for physicians and dentists.

695. Currently, the amended Convention of 13 December 1993 applies when taking care of a Luxembourg-insured patient, as well as when taking care of a patient insured within the EU, an EEA country, Switzerland, and any other country

664. Article 70, §3, CSS.
665. Article 105 of the Code of Medical Ethics request every physician to comply with the mandatory agreements negotiated between the associations representing the profession and the health and social security bodies or any other entity involved in regulating the profession.

with which Luxembourg is bound by a social security instrument.[666] The convention for physicians and dentists regulates a wide range of issues, including rules concerning associations of physicians; drafting of bills for medical fees; establishment of prescriptions, certificates, and other documents; declaration of admission and discharge letters in the case of inpatient treatment; direct payment of medical fee. The convention itself is supplemented by an annex and technical documents, which define forms for statements of medical fees, medical prescriptions, estimates, declarations of incapacity for work and technical elements in relation to standard forms and circulation of data with social security.

§3. Medical Fees and Nomenclature of Medical Fees

696. The services that are covered by social security are described in a fee schedule called 'nomenclature of acts and services' ('nomenclature des actes et services') of the concerned healthcare profession. The nomenclature tariff is fixed based on a detailed recommendation from the Nomenclature Commission. This Commission includes two representatives of CNS and two representatives jointly appointed by the Minister of Health and Social Security, as well as two representatives of AMMD and two representatives of the professional group concerned. The Nomenclature Commission may deal with any matter relating to its remit. It is also called to consider any proposal for the inclusion, modification or deletion made by the Minister of Health and Social Security, the Medical Council, IGSS, CNS, CSPCS or by the signatory parties, including AMMD.

After being published in the form of a Grand-Ducal Regulation, the statutory fee levels and its conditions are generally applicable. The fee schedule is mandatory and always applies. No physician may practise his profession outside of the social security system, as contracting is mandatory. The tariff applies thus to all physicians and all persons covered by the social security. It further applies in case of cross-border healthcare delivered to an insured person from another Member State of the EU, from Switzerland, from an EEA country or from any other country linked to Luxembourg through a social security agreement.

697. A nomenclature for physicians, as well as a nomenclature for dentists, set out the catalogue of medical and dental acts and services covered by sickness and maternity insurance. There is no distinction between medical services delivered by physicians within or outside of the hospital; the amount of the fee is always the same. The identification number of the fee and the amount of the fee are specified for each act or service.

In exceptional cases, to be assessed by CNS based on a detailed report by the attending physician, an act or service not included in the nomenclature may be reimbursed based on positive advice of CMSS, which sets a tariff by assimilating the

666. Convention entre la Caisse nationale de santé et l'Association des médecins et médecins-dentistes, conclue en exécution de l'article 61 et suivants du Code des assurances sociales, https://cns.public.lu/en/legislations/ammd_dent/cns-ammd-med-convention.html.

procedure with an existing procedure of comparable importance.[667] This mechanism implies requesting an individual decision and is, in practice, not frequently used.

698. Only the fees covered by the nomenclature are reimbursable to patients. The reimbursement rate is fixed by the statutes of CNS.[668] There is currently a distinction concerning the reimbursement level of services delivered by physicians within or outside of the hospital.

For outpatient treatment, the standard reimbursement rate is 88% of the fees set for adults. It is 100% for patients under 18 years of age. Patients generally must pay for such medical fees upfront. However, the deployment of a PID ('paiement immédiat direct') of medical fees started in September 2023. It is currently not mandatory for physicians to participate; deployment is currently in its early phase.

In the case of inpatient or semi-stationary treatment, the rate is 100% of the fees in the nomenclature of acts and services of physicians. Physicians may apply a so-called 1st class surcharge (forfait 1ère classe) of 66% of the nomenclature tariff of the concerned act or service in case the patient chooses a hospitalisation in a single room. Such a surcharge does not apply if the single room corresponds to a justified medical need certified by the physician. The 1st class surcharge is not reimbursed by CNS. The surcharge is typically covered by complementary voluntary health insurance. In most cases, medical fees in hospitals are covered through third-party payment, generally if the fees exceed a certain amount.

699. Pursuant to Article 36 of the Statutes of CNS, coverage of consultations or visits is generally limited to:

- one consultation or visit of a GP or of a specialist of the same discipline per twenty-four hours, unless there is an intervention by the emergency medical service;
- two consultations or visits of a GP or of a specialist of the same discipline per seven-day period;
- twelve consultations or visits of a GP or of a specialist of the same discipline per six months, unless such consultations or visits are delivered in a geriatric ward or in a hospital.

These limitations do not apply to prescription renewals, serial injections and dressings. Furthermore, exceeding these limitations may be granted through a prior authorisation or *ex post,* if a medical justification is accepted.

700. The convention for physicians and dentists allows charging of additional fees to patients in certain circumstances, if patients are informed in advance and consent. So-called personal convenience codes (convenance personnelle – CP) must be used for such billing. CP fees are not covered by health insurance.

CP codes CP1, CP2 and CP4–CP7 concern appointments at specific times at the request of the patient, immediate examination without appointment by a physician

667. Article 19, CSS.
668. Article 21, CSS.

usually working on an appointment-based system, emergency consultation without objective urgency and consultations by phone lasting over ten minutes.

CP3 concerns an appointment missed by the patient and not cancelled twenty-four hours in advance without providing a valid excuse; the physician generally invoices the tariff of a standard consultation.

701. Coverage of dental care is incomplete. According to the convention for dentists, such dental care is agreed upon with the patient and is delivered beyond the tariffs covered by social security. The code 'CP8' is mandatory; however, the tariff for charging additional fees under CP8 has not been fixed. In many circumstances, prior approval by CMSS is required.

702. Article 106 of the Code of Medical Ethics applies when a tariff is freely agreed upon. As a rule, if a procedure is not foreseen by the nomenclature and may be freely agreed upon, or if, in exceptional cases, a patient is not covered (no affiliation in Luxembourg or EU/EEA or specific agreement), Article 106 of the Code of Medical Ethics request physicians to determine fees 'with tact and moderation'. It furthermore requests to inform the patient before the procedure and to draw up an estimate covering all foreseeable fees and charges for the treatment requested or proposed. Written consent must be obtained by countersigning the estimate prior to starting the procedure.

703. If a physician proposes his patient to undergo a medical procedure for which the nomenclature prescribes a prior authorisation from the CMSS, the physician must inform thereof and take the necessary steps to obtain this authorisation. If a patient requests not to wait, the physician must inform the patient of the risk that the service is not reimbursed. In case the prior authorisation is refused by CMSS, and the patient decides nevertheless to undergo the procedure, the physician must give prior information about the fees charged at the patient's expense and a prior written agreement containing this information must be signed.

704. Article 107 of the Code of Medical Ethics further prohibits reducing fees below the conventional rates; however, free care may be provided to uninsured patients in need, to close relatives and to colleagues or employees of a physician.

705. A deposit of up to a maximum of 50% of the estimated costs may be requested to cover costs incurred prior to a procedure. In practice, deposits are frequent in dentistry (implants, etc.) as well as for hospital care given to patients from third countries or without a valid affiliation.

706. Medical fees are prescribed within two years of the delivery of the medical service. Furthermore, the right to seek reimbursement from the competent social security organism is prescribed within two years from the payment of the invoice.[669]

669. Article 84, CSS.

§4. SOCIAL SECURITY LITIGATION

707. To resolve disputes in relation to social security legislation, the CSS foresees specific administrative litigation procedures and specific Social Security Jurisdiction. This includes disputes concerning obligations imposed on a physician by the social security legislation.[670]

I. Social Security Supervisory Commission

708. The Social Security Supervisory Commission ('Commission de surveillance de la sécurité sociale') is an administrative organ under the supervision of the Department of Social Security. The Supervisory Commission has authority in matters concerning sickness and maternity insurance, accident insurance and long-term care insurance.

709. According to Article 72 of the CSS, the Social Security Supervisory Commission is competent with regard to respect for the nomenclature of fees. It may be called by a patient or the concerned physician after the president of CNS decides to refuse or partially refuse reimbursement because the nomenclature tariff has not been respected. It may likewise be called after a presidential decision refusing, for the same reasons, a direct payment of medical fees to a physician. Under Article 72, the Commission has full power to compel the necessary correction, either by granting reimbursement or by ordering repayment of a fee unduly paid by exceeding the official tariff. In case of disagreement with the decision, the parties may bring the matter before the Arbitration Council for Social Security within forty days.

710. According to Article 73 of the CSS, the Social Security Supervisory Commission is further competent for examining activity reports showing an 'unjustified deviation' from professional standards submitted to the Commission by the Director of the CMSS. The modalities thereof are governed by the Convention for Physicians and currently concern solely the screening of the emission of certificates of incapacity for work.

711. The Social Security Supervisory Commission may further examine facts reported by the President of the CNS or the President of a public sector sickness fund, which may constitute a breach of the physicians' obligations. Such breaches my concern: (1) failure to comply with legal, regulatory, statutory or contractual provisions that result in, or attempt to result in, an undue benefit at the expense of the sickness and maternity insurance scheme; (2) refusal of access to information, failure to reply or a false, incomplete or unreasonably late reply to any request for supporting documents, information or access to information by the competent social security institution or by CMSS; (3) acts which have the effect of hindering checks or the proper management of the competent social security institution; (4) failure to

670. Walch, M., *Les litiges opposant les prestataires individuels de soins de santé aux organismes d'assurance maladie et à leurs assurés*, BLQS, No. 16 (2004).

comply with administrative formalities imposed by legal, regulatory, statutory or contractual provisions; (5) refusal by the service provider to enter the details of each procedure or consultation in the shared health record, unless the insured has explicitly objected to it; (6) prescribing or performing unnecessary or unnecessarily costly services; (7) exposing the insured to excess fees that do not comply with legal, regulatory, statutory or contractual provisions.

712. If the Security Supervisory Commission considers that the violation of a physician's obligation is established, it must bring the matter before the Arbitration Council for Social Security, unless the dispute is resolved by a transaction between CNS and the concerned physician providing for compensation for the economic loss incurred.

II. Social Security Jurisdictions[671]

713. The social jurisdictions are composed of the 'Arbitration Council for Social Security' ('Conseil arbitral de la sécurité sociale') and the 'Superior Council for Social Security' ('Conseil supérieur de la sécurité sociale'). For judgments pronounced as a last resort, cassation may be introduced before the Court of Cassation.

714. The Arbitration Council for Social Security is composed of one president and two assessors. It is competent to rule in the first instance on disputes concerning social security benefits and other issues (affiliation, contributions, fines) on appeal before the Superior Council for Social Security if the subject of the dispute exceeds EUR 1,250. Cases must be lodged, on pain of foreclosure, within a period of forty days from the date of notification of the contested decision by simple application on plain paper, to be lodged at the head office of the Arbitration Council. Appeals to the Social Security Arbitration Board have no suspensive effect.

715. With regard to individual physicians, the Arbitration Council for Social Security is competent for matters brought to it by a party pursuant to a decision of the Social Security Supervisory Commission under Article 72bis, as well as by referral of the Social Security Supervisory Commission pursuant to Article 73.

671. Articles 545–546, CSS.

Selected Bibliography

Berthet, F., et al., *Luxembourg: HiT in Brief*, WHO Regional Office for Europe, European Observatory on Health Systems and Policies (2015).

Bock, H., *La conformité RGPD des médecins exerçant sous statut libéral et quelques réflexions sur des traitements de données liés au covid-19*, RLDS, No. 4, pp. 3–9 (2020).

Braum, S., *Euthanasie et assistance au suicide au Luxembourg: antécédents, contenu et effets de la nouvelle loi*, Ann. dr. lux., Vol. 19, pp. 219–236 (2010).

Carte sanitaire 2021, Observatoire national de santé (2022), https://sante.public.lu/fr/espace-obsante/carte-sanitaire.html.

Droit de la sécurité sociale 2023, IGSS (2023).

Feltz, A., *Responsabilité médicale : Les infections nosocomiales: vers une responsabilité sans faute?*, JurisNews Droit des Assurances et de la Responsabilité (2013/1).

Ferry, A. & Schiltz F., *La responsabilité médicale – rapport luxembourgeois*, in: *Journées panaméennes de l'Association H. Capitant, Responsabilités: aspects nouveaux*, Ed. L.G.D.J (2000).

Fondation bibliothèque du droit luxembourgeois (ed.), *La responsabilité médicale en droit luxembourgeois*, Ed. Bruylant (1992).

Lair-Hillion, M.-L., *Etat des lieux des professions médicales et des professions de santé au Luxembourg: rapport final et recommandations*, Luxembourg (2019).

Lauricella, P., *La prescription de l'action disciplinaire à l'encontre des professionnels inscrits au Collège médical*, RLDS, No. 1, pp. 38–44 (2019).

Leist, A., *Luxembourg*, in: Immergut, E., et al. (eds), *Health Politics in Europe: A handbook*, Oxford University Press (2021).

Loutsch, H., *Aperçu historique sur les origines du Collège Médical*, in: *Le Collège médical 1818–1968*, Imprimerie Coopérative Luxembourgeoise, Esch-sur-Alzette (1970).

Malmedier-Muehlschelegel, A. & Power, N.C., 'Mental Health Legislation in Luxembourg, a Small Country in Western Europe', 19(3) *BJPsych Int.*, 70–72: 2022.

McHale, J., 'Reforming the EU Clinical Trials Directive: Streamlining Processes or a Radical "New" Agenda?', 20 *Eur. J. Health L.*, (363), 375: (2013).

Merz-Spet, A., *Perte de chance et préjudice d'impréparation: responsabilité civile en cas de manquement au devoir d'information*, RLDS, No. 7, pp. 20–25 (2021).

Nati, R., *Etapes essentielles de l'organisation sanitaire, médicale et hospitalière au Luxembourg*, in: *Le Conseil d'État face à l'évolution de la société luxembourgeoise*, pp. 195–214, Conseil d'Etat (2006).

Nys, H., 'Towards a Human Right "to Be Forgotten Online"?', 18 *Eur. J. Health L.*, 469–475: 2011.

Nys, H., 'The Ambiguous Legal Status of Physician Assisted Suicide in Belgium', 7 *Journal für Medizin- und Gesundheitsrecht*, 191–194: 2022.

Nys, H. & Schwebag, M., *Illegal Practice of Medicine in the Benelux Countries. A Comparative Study.*, RLDS, No. 13, pp. 18–25 (2022).

Nys, H. & Schwebag, M., *The Mortier Case and What It Means for the Belgian and Luxembourg Legal Frameworks on Euthanasia*, RLDS, No. 15, pp. 22–27 (2023).

Patient Rights, Patiente Vertriedung, https://www.patientevertriedung.lu/?com=2I18I0I0I.

Pierrat, M., *Soins et respect de la volonté de la personne en fin de vie – Rapport luxembourgeois aux journées suisses de l'Association H. Capitant*, Ann. dr. lux., Vol. 19, pp. 189–218 (2010).

Ravarani, G., *La responsabilité civile des personnes privées et publiques*, 3e éd., Ed. Pasicrisie luxembourgeoise (2014).

Schiltz, P., *Le secret professionnel des médecins et autres professionnels de la santé*, RLDS, No. 16, pp. 1–20 (2023).

Schwebag, M. & Stoffel, D., *L'embryon humain en droit luxembourgeois*, RLDS, No. 3, pp. 21–23 (2020).

Schwebag, M., *Responsabilité civile en matière d'infection nosocomiale et d'infection au nouveau coronavirus*, RLDS, No. 7, pp. 1–10 (2021).

Schwebag, M., 'Implementation of the Cross-Border Care Directive in EU Member States: Luxembourg', 21(1) *EJHL issue*: 2014.

Schwebag, M., *Regard juridique sur le droit du patient de refuser des soins de santé*, RLDS No. 1, pp. 11–18 (2019).

Schwebag, M., *Le patient mineur et ses parents face aux soins de santé*, RLDS, Nos 9–10, pp. 11–23 (2022).

Schwebag, M., *L'encadrement national du droit d'accès au dossier patient au regard des dispositions du RGPD*, RLDS, No. 18, pp. 13–18 (2024).

Schwebag, M., *Médiation dans le domaine de la santé au Luxembourg,* Lettre des Médiations, No. 8 (2019), https://www.observatoiredesmediations.org/Asset/Source/refBibliography_ID-134_No-01.pdf.

Stoffel, D., *Etat des lieux de la bioéthique au Luxembourg: De l'avortement à l'euthanasie*, Cahier du droit luxembourgeois No. 22, Legitech (2014).

Stoffel, D., *La réforme de la réglementation du don d'organes au Luxembourg*, Droit, Santé et Société, N. 1/Vol. 20 (2017).

Vogel, G. & Rudloff, E., *Droit médical et hospitalier*, 2e éd., Promoculture (2021).

Index

The numbers refer to paragraph numbers.

Abortion. *See:* Termination of pregnancy.
Academic title, professional title, 144–146
Advance directive. *See:* Palliative care.
Association of physicians, 649–655
Authorisation to practise, 113–135
  general conditions, 115–121
  duration and lapsing, 125–127
  judicial review, 131
  suspension, revocation, 128–130
  temporary authorisation (traineeship, replacement), 122–124
  See also: Temporary service provision notification.
Autopsy, 641–643

Blood and blood components, 586–589
Biomedical research. *See:* Research.
Birthing house, 42, 683
Burial, cremation, and mortal remains, 644–646

Child abuse, 340
Childcare, 28, 36, 506–508
Clinical trials. *See:* Research.
Code of medical ethics, 141, 148, 173, 175–176, 182, 234, 241, 271, 287, 310, 348, 647, 649, 650, 694, 702, 704
Complaints, 16, 177, 195, 231, 315, 344, 368, 379–382, 497
Commuters, 5, 50, 51, 111
Constitution, 90–93
Consent. *See:* Informed consent.
Continuity of care, 141, 252, 261, 271, 307, 329, 562, 652, 677
Convention for physicians and dentists, 694–695
Cross-border healthcare, 48–51, 62, 86, 317, 363, 696
Curatorship ('curatelle'), 463, 466, 468, 477

Death, death certificate, 638–640
Decker-Kohll, 49, 86
Dental medicine, 117, 150, 152
Diagnostic error, 202
Digital Health (eHealth)
  eHealth Agency, 590–593, 595
  electronic healthcare record (DSP), 40, 406, 564, 590, 592, 594–597
  telemedicine, 237
Directorate of Health, 57, 58, 109, 508, 509, 572. 638, 639, 646
Duty to inform, 205, 283–294

Electronic Healthcare Record (DSP), 40, 406, 564, 590, 592, 594–597
Euthanasia and assisted suicide, 410–450
  actual request, 414–423
  advance request in end-of-life provisions, 424–432
  definitions, 411–412
  life insurance contracts, 450
  notification and control, 433–446
  objection of conscience, 447–449
Extended intervention, 284

Free choice of provider, 253–259

Gametes, 522–525, 576, 582, 637
GDPR, 308, 351–354, 357–359, 366, 369, 381–383, 385, 616
Genetic testing, genetic counselling, 513–518
Good Repute, 115, 119, 129

Index

Healthcare; healthcare provider (definitions), 238
Health Scientific Council, 107, 270, 289
Health Insurance, 64–72
Higher Council for Certain Health Professions, 673
Hospital
- definition, 674
- ethics committee, 226
- financing, 67
- historical background, 25–28
- interhospital management committee, 30, 220
- liability, 209–210
- hospital antenna, 31, 684, 685
- hospital medicine, relations with physicians, 677–681
- organisation and governance, 675–676
- overview and hospital landscape, 28, 31
- permanent commission of the hospital sector (CPH), 30

Hospitalisation without consent of persons with mental disorders, 472–505
- involuntary treatment, 487–488
- judicial placement order, 500–505
- legal conditions and requirements, 476–479
- long-term placement, 485
- observation period, 480–482
- oversight, 494–499
- permission to leave, 489
- request of a third party, 475–499
- visits, 490

Human bodily material, 549–589
Human dignity, 75, 91, 93, 240–245, 389

Illegal practice of medicine, 136, 149–162
Immediate direct electronic payment (PID), 67, 70
Informed consent, 283–294
- adequate prior information, 285–289
- burden of proof, 291
- consent form, 291
- shared decision-making, 293

Involuntary placement. *See:* Hospitalisation without consent of persons with mental disorders.

Liability,
- civil, 196–214
- criminal, 215–218
- damage and causation, 202, 211–213
- failure to inform, 205–206
- fault (obligation of means), 201–203
- hospital, 209–210
- insurance coverage, 142
- prescription period, 214
- recommended vaccination, 547, 548
- safety obligation (strict liability), 204

Long-term care, 21, 45–47, 61, 63, 64, 227, 239, 396, 689–690
Loss of chance, 206, 213

Mandatory care, 297–298
Mandatory contracting with social security, 692–693
Matters reserved to the Law, 93, 99, 668
Mediation, 315–318
Medical coordinator, 148, 220, 675, 681
Medical council, 30, 676
Medical houses, 37, 141
Medically assisted procreation, 519–525
Medical emergency, 294, 471
Medical College, 163–193
- annual contribution, 170
- composition and functioning, 165–170
- rules of conduct (deontology), 173–176
- discipline, disciplinary action, 177–193
- registration, 171–172

Medical data. *See:* GDPR and Patient file
Medical fees, 67, 70, 151, 650, 654, 695–706, 709
Medical file. *See:* Patient file
Medical laboratories, 43
Medical secrecy, professional secrecy, 319–346
- infringement, 346
- mediation, 318
- patient consent/waiver of secrecy, 330–332
- reporting to judicial or police authorities, 339–343
- scope, 321–328
- shared professional secrecy, 329
- statutory obligations to disclose, 344–345
- testimony, 338

Medical profession
- access, 108–137
- overview, 35–42
- emergency medicines, 663
- practice of medicine, 136–148
- titles, 144–146
- training, 108–109

recognition of diplomas, 112
Ministry of Health and Social Security, 30, 56, 57, 60–62, 548
Minor patient, 297, 313, 340, 451–461, 537–539, 577, 629
Midwives, 41–42, 68, 321, 322, 669

National Ethics Commission (CNE), 80, 224–225, 390, 521, 523, 524, 637
National Health Laboratory (LNS), 32, 43, 514–516, 642
National Health Observatory, 59
National Information and Mediation Service for Healthcare, 195, 273, 316, 345
National Research Ethics Committee (CNER), 222, 228–230, 602–607, 609, 623, 633
No-fault liability, 197, 548
Nomenclature of medical fees, 696–706
Nosocomial infections, 204, 210, 220

Objection of conscience, 447–449, 540
Occupational health, 509–510
Open regime – closed regime hospital, 199, 678–679
Order of other professions. *See:* Superior Council of Certain Health Professions.
Order of physicians, dentists, pharmacists, and psychotherapists. *See:* Medical Council.
Organ donation, removal, and transplantation, 549–589
Oviedo Convention, 80, 525, 599, 604, 637

Palliative care, 392–409
advance directive, 400–406
cessation (withdrawal) of treatment at the patients request, 399
cessation or refusal of treatment without prospect by a physician, 407
definition, 395
in hospital, 393
pain relief with life-shortening effects, 398
palliative care entitlement, 397
presumed patient will, 400–406
Paramedical health professions, 68, 668–673
Patient companion, 262–264
Patient file
access to the patient file and to medical data, 305–309
access after the death of the patient, 312–313
conservation, 310–311
copies of the patient file, 308
definition, 299
hospital patient file, 314
right to a patient file, 300–304
electronic healthcare record (DSP). *See:* Digital health (eHealth).
Patient obligations, 246–252
Patient organisations and patient representation, 52–54
Patient rights, 234–318
right to a patient companion, 262–264
right to appoint a person of trust, 265–267
right to privacy, dignity, and respect of religious and philosophical values, 240–245
right to free choice, 253–259
right to information, 272–282
right to informed consent, 283–294
right to lodge a complaint, 315–318
right to palliative care. *See:* Palliative care.
right to equal access to quality care, 268–271
rights related to the patient file. *See:* Patient file.
Person of trust, 265–267, 333–337, 400–406
Perinatal care, childcare and school medicine, 507–508
Pharmacist, pharmacy, 44, 656–663
Presumed patient will, 400–406
Prevention, preventive medicine, 506–512
Protective regime, 462–469
Psychotherapist, 664–667
Psychiatric patient. *See:* Hospitalisation without consent of persons with mental disorders.

Quality and safety, 81, 139, 219–221, 268–271

Recognition of foreign diploma, 112, 665
Reference doctor scheme, 40
Refusal of care by a physician, 260–261
Refusal or withdrawal of consent, 295–298
Research

general authorisation process, 600–607
clinical trial on medicinal products, 608–632
ethics boards, 228–232
human bodily material, 634–637
medical experiments on patients, 238
medical devices, 633
tissues and cells, 575
Result or safety obligation (strict liability), 204

Second opinion, 255
School medicine, 507–508
Shared decision-making. *See:* Informed consent.
Social Security Medical Board (CMSS), 49, 62, 344, 397, 697, 701, 703, 710, 711
Superior Council of Certain Health Professions, 15, 92, 104, 164

Telemedicine. *See:* Digital health (eHealth).
Temporary service provision notification, 132–135
Termination of Pregnancy, 526–544
Therapeutic exception, 281
Therapeutic freedom, 148, 203, 269, 449, 675, 677
Third party payment, 67–69
Tissues and cells intended for human applications, 573–585
Tutelage ('tutelle'), 463, 466–468

Vaccination, 545–548

www.ingramcontent.com/pod-product-compliance
Lightning Source LLC
Chambersburg PA
CBHW070245030525
26096CB00033B/1271
9789403512396